UNDERSTANDING
THE TALMUD

BY

ERNEST R. TRATTNER, M. A., Litt. D.

GREENWOOD PRESS, PUBLISHERS
WESTPORT, CONNECTICUT

Library of Congress Cataloging in Publication Data

Trattner, Ernest Robert, 1898–
    Understanding the Talmud.

    Reprint of the ed. published by T. Nelson, New York.
    Bibliography: p.
    1. Talmud--Introductions.   I. Title.
BM503.5.T7 1978   296.1'206   77-27887
ISBN 0-313-20253-2

Reprinted in 1978 by Greenwood Press, Inc.
51 Riverside Avenue, Westport, CT. 06880

Printed in the United States of America

10 9 8 7 6 5 4 3 2 1

TABLE OF CONTENTS

FOREWORD

PART ONE

TABLE OF CONTENTS

FOREWORD

WHERE CAN I FIND a book which will tell in simple language the story of the origin and development of the *Talmud?*

You hold the answer in your hand. Not the whole answer because no one book could possibly sum up every smallest detail of a vast spiritual process which has expressed itself in unbroken continuity over a thousand years. Like a great continental river the historical development of the *Talmud* has wound in and out among the civilizations of antiquity.

Such a book, as this present volume purports to be, could not have been written one hundred years ago. Not because there was any lack of a healthy desire to explain the story of the *Talmud* but because the great advances of modern scholarship, which constitute the glory of scientific research, were only in their infancy at the opening of the nineteenth century. In other words, the answer, as we now have it, was undergoing the process of being worked out; for the very nature of the *Talmud* makes investigation of its growth difficult. But just as the science of modern chemistry came forth from the confused studies of the alchemists, so has the modern understanding of this great subject emerged beyond the barriers of the past.

With the opening of the nineteenth century a new era dawned. There was a group of investigators who were determined to unravel the tangled skein of those traditions which cluster around the name, *Talmud.*[1] These men pos-

---

[1] Outstanding among these pioneers were Nahman Krochmal (1785–1840), Leopold Zunz (1794–1886), Abraham Geiger (1810–1874), Isaac Hirsch Weiss (1815–1905), Wilhelm Bacher (1850–1913), Claude Montefiore (1858–1938), Solomon Schechter (1850–1915), Jacob Z. Lauterbach (1873–1942).

sessed a familiarity with its massive literature. Consequently, when they undertook this project they were well
equipped for it.

The origins of the Jews and their religion are better
known to mankind than that of any other people and its
faith. This, of course, is due to the Old Testament which
entered deeply and significantly into the lives of men and
women over the centuries. The Old Testament tells the
story of the early beginnings of the Jewish people from the
time of the Creation at approximately 3760 B.C.; and it ends
with some details of the Maccabean insurrection during the
reign of King Antiochus IV (175 B.C.–163 B.C.). This covers
a period of more than thirty-five hundred years. The fact
that Christianity eventually made all the Hebrew literature
a vital part of the sacred Scriptures of the churches explains,
in large measure, the widespread information about Judaism in its Biblical setting.

However, outside of the pages of the Bible the world
knows little about the development of the Jewish religion,
and what little is known is often untrue. In other words,
knowledge about Judaism is usually confined to the Biblical
period which embraces only one section or division of the
entire story. What happened to Judaism in the long ages
since the records of the Bible were closed has unfortunately
been a blank in the mind of the average person.

Interestingly enough, the investigations into the history
of the *Talmud* touched off a tremendous Christian enthusiasm in behalf of the new information that was now being
brought to light.[2] It was not a question of knowing more
about the Hebrew Old Testament (there were many books
on that subject), but an eager readiness to lay hold of something quite different, namely: the correct knowledge of the

---

[2] Among the illustrious Christians whose pioneer achievements matched
those of the Jewish experts in this field the following names loom large:
Herman L. Strack (1848–1922), Crawford H. Toy (1836–1919), George
Foote Moore (1851–1931), R. Travers Herford (1860–1950), W. O. E.
Oesterley (1866–1950), Herbert Danby (1889–1953). *See* Bibliography,
p. 203.

development of religion after the Old Testament period ended. A stretch of approximately four hundred years intervenes between the close of the Old Testament and the New Testament. What happened during those four centuries leading up to the birth of Christianity? And what happened to Judaism in the ages following Christianity's establishment?

Those who have studied the Bible are aware that something like a unified portrait shapes itself in an almost sculptural sense out of all the varied historical experiences contained in the Old Testament. What is equally true is that another portrait emerges from an altogether different set of circumstances (with new types and forms of literature) which developed after the close of the Biblical period. When the curtain of history comes down on the vast stage of the Old Testament it merely marks the end of Act I. But Judaism is not a one act play. What is hard for people to remember is the fact that the story did not end abruptly on the last page of the Old Testament. In other words, the Jewish religion did not go out of existence. To understand what happened after the completion of the Bible is the purpose of this book.

The *Talmud* is the Oral Law of Judaism reduced to written form. Consequently, one cannot understand the *Talmud* without gaining insight into the origin and development of the Oral Law. Our first task, therefore, is to understand the history of the Oral Law; for it is impossible to comprehend the *Talmud* by ignoring that phase of it. To begin with, one ought always draw a distinction between Judaism and the Hebrew religion. They are not the same. The Hebrew religion constitutes the faith and the practice of the Jewish people of the Biblical age whereas Judaism is the faith and practice of the Jewish people in the ages known as "post-Biblical." It was the Oral Law, perhaps more than any other factor, which created the difference. And that is why the Jews placed the *Talmud* on a basis equal to that of the Bible.

The Oral Law had its origins in Babylonia. It came about in this way: In the sixth century B.C. act one ended when King Nebuchadnezzar's armies destroyed Jerusalem. The theater of Jewish life was now quickly shifted from Palestine to far-off Babylonia. It was a dramatic transfer of activity from the west to the east; and it profoundly changed the old Hebrew religion into Judaism, a change from the simple belief of those living in the Judean hills into a universal faith.

The exiled Jews brought the heritage of the Old Testament with them into Babylonian captivity. To it they added the Oral Law. Of necessity this had to be, otherwise they could not have managed to alter their religion to fit the newer circumstances. In other words, the Oral Law grew during the Babylonian Exile as the answer of the Judean captives to survival. Once having called the Oral Law into existence it was the chief instrumentality in holding the Jewish people together in the long course of their unique experiences.

While the heritage of the Old Testament (act one) is everywhere appreciated, the purpose of this present book is to help the reader understand still another heritage: the one which extends beyond the Holy Scriptures. It is this other heritage—the second act—which has a beauty and value that is only half suspected even by those who are familiar with the story of the Bible.

UNDERSTANDING THE TALMUD

Part One

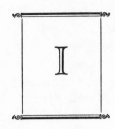

INTRODUCTION—THE BEGINNINGS
OF THE TALMUD

THE BABYLONIAN CONQUERORS permitted the Hebrews to carry but few possessions when they drove them into exile across the vast arid stretches of the desert. Among those things which the captive Hebrews brought to their new home in Babylonia the most precious was that sacred code which had been called by their forefathers the "Torah" (Pentateuch).[1]

Obviously these Hebrew writings (the Torah) had originated in Palestine long ago; they were designed as the religious and legal code for the people who lived on that small strip of land. But now, as a result of the destruction of their capital city, Jerusalem, the Hebrews found themselves hundreds of miles away from their national home. What distressed them was the fact that they could no longer carry out their sacred laws on foreign soil. Consequently, there arose a desperate need for a reinterpretation of their ancient religio-legal system so that there could be evolved out

---

[1] The Pentateuch is frequently designated as The Five Books of Moses, namely: Genesis, Exodus, Leviticus, Numbers, and Deuteronomy.

1

of the old laws (Pentateuch) a new set of ideas to meet the new conditions. Thus the very nature of the Babylonian Exile forced upon these captive Hebrews the necessity of rethinking their entire system of religion and jurisprudence. The fascinating elements of this rethinking process became the germinative seeds which eventually led to the origin of the *Talmud*.

❋   ❋   ❋

The first and most important task of the exiled people was to rearrange the fixed nature of their written code. They did this by evolving the concept of another law given by God to Moses on Mt. Sinai at the same time he gave their ancestors the written code. This parallel divine revelation came to be known as the "Oral Law." Belief in this Oral Law was based upon scriptural authority (Exodus 34.27): "And the LORD said to Moses, 'Write these words; in accordance with these words I have made a covenant with you and with Israel.' " [2]

The interpretation of this modest little text succeeded in adding an entirely new dimension to Scripture, and, of course, to the lives of these exiled people whose daily existence had been closely regulated by this sacred code "Write these words": Why the plural "these" if not to imply that two laws were given? Something additional was needed whereby the written law could be invested with new meanings. By searching their scriptures these Babylonian Jews were capable of forging for themselves the supreme instrument for their survival: that is, they had the right to interpret their Scriptures. This was an unheard-of thing in those far-off days; for in pagan religions, only the priesthoods were in charge of holy writings and "sacred" traditions. Scriptures of heathen peoples were strictly secret; no ple-

---

[2] The English word "tenor" used in some of the English translations of the Bible instead of "in accordance with" is a translation of the Hebrew phrase (*Al Peh*) meaning "by the mouth"—hence the Jews upheld the theory that the Oral Law was to be transmitted only by mouth. For centuries it was forbidden to write down any part of it.

bian had any access to them and had no right to interpret them. To a large extent this was true of the pre-exilic Hebrews. The sacred codes which make up the Pentateuch (Torah) had been the possession of the Jerusalem priesthood. But the experience of these people in captivity dramatically changed this situation; and that is why the Babylonian Exile became a turning point of greatest significance in world history; it was the cradle of new ideas and progressive forces.

In all probability these newer ideas would not have developed as rapidly as they did had not Cyrus, King of Persia, dealt Babylonia its death blow in 538 B.C. Shortly thereafter a royal Persian decree was issued permitting the exiled Jews to return to Palestine. The Bible records several waves of emigration going up from Babylonia to Judea. But the groups which returned to their homeland did not constitute large numbers; the majority of Babylonian Jews had by now adjusted themselves to Babylonian life and were comfortably settled in their new mode of living. Nonetheless these Babylonian Jews, having forged the concept of Biblical interpretation, were eager to see that the re-establishment of the Jewish commonwealth would embody those newer progressive principles they had come to cherish. Many elements which had been a vital part of the pre-exilic religion were now regarded as obsolete. For this reason the Babylonian community sent Ezra the Scribe to Palestine as the leader of an important mission.

Ezra arrived in Jerusalem as the head of a very large caravan in 457 B.C. Those things which he accomplished in the Holy City, in order to bring his Palestinian brethren within the newer framework set up by Babylonian Jewry, are a part of the Biblical record.[3] Perhaps the most important of his accomplishments was the inauguration of an Assembly which possessed the right to interpret the laws of the Pentateuch in the light of those progressive oral traditions which

---

[3] These records are contained in the Books of Ezra and Nehemiah which were originally one document.

had begun to evolve in Babylonia from the very earliest
days of the captivity.

*   *   *

Over the years the "Men of the Great Assembly," that came
to be their official title, regulated the affairs of the Jewish
people as the supreme religious and legal authority, not only
for Palestine, but for Jews wherever they were living in
lands remote from Judea. These spiritual leaders of the people were mostly scribes; they were expert Biblical scholars
who were specialists in the sacrosanct Written Law (Torah)
and yet were authorized to interpret and modify its many
archaic regulations to conform to the changing needs of the
times.

The history of the *Talmud* rightly begins with the Men of
the Great Assembly; the *Talmud* is their offspring, being
the literature which records the interpretations, changes,
and the modifications which they set in motion whereby the
religion of the Jewish people underwent profound altera-
tions. While none of the activities of the Great Assembly is
recorded in the Old Testament, the *Talmud* carries numerous references to the many things these men accomplished
in strengthening Judaism. These scribes were essentially
men of the synagogue. It is they who developed the synagogue as the institution of the laity as opposed to the one
great central Temple at Jerusalem which the priests regarded as their monopoly. And while it is true that the
Babylonians had called the synagogue into existence, it was
the Men of the Great Assembly who fostered it and made
it the home of those progressive oral traditions which came
to be known as the "Oral Law." [4] These men conferred upon
the synagogue the title *Beth ha-Midrash,* which literally
means the "House of Interpretation."

The Assembly continued its existence from the days of
Ezra the Scribe until the time of Alexander the Great (the

---

[4] In the Gospels the Oral Law is referred to as the "tradition of the
elders." (*See* Matthew 15.2, Mark 7.3-5.)

Greek period). When the Assembly died, due to the cataclysmic changes of that age, it was succeeded by the Sanhedrin. Talmudic literature is filled with the story of this newer council—the Sanhedrin—and yet perhaps no other jurisdictional body has been subjected to such wide-scale misunderstanding. Actually, as we now know the facts, the Sanhedrin was divided into two chambers: the upper house being composed of the priests and members of the aristocratic and wealthy classes, and the lower house made up largely from those people who had inherited the progressive oral traditions of the scribes. The leaders who followed the policies of the upper house came to be known as Sadducees, whereas those who composed the lower house were known as the Pharisees.

The many points of difference between the two houses form a most fascinating chapter of inter-Testament history. Much that has been written about the Pharisees and the Sadducees is sheer nonsense. What is true, however, and what constituted their main difference was the fact that the upper house denied the validity of the Oral Law, whereas the lower house vigorously championed it. In addition to this conflict over the status of the Oral Law, there were serious tensions between the growing prestige of the synagogues as against a diminishing respect towards the Temple and its decadent priesthood.

Eventually the question had to be settled as to who possessed the supreme authority in Judaism:—the priests or the lay-sages. For generations the battle over this problem seesawed. But the advancing power of the Pharisees left no doubt as to the eventual outcome. It had long been recognized that a higher form of Judaism—the Judaism that had been evolving in the synagogues—would some day predominate. Just how or when no one knew. After all, the Temple with its priesthood and elaborate ritual of animal sacrifice was a form laid down in the Divine Legislation (Pentateuch). The Pharisees no less than the Sadducees recognized that. But what the Pharisees possessed and the Sadducees lacked was a strong tradition of interpretation geared into the Pentateuch which could claim on the one hand that the Five Books of Moses (Torah) was a divinely perfect legislation, and yet proceed to give the Torah a kind of "advanced" meaning that would harmonize its obsolescence with a changing civilization. Because the Sadducees had rejected Scriptural interpretation as the key to the expansion of the law, they were incapable of meeting the forces of history as those forces were moving swiftly towards the great crisis of 70 A.D.

*   *   *

It was in the early spring of that fateful year, 70 A.D., that the Roman armies under Titus began to besiege Jerusalem. By midsummer they had breached its walls and swarmed within. The Romans immediately set fire to the entire city. Devoured by flames, the whole of Jerusalem, together with its great Temple, was burnt to the ground.

The Sadducees were completely lost. They had no program for continuity or survival. All their policies had been built around the fixed nature of the Pentateuch with its priests, its Temple, and the Jewish National State. Not so the Pharisees. They were prepared to meet the situation with great spiritual strength, ingenuity, and resourcefulness; for they were in possession of both the Oral Law and the Synagogue, which were capable of continuity irrespective of whether the National Jewish State existed or not.

With the Temple laid in ashes, and the upper house of the Sanhedrin wiped out, the re-organization of Judaism took place in a little seacoast town in southwestern Palestine called Jamnia. Here the Pharisees—the members of the lower house of the Sanhedrin—set up a continuing authority under the powerful personality of Jochanan ben Zakkai, who had long been their recognized leader in the last years before the holocaust of 70 A.D.

Since the days of Ezra, the Divine Law (Torah), both in its written and oral expression, had been the compelling center of gravity around which the progressive forces of Judaism had revolved. Now more than ever, the Oral Law came into its own; and this, of course, added impetus to the growth of the *Talmud*. With the destruction of the Temple, many old-time designations vanished. No longer did the Jewish people continue to use the words Pharisee and Sadducee. Even the reconstructed council over which Jochanan ben Zakkai presided was not called Sanhedrin but *Beth Din* meaning "Court.

Jamnia, therefore, and not Jerusalem, became the center of Judaism. As one of the great places of the *Talmud* the fame of this small village may be compared to the significance of Independence Hall in the formative period of American history. Here, within the walls of Jamnia, there arose a new personality—the rabbi, the authoritative religious layman.[5] The rabbi was the immediate product of the new order and at the same time the direct inheritor of Pharisaic Judaism. And inasmuch as Pharisaic Judaism had championed the growth of the Oral Law, it is understandable why the *Talmud* is frequently called "rabbinic literature."

* * *

Jochanan ben Zakkai chose as his successor for the High Court (*Beth Din*) Gamaliel II who was given the official title "Patriarch." He was the grandson of Gamaliel I at whose feet Paul had studied the Written and Oral Law.[6] Immediately upon assuming his official duties Gamaliel II turned his attention to the problem of achieving for Judaism: (1) a greater central authority, and (2) a more precise definition of the religio-legal rules of Judaism especially now that the Jewish people had to get along without a Temple, a priesthood, and a National State of their own. These

---

[5] The word rabbi is derived from the Hebrew noun *Rav* which means "great" or "distinguished." As the authoritative teacher of the law (both in its written and oral form) he became the head of the Jewish community wherever Jews established a synagogue.

[6] Gamaliel I is mentioned twice in the New Testament (Acts 5.34; 22.3).

religio-legal rules came to be known as *Halakah* and they form a very large part of the *Talmud*. Some Halakic rules are quite old, going back to the times of Ezra and the early days of the men of the Great Assembly. But the bulk of the *Halakah* as we find it in the *Talmud* is made up of those rules which developed with great rapidity from the time of Gamaliel II until the *Talmud* was brought to a conclusion in the sixth century A.D.

The destruction of the Jewish National State and the burning of the Temple necessitated tremendous changes of a structural nature. Many old regulations had to be abolished. The High Court at Jamnia also took upon itself the power to suspend certain Biblical laws which were either obsolete or incapable of being fulfilled due to changed conditions. Of the many prohibitions abrogated by the rabbis none benefitted Judaism more than setting aside the age-old tradition against putting the Oral Law into written form. Despite the fact that for centuries it was regarded as a serious transgression of Judaism to commit any part of the Oral Law into writing, the demands of the new age were entirely too compelling to be denied. The time had now come when the memory of the sages (even as it was trained in those days) could no longer hold the vast accumulation by oral transmission. Since the destruction of the Temple, the growth of the Oral Law, and the extensions of its principles, mushroomed into a huge bulk. Individual teachers, jurists, and disciples resorted to jotting down various aspects of the Oral Law as aids to memory. From such beginnings as these arose the vast literature of the *Talmud*.

THE TALMUD: THE STORY OF
THE MISHNAH

THE *Talmud* is the Oral Law of the Jewish people reduced
to written form. Much of it is anonymous; and it has
come down to us in two distinct parts. The first and oldest
part is called the *Mishnah*—being the text of the *Talmud*.
The second part is called the *Gemara*—being the commentary upon the text.[1]

At first this writing was done surreptiously and in defiance of tradition. But the crying need of getting some portions of the Oral Law into written form became such a
recognized necessity that within a few years after Jochanan
ben Zakkai established the Academy-Council (*Beth Din*),
at Jamnia there were floating about Palestine a number of
private collections of this or that aspect of the Oral Law.
This, to be sure, was a calculated disregard of the rigid prohibition against writing down any part of it. So widespread
had become the infraction of the law that it had to be justified. And justified it was by the principle:—"It is better

---

[1] The word *Mishnah* means "repetition" because the Oral Law had to
be memorized and repeated from generation to generation with verbal
accuracy.

9

that one letter of the Torah be uprooted than that the whole
Torah be forgotten." [2]

Once having broken the prohibition against writing, a
number of the most distinguished sages felt free to draw up
their own digests of the Oral Law. These digests were uneven in their scope and authority, and in many parts even
discrepant. Naturally they were based upon old materials.
It is said that even the arrangement of this material into
six categories had been determined long ago by Hillel himself. Among the many digests claiming the attention of people there were already two that had now achieved great importance:

1. the *Mishnah* of Rabbi Akiba and 2. the *Mishnah* of Rabbi
   Meir.

It was inevitable that a time would come when all these
private *Mishnah* collections would have to be gathered together, properly organized, edited, and issued as a single
code. The times now needed some one who could clarify
the entire system of the Oral Law. What with different
rabbis using various collections the need for a standardized
version that could give the right answer to any one who
wanted to know the law on a given subject became an im-
perative necessity. Although several important rabbis had
tried their hands at the task of compiling the standardized
Mishnah it was not until Rabbi Judah, "the Prince" (132–
217 A.D.) became patriarch that the work was successfully
achieved.

Who was this great rabbi called "the Prince"? How did
he manage to succeed in a field where others had failed?

Being of the House of Hillel he inherited his position as
patriarch of the Jews upon the death of his father, Gamaliel
II. From his youth he had demonstrated extraordinary powers of both scholarship and statesmanship which distinguished him through a long life of service to his people.
"I have learned much from my teachers," he once said with

---

[2] *Talmud*, tractate *Temurah* 14b

characteristic humility; and then he added: "I have learnt even more from my friends, but I have learnt most from my pupils." The eminence of Judah's position, combined with his great wealth, enabled him to gather together a large staff of scholars to assist in the sacred task of collecting, arranging, grouping, and editing the Oral Law. Such a massive effort required an unusual organizing skill which Rabbi Judah shared with the sages of his *Beth-Din* who were just as eager as he to see uniformity established.

When Rabbi Judah finally redacted his *Mishnah* it appeared in six categories (or "Orders"). This sixfold arrangement was used because that had been the manner in which the Oral Law had been discussed in the academies since the days of Hillel and Shammai. These Six Orders (they may just as well be called six "categories" or six "divisions") were divided into tractates as follows:

SEEDS (*Zeraim*). This Order deals with the ritual laws relative to the cultivation of the soil. It contains eleven tractates:

1. Blessings (*Berachoth*). Liturgical rules.
2. Corner (*Peah*). Corners and gleanings of the fields. Forgotten sheaves, olives, and grapes left for the poor. The laws of this tractate are based upon Leviticus 19.9-11 and Deuteronomy 24.19-22.
3. Doubtful (*Demai*). What to do about doubtful fruits— that is when an uncertainty exists about produce which has not been tithed.
4. Mixtures (*Kilayim*). Deals with prohibited mixtures in animals, plants, and garments based upon Leviticus 19.19 and Deuteronomy 22.9-12.
5. Sabbatical Year (*Sheviith*). This tractate deals with the land during the seventh year, the year in which the land is to rest. The laws of this tractate are based upon Exodus 23.10-12; Leviticus 20-23, 25.2-8; Deuteronomy 15.1-4.
6. Heave Offerings (*Terumoth*). This tractate goes into detail about many aspects of the heave offering. It enumerates five classes of persons who may not make the heave offering. It lays down the rules indicating from what sacrifices the heave offering may not be taken. Cases in

which the heave offering is valid, and cases where it is
invalid, etc. The laws of this tractate are based upon
Numbers 18.8, 12, 24, 26; Deuteronomy 18.4.

7. Tithes (*Maaseroth*). This tractate deals with the tithes to
be given to the Levites. It concerns itself also with those
products which are not subject to tithes. The laws set
down here are based upon Leviticus 21.3-33; Numbers
18.21-26.

8. Second Tithe (*Maaser Sheni*). That which remained after
the first tithe was taken was called the "Second Tithe."
It was to be taken to Jerusalem and there consumed by
the landowner and his family. The laws of this tractate
are based upon Leviticus 27.30; Deuteronomy 14.22-29,
26.12.

9. Dough (*Challah*). This tractate deals with those cereals
which fall into the category of *Challah*—that is the priest's
share of the dough. Laws pertaining to the required quantity to be given by the baker to the priests. The laws of
this tractate are based upon Numbers 15.18-21.

10. Uncircumcised (*Orlah*). In this tractate the word "uncircumcised" has a special meaning. It means that which is
rejected (in an agricultural sense). Here it is based upon
the law of Leviticus 19.23-26 which forbids the eating
of the fruit of a young tree during the first three years
after planting.

11. First Fruits (*Bikkurim*). This tractate refers to the products mentioned in Deuteronomy 8.8—wheat, barley, grape,
fig, pomegranate. olive, and dates. The tractate treats of
those who are eligible to bring First Fruits as offerings
to the Temple. Also, it gives the rules when these fruits
are to be brought and in what seasons. Ceremonials in
connection with their presentation are also considered.
This tractate is based upon the Biblical legislation laid
down in Exodus 23.19; Deuteronomy 26.1-12.

FESTIVALS (*Moed*). All the tractates of this Order deal with the
rules and regulations regarding the Sabbath, high holydays,
and festivals. It contains twelve tractates:

1. Sabbath (*Shabbat*). Deals with Sabbath laws, predominantly the prohibitions against all forms of labor. The

laws of this tractate are elaborations of many Biblical laws. (*See* Exodus 16.22-30; 20.10; 23.12, etc.)

2. Combinations (*Erubin*). This tractate concerns itself with ways in which localities can be artificially combined so as to extend or enlarge the Sabbath boundary.

3. Passover (*P'sachim*). Sets forth the laws regulating the Passover.

4. Shekels (*Shekalim*). Its main subject is the Temple tax based upon Exodus 30.12-16.

5. The Day (*Yoma*). Deals with all that concerns the ritual of the Day of Atonement as celebrated in the ancient Temple. The rules and regulations contained in this tractate are based upon Leviticus 16.3-34; Numbers 29.7-11.

6. Booths (*Succa*). The laws concerning the Festival of Booths (or Tabernacles) are dealt with here. Their Biblical origin is given in Leviticus 23.34-43.

7. Egg (*Betzah*). This tractate derives its title from its opening word. However, it is also known as "holyday" which better indicates the nature of its contents. It concerns itself mostly with the different kinds of work allowed or prohibited on holydays. The Biblical laws underlying its regulations are based upon Exodus 12.16; Leviticus 23.3-36.

8. New Year (*Rosh Hashana*). Questions of the calendar are discussed here; but more especially the laws pertaining to the Jewish New Year. The basic Pentateuchal legislation upon which this tractate is based can be found in Leviticus 23.24; Numbers 29.1.

9. Fasting (*Ta'anith*). This concerns public fasts. The laws regarding them are discussed together with the liturgical directions.

10. Scroll (*Megillah*). This tractate is concerned with the reading of the Book of Esther and the observance of the Festival of Purim.

11. Minor Festival (*Moed Katan*). Deals with the regulations concerning the "intervening days" of Passover and Tabernacles. At the end of this tractate there is a section on mourning customs.

12. Festival Offering (*Chagigah*). Treats of private offering during the pilgrimage festivals. Based upon the Biblical laws of Exodus 23.14; Deuteronomy 16.16-18.

WOMEN (*Nashim*). This Order discusses marriage, divorce, and other phases of family life. It contains seven tractates:

1. Sisters-in-Law (*Yebamoth*). This tractate is concerned largely with regulations of Levirate marriage based upon Deuteronomy 25.5-10.
2. Marriage Deeds (*Kethuboth*). This tractate has for its subject rules, laws, and regulations pertaining to marriage deeds and marriage settlements. Divorce is also treated.
3. Vows (*Nedarim*). Deals with vows and their annulments, basing such rules upon Numbers 30.3-16.
4. Nazirite (*Nazir*). Treats of the laws concerning the Nazirite with reference to Numbers 6.2-21.
5. Adulteress (*Sotah*). Concerns itself with the "faithless wife." It gives the rules of procedure in case of a wife either actually or supposedly unfaithful. Numbers 5.11-31 is the basis for the laws of this tractate.
6. Divorces (*Gittin*). Contains rules relative to bills of divorce: the procedure involved in delivering them, their preparation, attestation, etc. All these regulations are built upon Deuteronomy 24.1-5.
7. Betrothals (*Kiddushin*). This tractate devotes itself chiefly to a consideration of the various modes of betrothal and the conditions which must be fulfilled to make a marriage valid.

DAMAGES (*Nezikin*). This Order deals largely but not exclusively with injuries and claims for damages. It contains ten tractates:

1. First Gate (*Baba Kamma*). This first tractate of the "gates" deals with compensation on damages. The regulations provided here have their source in Exodus 21.28-37, 22.1-6.
2. Middle Gate (*Baba Metzia*). Treats of man's responsibility with regard to the property of his fellowman. It covers the subjects of found property, trusts, buying, selling, lending, hiring, renting. The decisions of this tractate are based upon Exodus 22.6-14, 24-27; Leviticus 25.14, 35-38; Deuteronomy 22.1-4.
3. Last Gate (*Baba Bathra*). Deals with real estate, commerce, laws of tenantry, joint tenants, inheritance, and

division of property. The laws of inheritance are based upon Numbers 27.7-11 as interpreted by tradition.

4. Courts (*Sanhedrin*). Deals with the constitution and procedures of courts of justice and the administration of criminal law.

5. Stripes (*Makkoth*). Concerns itself with crimes punishable by stripes. Discusses false witnesses, cities of refuge, etc. The 39 stripes of corporal punishment have a Biblical basis in Deuteronomy 25.1-3. The punishment of false witnesses has its basis in Deuteronomy 19.16-19. The laws of the cities of refuge derive from Numbers 35.10-32. Also of value to this tractate are the laws of Deuteronomy 19.1-13.

6. Oaths (*Shebu'oth*). Different kinds of oaths are considered in relation to their judicial validity. All these considerations are based upon Exodus 22.6-10; Leviticus 5.4-6, 6.2-4.

7. Testimonies (*Eduyoth*). Here is gathered together the testimonies of many sages. Oral laws and decisions which trustworthy teachers derived from their elders are given in detail. Also the opposing opinions of Hillel and Shammai are recorded on a variety of subjects.

8. Idolatry (*Abodah Zarah*). Contains the regulations which should govern Jews towards idolatry and contact with pagan peoples.

9. Sayings of the Fathers (*Aboth*).[3] Contains a collection of ethical maxims of the rabbis. It is the one tractate in the *Mishnah* that deals with moral conduct instead of legal requirements.

10. Decisions (*Horayoth*). Deals with the problems arising out of wrong decisions. It is based upon Leviticus 4 and 5.

SACRED THINGS (*Kodashim*). This Order contains regulations and laws concerning sacrifices, priestly contributions, and other matters pertaining to the ancient Temple and its ritual. It is made up of eleven tractates:

1. Sacrifices (*Zebachim*). Treats of animal sacrifice, regulations for killing sacrificial animals. Valid and invalid sacrifices. How priests partake of them, etc. The Biblical

---

[3] For full text of *Aboth see* pp. 161ff.

basis for much of this tractate is to be found in Leviticus 1-4.

2. Meal Offerings (*Menahot*). Deals with the meal offering and its ingredients. Also discusses peace offerings, the wave offerings, the shewbread, the pentecostal bread, and the drink offering. The Biblical basis for this tractate is Leviticus 2.

3. Profane Things. (*Chullin*). Deals with regulations concerning the slaughter of animals for ordinary domestic (nonsacrificial) use. The dietary laws are elaborated.

4. First-born (*Bekoroth*). The first-born of animals are considered. Blemishes on the first-born which make them unfit for sacrifice. The first-born among animals leads to a discussion of the first-born among men, consequently the rights of the first-born son in regard to inheritance. The Biblical legislation which supports this tractate can be found in Exodus 8.12-14, 13.2, 12; Numbers 18.15-19; Deuteronomy 15.19-21.

5. Evaluations (*Arakin*). Rules for determining the amount which must be given to redeem one pledged to God. Persons or things dedicated to the Lord by a vow are estimated in order to be redeemed according to Biblical principles laid down in Leviticus 27.2-27.

6. Exchange (*Temurah*). Deals with the laws regarding the substitution of a nonsacred animal for one already dedicated to the altar. Ways in which sacred things are exchanged. Exchange in case of a sin offering, etc. (*See* Leviticus 27.10-27.)

7. Excisions (*Kerithuth*). Treats of offenders being "cut off" from the Lord if their sins were wantonly committed. How guilt offerings and sin offerings are to be brought in the event the offense was inadvertently committed. The Biblical origin for the penalty of excision (*karat*) is based upon the following: Genesis 17.14; Exodus 12.15; Leviticus 27.10-27.

8. Trespass (*Me'ilah*). When things, which belong to the Temple or altar, are used for secular purposes there is involved a sacrilege. This tractate gives many regulations concerning such trespasses. (*See* Leviticus 5.15-17.)

9. Daily Sacrifice (*Tamid*). Gives details relating to the

ritual of the daily burnt offering. Based upon Exodus 29.38-42; Numbers 28.2-8.

10. Measurements (*Middoth*). Gives measurements and descriptions relative to the size, shape, and structure of the Temple. Valuable knowledge is preserved in this tractate relative to the Temple's separate parts such as its many courts, porches, and chambers.

11. Birds' Nest (*Kinnim*). Treats of sacrifices of fowl. Dove offerings (pigeons) which were brought by indigent women after confinement. Also the use of doves (instead of lambs) by such of the poor who had committed any of the trespasses listed in Leviticus 5.1ff. (*See also* Leviticus 1.14, 12.8, 14.22-31, 15.14-30; Numbers 6.9.)

PURIFICATIONS (*Toharoth*). All the tractates of this Order deal with the subject of uncleanliness and the laws governing impurity. There are twelve tractates:

1. Vessels (*Kaylim*). Ritual uncleanness is the subject of this tractate as it applies to beds, furniture, garments, and utensils of various kinds. The underlying religio-legal structure is based upon Leviticus 11.33-36. (*See also* Numbers 19.14ff, 31.20ff.)

2. Tents (*Ohaloth*). Treats of defilement through a dead human body or through the dead body of an animal which may arise in connection with tents and any other habitations. Different degrees of uncleanness considered, the highest being that of a corpse which defiles everything in the same room. The regulations of this tractate are based upon Numbers 19.14-23.

3. Leprosy (*Negaim*). Concerns itself with leprosy in its various degrees, and the infection of clothing and dwellings in contact with it. Signs of leprosy. Purification of a leper, etc. Based upon Leviticus 13 and 14.

4. Heifer (*Parah*). Directs how the "red cow" (heifer) is to be burned and its ashes mixed with water so that the compound may be used to sprinkle and cleanse any one who becomes unclean. Deals with the required age of the red heifer, characteristics, preparation for slaughter, etc. The whole procedure was surrounded by very strict ceremonies. Based upon Numbers 19.

5. Purifications (*Toharoth*). This tractate concerns itself with all those lesser degrees of uncleanness which last only until sunset. Based upon Leviticus 11.24-28.

6. Reservoirs (*Mikwa'oth*). Deals with baths, cisterns, wells, reservoirs, ponds, ditches, or any pool of water, if to be used for ritual purification. The Pentateuch prescribes a bath for lepers (Leviticus 14.9) and for persons suffering from other diseases (Leviticus 15).

7. Menstruant (*Niddah*). Deals with the separation of women during their menstrual period. Also ritual uncleanness after childbirth. Regulations governing the woman's purification after menstruation and her ritual bath. The laws of this tractate are based upon Leviticus 12.2-8, 15.19-31.

8. Preparations (*Makshirin*). Deals with liquids that may pollute seeds, fruits, and other foods. The liquids may be of seven kinds:—dew, water, wine, oil, blood, milk, and honey. Water is understood to include discharges of the eye, ear, and other organs. The regulations of this tractate are based upon Leviticus 11.34-39.

9. Sufferers with Gonorrhea (*Zabim*). Deals with the impurity attached to persons afflicted with running issues. Anything upon which the sufferer sits, lies, or rides is unclean. Discusses various forms of contact which render other persons unclean. Treats of washing, bathing, and purification. Based upon Leviticus 15.2-18.

10. Immersed at Daytime (*T'bul Yom*). Laws affecting a person who has already taken the ritual bath but has to await the coming of sunset before he can be regarded as completely free from defilement. (*See* Leviticus 15.5, 22.6-8.)

11. Hands (*Yadayim*). Treats of washing of hands ritually according to the Oral Law. The quantity of water necessary to cleanse the hands. Kinds of water which may not be used. Things which render the hands unclean.

12. Stalks (*Uktzin*). Deals with the question how far the roots, hulls, and stalks of fruits and plants may be considered as "connectives"—that is, capable of conveying impurity when touched by anything unclean. For, if such a part suffers uncleanness, it then conveys defilement to the edible parts. There are no Biblical laws supporting the regula-

tions of this tractate. It is wholly a product of rabbinical
thinking.

* * *

Fortunately, Rabbi Judah's *Mishnah* preserved some very
old material of the Oral Law. We have already seen how
many traditions, even though they were not written down,
go back as far as the days of Ezra and the Men of the Great
Assembly. For the most part these hoary traditions, which
Rabbi Judah assiduously gathered from older collections,
were considered too sacred to be tampered with. This explains in part why the *Mishnah* preserves much that had
long been obsolete even to the Jews of Rabbi Judah's generation. His work manifests a veneration for tradition which
has always been an important insistence of Judaism. The
determination to preserve every aspect of the Oral Law,
even as it pertained to the nonexistent Temple, was a part
of a persistent hope of national restoration. More than half
the *Mishnah* deals with the procedures, rules, laws, and regulations of the Temple which had been destroyed in 70 A.D.
(Curiously enough, in retrospect the old Temple though in
ruins exerted upon the Jewish people a tremendous influence; it became the symbol of their great past.) Thus, although the Temple had been demolished over one hundred
and forty years before the *Mishnah* was redacted, nonetheless so powerful was the romanticism towards it that every
aspect of its ritual was carefully preserved. For this reason
it is possible for a master of the *Mishnah* to pick out the
earlier parts of the material, for they are able to be distinguished because of their ancient modes of expression.

This shaping together of various old collections into one
orderly code is not the only reason why Rabbi Judah's *Mishnah* became authoritative. One of the most significant reasons for the conspicuous success of his work can be attributed to the fact that Rabbi Judah was the patriarch of the
Jews—that is, the hereditary ruler whose authority and prestige were recognized by Rome. But even this would not

have carried his *Mishnah* to such exalted heights had it not been for the fact that he engaged many sages for the undertaking of this sacred task. These scholars were consulted at each step of the way as the great work progressed. It is because many sages, not merely one, were the architects of this edifice that Rabbi Judah's *Mishnah* was universally adopted shortly after it made its appearance approximately about 217 A.D. In all probability the major part of the redactional work took place in a city called Bet She'arim located in the Galilee section of Palestine; for it was here that Rabbi Judah had established the seat of his patriarchate during the most significant years of his spiritual leadership.[4]

The shaping of the *Mishnah* took place during the years that Christianity was developing its New Testament. These were the years (the first and second century) when all peoples, who were in any manner touched by the ancient Judaic traditions, felt that it was necessary to possess some authoritative literature in addition to the Old Testament. Christian leaders satisfied this yearning among their people with the New Testament at the same time that Jewish leaders were satisfying a similar yearning among their people with Jewish literature called the *Mishnah*. In other words, the *Mishnah*—not the Gospels—became the new testament of the Jewish people. Now that the Oral Law had made its appearance in written form its authority became immediately available to all. Thus the rules, customs, and interpretations which had developed over the centuries achieved a status equal to the Pentateuch (Torah). In many respects it was claimed that the *Mishnah* was more important than the Pentateuch (just as the claim was being set forth by Christians that the New Testament was in many respects more important than the entire Old Testament). Of course, the reason for these claims is not hard to understand. A liv-

---

[4] However, the last seventeen years of his life he spent at Sepphoris for health reasons because of its high altitude and pure air. Work on the *Mishnah* was accomplished here too. Rabbi Judah's presence in Sepphoris made it an important center for Judaism. At one time Sepphoris had been the capital of Galilee.

ing tradition inevitably comes to be considered more important than an archaic one, especially if that living tradition
claims to be the authentic continuity of the old. Thus the
Christians were claiming that the New Testament was the
rightful heir and essential complement of the Old Testament in the same manner that the rabbis were claiming
that the *Mishnah* occupied that position. Unlike the Gospels, which constituted a break with the traditional legal
system of Judaism, the *Mishnah* was unquestionably its authoritative continuation.

One of the major reasons why the *Mishnah* was reduced
to written form was the desire to offset the powerful propaganda of Christianity which was luring thousands of Jews
to the new faith. The sages of the *Mishnah* felt that they—
and not the writers of the Gospels—stood in the direct line
of Biblical succession, and that it was their solemn Jewish
duty to carry out in expanded form the true Mosaic tradition. Seeing that Christianity had definitely parted from
Judaism there now existed a need for some written medium
which could affirm the old faith and repudiate heresy—particularly in view of the fact that Christians were now claiming the Old Testament as their own. Moreover, the Christians were also saying that they (and not the Jews) were
God's chosen people. In the face of these Christian claims
the founders of the *Mishnah* insisted that the Jews were
still the true Israel not only according to the flesh but also
according to the spirit.[5]

Being a code of laws the *Mishnah* is brief and terse; and
inasmuch as it is made up of strands from many sources
there is considerable variation in its contents, style, form,
and character. In other words, the *Mishnah* does not follow
a single literary pattern. Had he chosen to do so Rabbi
Judah could have easily worked over the source materials
and reduced his *Mishnah* to a single standard of literary

---

[5] It is interesting to read Paul's contrary words coming from the heat of
this controversy: "For he is not a real Jew who is one outwardly . . . He
is a Jew who is one inwardly" (Romans 2.28, 29).

style. But he did not choose that method of handling the sources. Rather than recast these old laws and regulations in his own terms he adhered to the principle of retaining the old in the very words in which they had been repeated orally for generations. Following this principle of the retention of the old, it is interesting to note that Rabbi Judah incorporated many traditional laws even when those rules or regulations had later been repudiated. So great was his sense of fairness, because of his reverence of the Oral Law, that he did not omit or suppress the views of any sage even though the ruling in question had been declared wrong by the highest authorities. Divergencies of opinion as well as opposing legal views were considered a significant part of the Jewish heritage and an exceedingly important element in preventing an unwarranted religious dictatorship.

Obviously the *Mishnah* is not systematically written according to twentieth century standards, nor was the arrangement of its materials designed to catch the interest of the modern reader. Consequently, it takes considerable time and scholarship to be able to grasp its style and method of presentation. (For this reason one ought not attempt a study of the *Mishnah* without the aid of a competent master.) Yet the *Mishnah* is more than a legal code, for its underlying structure is religious. This can be seen in the opening tractate called "Blessings," constituting the first section of the Order, SEEDS. This opening tractate deals with the prayers which are man's dues to God—dues which must be paid before a person is free to go about his daily tasks. To be sure the Order, SEEDS treats the laws governing the dues which a man must separate from his crop before it is free for common use. These crop dues he is to give to the priests and Levites. But, interestingly enough, all the Mishnaic regulations embodied in the Order, SEEDS relative to "crop dues" are preceded by the laws governing prayers which are man's due to God. And such prayers include all the benedictions over food which a man must pronounce before he is allowed to partake of it. Thus the spirit of the *Mishnah* based upon the Bible carries forward in expanded form the religio-ethical-legal spirit of the Old Testament. This accounts for the high moral tone of the *Mishnah* which is everywhere impressed in its Six Orders.

For one who is seeking in the *Mishnah* for something more than a precise formulation of ancient laws, the most important tractate is that small but highly valuable section called *Aboth* ("Sayings of the Fathers").[6] It forms a little Book of Ethics placed in the very center of the *Mishnah* telling us in no uncertain language that the soul of the law is the law of the soul. The "sayings" which comprise this tractate are maxims on morals handed down in the names of sixty illustrious sages of the law who lived between 300 B.C. and 200 A.D. *Aboth* is indeed the gem of the *Mishnah* and its wondrous luster has captivated the hearts of men and women in all ages. One would indeed have to be possessed of a determined antiquarian interest to plod through all the heavy religio-legalistic matters that compose the bulk of the Six Orders of the *Mishnah*.[7] Much of what is set down there has passed out of the thought and practice of Judaism. It would, of course, be just as erroneous to evaluate Judaism of today by the obsolete laws of the *Mishnah* as it would be to judge Judaism by the archaic legislation embedded in the Bible. But this does not apply to tractate *Aboth*. For here is a section of the *Mishnah* which has entered deeply into the minds of men over the centuries. There is nothing of a legalistic nature in *Aboth*. As the oldest collection of ethical maxims of the great sages its concern is almost entirely with the subject of moral conduct. If one wishes to understand the true spiritual-ethical atmosphere of the Jewish people at this time (the atmosphere which Jesus and his disciples breathed) he should read

---

[6] Inasmuch as Jewish sages (rabbis) were called "Fathers" it can readily be seen that here is to be found the origin of the Catholic Church's use of that term for its clergy.

[7] An excellent English translation of the entire *Mishnah* (London 1933) may be obtained from the Oxford University Press. The translation is the work of the distinguished British scholar, Rev. Herbert Danby.

Aboth.[8] It represents the distilled essence of the wisdom, teaching, and experience of the rabbis. No wonder that the whole tractate of *Aboth* was incorporated into the Prayer Book of the synagogue. This is in itself a unique phenomenon, for at no time did the Jewish people ever incorporate a complete work of any kind into the body of the Prayer Book—not even the Book of Psalms.

---

[8] *Aboth* comes from approximately the same period as the Gospels. What the Sermon on the Mount has meant to Christians in all ages that is what *Aboth* has meant to Jews. (*See* pp. 15, 161.)

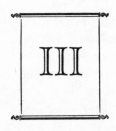

THE GEMARA—ORIGIN AND GROWTH

IT HAS OFTEN BEEN SAID that a law code is the clock that
tells what time it is in the civilization of a people. If this
be true it can easily be seen that the hands of the Judaic
clock, as indicated by the *Mishnah,* had moved a long ways
from the Biblical legislation laid down in the Pentateuch
. . . And now those hands were destined to move again.

✳   ✳   ✳

No sooner had the *Mishnah* become the authoritative code
of Judaism when the need arose to interpret its laws. Like
the Bible before it, the *Mishnah* now became the predom-
inant object of constant study, research, and exposition.
What with a rapidly changing society it was no more possible for the *Mishnah* to meet all conceivable cases than it
had been for the Pentateuch to be all comprehensive. The
rabbis and their academies were called upon to settle new
cases for which there was often not a single answer to be
found in the *Mishnah.* Fresh problems were arising, some of
a purely legal nature and some religious. All these were
brought to the academies for decision. To provide for new
situations, to regulate and settle questions bearing upon all

phases of public and private life, it became necessary to expand and interpret the laws of the *Mishnah*. To this end newer methods of interpretation were evolved. As the study of the law proceeded it continually yielded new meanings. And so there developed a considerable number of "Rules of Interpretation" that went far beyond the original Seven Rules laid down by Hillel.[1]

So great was the reverence towards Jewish law that even the most obsolete aspects of it were discussed and expounded as though they had relevance and validity. The old was never discarded. The growth of Jewish law may be compared to the geological formations of the earth in which every new stratum merely covered but did not remove the old layers. This phenomenon--the relationships of the old to the new—was made possible by the sages who used their ingenuity to develop rules of interpretation which could read newer meanings into the older laws. The problem of how to find new decisions for unprecedented cases was solved in this manner. And above all, the proper sanction was given to new regulations. In their own way the rabbis showed that they possessed the capacity to respond to changing conditions and yet hold on to permanent truths. The old within Judaism always retains its unmistakable identity. For this reason one must be cautious not to identify the ongoing process of the Jewish Religion with those aspects of it which are admittedly primitive or obsolete.

*   *   *

So much of the *Mishnah* is very brief and concise in style that of necessity the whole code had to be subjected to interpretation, not only with the idea of keeping alive the true understanding of the Mishnaic text, but with the further objective in view of applying the knowledge of its basic laws to new conditions. Consequently, vast materials of a

---

[1] These additional rules were called "Hermeneutic Principles." (*See* p. 191.) Interpretation was always the effective instrument in adapting Jewish law to meet new and unprecedented situations.

commentary nature arose. This new body of religio-legal thinking came to be called *Gemara*—for this was the general name applied to all this new juristic activity which regarded itself as an explanation of the *Mishnah*. Because of its nature as a commentary the *Gemara* is full of debate, opinion, questions and answers. Passage after passage of the *Mishnah* is quoted and then followed by broad discussion until a decision is finally reached. For example, here is a specimen illustration taken from the opening discussion of the tractate *Baba Metzia* which is a part of the ORDER DAMAGES (*Nezikin*).

THE MISHNAH TEXT: Two persons appear before a court. They hold a garment. One of them says "I found it." And the other says "I found it." One of them says "It is all mine" and the other says "It is all mine." Each must take an oath that he claims not less than one half of it. Then the value of the garment shall be divided between them. If one says "It is all mine" and the other says "Half of it is mine" then he who says "it is all mine" must take an oath that he claims not less than three quarters. He who says "half of it is mine" shall swear that his claim is not less than one quarter. The former then receives three quarters of the value of the garment and the latter receives one quarter.[2]

If two ride on an animal, or one rides and the other leads it, and one of them says "It is all mine," and the other says "It is all mine" then the one shall take an oath that he claims not less than half of it; and the other shall take an oath that his share in it is not less than half. The value of the animal shall then be divided between them. If both admit each other's claims, or if they have witnesses to establish their claims then they may divide it without taking an oath.

THE GEMARA COMMENTARY:[3] What need is there for the *Mishnah* to give two pleas of the litigants and state:—"One

---

[2] Thus each gets one quarter less than he originally claimed.

[3] The *Gemara* commentary on this one *Mishnah* text ranges over forty-eight pages of solid reading matter as the reader can see for himself if he will consult the authorized English translation of this tractate as it appears in the Soncino Edition (London 1935). It is not necessary for our present purpose to quote the entire length of this *Gemara* commentary. Only a

of them says I found it and the other says I found it. One of them says it is all mine and the other says it is all mine"? Surely one plea would have been sufficient. Actually it is only one plea. One says I found it, and therefore it is all mine—and the other says I found it, and therefore it is all mine. But why not just state "I found it" and it will be understood that the intention is to claim the whole garment? The term "I found it" might have been explained as denoting "I saw it," the mere seeing of the garment entitling him to claim it as his possession. Therefore the plea "it is all mine" is added, so as to make clear that seeing alone does not constitute a claim. But how could it be thought that one who has only seen the garment could plead "I found it"? Does not *Rabboni* say that the phrase "and you find it" (Deuteronomy 22.3) means "you have taken hold of it"? It is admitted that the Scriptural use of the term "find" implies having taken hold.

But the *tanna* (the sage) uses popular language, in which, on seeing something, one might use the term "found it"—the belief being prevalent that one acquires a lost article by sight alone. For this reason it was necessary to add the plea "It is all mine" and thus to indicate that the mere seeing of an ownerless object constitutes no claim to possession. But even so, would it not have been sufficient to state "It is all mine" without the plea "I found it"? Had the *Mishnah* stated only the plea "It is all mine" I might have said that elsewhere in the *Talmud* the term "found" is used to mean "seen"; and the conclusion would have been drawn that mere sight constitutes a claim to possession. For this reason the *Mishnah* states first "I found it" and then "it is all mine," so that we may gather from the additional clause that mere sight does not constitute a claim to possession.

But how could you say that the two pleas are really one? Is not each plea introduced by the words: "One of them says I found it and the other says I found it—One says it is all mine and the other says it is all mine"? To this Rabbi Papa and Rabbi Shimi ben Ashi—or, as some say Kadi, replied:— The first plea applies to a case of finding, but the second plea applies to a case of buying and selling. And it is necessary to

small portion of it will be given here, but enough to give the reader an understanding of the nature of the *Gemara*.

have the two cases. For if the *tanna* (the sage) had dealt solely with the case of finding I might have said that only in such a case would the rabbis impose an oath, because each disputant might permit himself to claim the garment by saying to himself: "My neighbor loses nothing through my action as it cost him nothing to acquire the garment, I shall go and take hold of it and share it with him." But in the case of a bought article, where this argument does not apply it might be assumed that no oath was to be imposed. On the other hand, had the *tanna* (the sage) dealt solely with a case of buying and selling, it might be assumed that only in such a case would the rabbis impose an oath, because each disputant might permit himself to claim the garment by saying to himself, "My neighbor has paid the price and I am prepared to pay the price; seeing that I need it I shall take it, and let my neighbor take the trouble to go and buy another garment." But in the case of a found article, where this argument does not apply, it might be assumed that no oath was to be imposed. Therefore both cases are necessary . . . But does not Rabbah the son of Rabbi Huna maintain that Symmachus' decision applies also to a case where both parties are certain and definite in their claims? For Symmachus expressed the view only in a case where a verdict in favor of one would involve a loss to another; but where no actual monetary loss is involved he would take a different view . . . For the oath imposed upon disputants is only rabbinical, not Biblical. This is expressly maintained by Rabbi Johanan. For Rabbi Johanan says: This oath is an institution of the sages, intended to prevent any one from going out and seizing a neighbor's garment, declaring it to be his own . . . But according to Rabbi Shesheth there is a difficulty about our Mishnaic text. Rabbi Shesheth may reply: "The oath requirement in the *Mishnah* is an institution of the rabbis and not Biblical." However his opponent will say: "Yes, it is an institution of the rabbis: but if you maintain that according to Biblical law the offer of 'Here they are' carries with it an oath, then it is right that the rabbis imposed an oath upon the litigants, for they follow herein the principle underlying the Biblical law. But if you say that the offer of 'Here they are' exempts, according to Biblical law, the debtor who made it from taking an oath, then how can the rabbis impose an oath which is unlike any Biblical oath?"

The above specimen shows us how the *Gemara* introduces citations from old debates like those of Rabbah the son of Rabbi Huna when he appealed to Symmachus' decision. Whenever necessary the *Gemara* will not hesitate to quote the interpretation of some great teacher. Our specimen illustration does exactly that when it brings in the words of *Rabboni* to bear upon the interpretation of Deuteronomy 22.3. Very frequently too, the *Gemara* will introduce supplementary matters which have nothing to do with the strict legal aspects of the subject under discussion. These nonlegal matters, which constitute a most fascinating digression, amount to about one third of the bulk of the *Gemara*. The general term used for all these nonlegal interests is *Haggadah*, which embraces such things as history, legend, parables, folklore, and bits of scientific information upon a variety of topics like medicine, astronomy, and mathematics. *Haggadah* is a whole vast world in itself; and while it is enmeshed with the *Halakah* (the legal side) of the *Gemara*, it merits separate treatment because much of it is relevant to twentieth century man.[4]

The *Gemara*—like the Bible and the *Mishnah*—is made up of a great deal of accumulated material. Its literary history follows closely upon the pattern of the *Mishnah*, namely: centuries of oral transmission followed by efforts to reduce these materials to written form. Not one author, nor several authors, but many successive generations of authors labored to make the *Gemara* what it finally became. The manifold additions which the *Gemara* adds to the *Mishnah* have made the entire literature of the *Talmud* (which, of course, embraces both *Mishnah* and *Gemara*) a most imposing legal edifice.

---

[4] Because of the importance of the *Haggadah* in the *Talmud*, a whole chapter is being devoted to it in this book. (*See* pp. 57-97.)

Our second specimen of the *Gemara* is taken from tractate *Yoma* which appears in Order FESTIVALS (*Moed*). As the *Talmud* was originally not printed in book form but only on scrolls of parchment written by hand, the method used was to present the *Mishnah* text approximately in the middle of the manuscript page and then surround the text by its *Gemara* commentary. In subsequent ages there grew up commentary after commentary upon the *Gemara* in which the Mishnaic text became engulfed. With this understanding let us now proceed to the *Gemara* commentary under consideration which is based upon the *Mishnah, Yoma* 8.6, 7.

MISHNAH TEXT: If one is seized by a ravenous hunger he may be given to eat even unclean things until his eyes are no longer dull. If one was bit by a mad dog he may not give him to eat the lobe of its liver. But Rabbi Matthia ben Heresh permits it. Furthermore did Rabbi Heresh say: If one has pain in his throat he may pour medicine into his mouth on the Sabbath because it is a possibility of danger to human life—and every danger to human life suspends the laws of the Sabbath. If debris fall on some one, and it is doubtful whether or not he is there, or whether he is alive or dead, or whether he be an Israelite or a heathen, one should open even on the Sabbath the heap of debris for his sake. If one finds him alive one should remove the debris. And if he be dead one should leave him there until the Sabbath Day is over.

THE GEMARA COMMENTARY: [5] Our Rabbis taught: one must remove debris to save a life on the Sabbath, and the more eager one is, the more praiseworthy is one; and one need not obtain permission from the *Beth Din* (court of religious authorities). How so? If one saw a child falling into the sea, he spreads a net and brings it up, the faster the better. He need not obtain permission from the *Beth Din* though he thereby catches fish in his net. If he saw a child fall into a pit, he breaks loose one segment of the entrenchment and pulls it up, the faster the better; and he need not obtain permission

---

[5] Only a portion of the *Gemara* Commentary is given here in order to present the sense of the principles involved.

of the *Beth Din,* even though he is thereby working to make a step (stairs). If he saw a door closing upon an infant, he may break it, so to get the child out, the faster the better. And he need not obtain permission of the *Beth Din,* though he thereby consciously makes chips of wood. One may extinguish and isolate the fire in case of a conflagration, the sooner the better. He need not obtain permission from the *Beth Din,* even though he works to subdue the flames. Now all these cases must be mentioned separately; for if only the case of the infant falling into the sea had been mentioned one would think that it is permitted there, but does not apply in the case of falling in the pit, etc. etc. . . . Rabbi Ishmael, Rabbi Akiba, and Rabbi Eleazar ben Azariah were once on a journey with Levi ha-Saddar with the son of Rabbi Azariah following them. Then this question was asked: Whence do we know that in the case of danger to human life the laws of the Sabbath are suspended? Rabbi Ishmael answered and said: "If a thief is found breaking in." [6] Now if in the case of this one it is doubtful whether he has come to take money or life; and although the shedding of blood pollutes the land, so that the *Shekinah* (the Divine Presence) departs from Israel, yet it is lawful to save oneself at the cost of his life. How much more then may one suspend the laws of the Sabbath to save human life! . . . If circumcision which attaches to one only of the two hundred and forty-eight members of the human body suspends the laws of the Sabbath how much more shall the saving of the whole body suspend the Sabbath! [7] . . . Rabbi Jonathan ben Joseph said: "Because it is holy for you" [8] meaning that the Sabbath is committed to your hands, not you to its hands . . . Rabbi Simeon ben Menassia said: "Wherefore the people of Israel shall keep the sabbath." [9] Obviously Scripture implies that to violate the laws of one Sabbath is permissable so that one may keep many Sabbaths.

---

[6] These words are from Exodus 22.2 and they are quoted by Rabbi Ishmael to indicate that in such a case, in spite of other considerations, it would be lawful to kill the thief.

[7] The point is that circumcision according to the Jewish religion must take place on the eighth day even if that day falls on the Sabbath thereby suspending the law of the Sabbath which prohibits work on that day.

[8] Exodus 31.14.

[9] Exodus 31.16.

Although the foregoing specimens are admittedly inadequate in a literature so vast, nonetheless the reader can easily see that the *Gemara* is not an independent work. Indeed, it is so wedded to the *Mishnah* text that both (*Mishnah* plus *Gemara*) are considered two sides of one and the same shield. That is why one term—*Talmud*—includes both.

Frequently the *Gemara* takes on the nature of a lecture hall. This can be felt in the very language of the *Gemara* whose vocabulary and idiom bear the stamp of colloquial usage. The *Gemara* is a heterogeneous mixture of contents and style where the discussions are sometimes smooth and calm—but also at times raucous with argument ending in stormy assertion and refutation. All this enables us to look into the world of the *Gemara* where its sages were trying to make clear to themselves the knowledge of their predecessors in order to apply the Mishnaic wisdom of former generations to the problem of their own age. For this reason the *Gemara* is full of notes—a veritable collection of detailed minutes in the elaborate discussions which filled the academies generation after generation. But the *Mishnah* was not only the text for lectures in the Jewish academies it was also the authoritative code for every Jewish house of worship (synagogue). And even more than that. The *Mishnah* became the authoritative code for every Jewish court which administered the civil and criminal law.

What is difficult for the modern reader to understand is this courtroom aspect of the *Gemara*. This brings up an interesting question: Were the rabbis also judges? Yes, they were. In the Jewish Religion no distinction was made, until comparatively recent times, between ceremonial law, civil law, moral law, and criminal law. All law was regarded as religious law going back in its origin to the revelation at Sinai. In the Bible all law is treated as religious law—and this holds true for the *Mishnah* and the *Gemara*. Furthermore, the modern reader must be prepared to understand that the Jewish people occupied the unique status of being a state-within-a-state during those centuries in which the

Mishnah and the *Gemara* were reduced to written form. The suzerain power, whether it was Rome, or Parthia, or Persia, granted the Jews large-scale autonomy which enabled them not only to carry on their own religion but permitted them to regulate their own internal affairs. This double system of government allowed the Jews their own jurisprudence in all phases of private and public life. Patriarchs, such as Rabbi Judah "the Prince," were temporal as well as spiritual rulers and their authority was recognized by the government. And when the patriarchs no longer ruled the Jews then their successors—those men who were called exilarchs—enjoyed a somewhat similar status; for exilarchs were likewise regarded as Jewish royalty because they too claimed that they could trace their descent from King David just as the patriarchs were supposed to do. Yet, it was unquestionably the large scale autonomy given to the Jewish people that encouraged the development of both the *Mishnah* and the *Gemara*. As products of self-governing communities this literature must be understood in terms of the social, political, and economic climate which nurtured its growth.

The history of the *Gemara* is full of names, places, academies, and rabbis. It is a remarkable galaxy of sages who appear before us in this vast commentary which covers a period of approximately three centuries (200–500 A.D.). They were men of varying backgrounds, origins, experiences, and temperaments which account in a large measure for the heterogeneous nature of the *Gemara*. But that is just what we should normally expect from such a variety of independent thinkers. Far from being vexed by this display of differences we ought to be grateful for a literature that deliberately sets out to preserve freedom of expression, investigation, and opinion in the domain of religion which is notoriously intolerable of dissenting views. Despite the variety of their ideas, the rabbis so cohere in their main principles that cumulatively they achieve a broad harmony. Thus the unity developed by the Jews in Babylonia during the period of the *Gemara* led to a phenomenal expression of allegiance to religion. It was this allegiance to significant spiritual principles which no extraneous or secular loyalty could divide.

Gemara history is always vividly, passionately alive. Despite its dependence upon the *Mishnah* it confronts us with an important transformation of mental outlook. This transformation can be stated as follows: The Judaism of both the Bible and the *Mishnah* was largely limited to Palestine and to the cultural homogeneity of the Jewish people as it existed in that one little country during Biblical and Mishnaic times. However with the development of the *Gemara,* especially as it flourished in Babylonia, it was now being demonstrated that Judaism could adapt itself to any country, to any type or form of civilization or to any condition of society. How this transformation was brought about can be understood in terms of at least three profound historical forces which brought the *Gemara* into existence.

1. The House of Hillel located in Palestine came to an end which means that the authority of the patriarchate died out.

2. Palestine as a center for the Jewish people declined because of a chronic state of warfare fomented by Rome which had steadily driven the inhabitants of the Holy Land into poverty, ineffectiveness, and obscurity.

3. The great Palestinian academies, located in such towns as Tiberias, Sepphoris, Acre, Lydda, were destroyed.

Due to wars, the shifting of populations, and widespread social upheavals it became the major concern of the rabbis to hold their people to an orderly way of life. Certainly this could not have been done by invoking Roman law or Parthian law or the law of any pagan nation at that time. It could only be done in conformity with traditional Jewish laws and regulations based upon Scripture. That is why the rabbis found it necessary to define the rules (*Halakah*) more precisely. They were aiming at a religio-ethical control of Jewish masses which would prevent them from plunging headlong into barbarism. In other words, the rabbis felt that lacking the guidance of the *Halakah*, life for the Jew would be as unsafe as a sea voyage without a compass.[10] That the founders of the *Gemara* had a sure instinct for the preservation of the Jewish people is attested by the fact that the Jews survived those explosive and revolutionary centuries during which Rome rose to her eminence and died in ignominy and shame.[11]

Roman rule, which had been harassing Palestinian Jewry for centuries, eventually resulted in the closing down of the great academies in that ancient homeland. This explains why the Palestinian *Gemara* exists today in only a fragmentary condition. It reflects the disturbed state of affairs that brought the historic Jewry of the Holy Land to a standstill. Not that the Jews ever willingly yielded their title to the land of their fathers. Active measures were always taken to resist Roman paganism and brutality. But a time came when Palestine was laid in such utter ruin that this inevitably led to a shifting of the intellectual and spiritual center of Judaism to another land. That other land was Babylonia which gave birth to the massive Babylonian *Gemara*. (In actual size the Babylonian *Gemara* is about four times larger than its Palestinian counterpart.)

*   *   *

And now for the second time in the history of Judaism the land of Babylonia became important.

Ever since the days of the old Exile, segments of the Jew-

---

[10] It is interesting to note that at the time the rabbis were developing the Halakic aspects of Judaism (thereby making Judaism an "actional" religion filled with observances) the church fathers were developing the creeds of Christianity (thereby making Christianity a "faith" religion filled with articles of belief). Thus the "legalism" of the rabbis was matched by the "creedalism" of the church fathers. Both sides possessed deep-seated convictions that they were showing mankind how best to conform to God's revelations.

[11] Pagan Rome had twenty-six emperors who sat uneasily on their thrones between 235 A.D. and 285 A.D. Only one died a natural death.

ish people uprooted by Nebuchadnezzar had chosen to remain permanently in Babylonia. There were those who returned with Ezra to rebuild the ancestral home in Judea; but for the most part the Jews who were brought to Babylonia as captives remained to become prominent citizens of that eastern empire. Not much is known of Babylonian Jewry between the times of Ezra and the period of Rabbi Judah the Prince which covers a span of six hundred years. But this much we do know: there had existed since the days of the Exile a strong and continuous Jewry on Babylonian soil which had never broken its ties with the recognized spiritual authority emanating from the ancestral homeland. Unlike the Jewries of other countries, Babylonian Jewry was the most loyal, the most orthodox, and the most vitally concerned with the correct expression of Judaism.[12]

It is therefore to Babylonia that we now turn our attention for the larger and fuller development of the *Gemara*—the Babylonian *Gemara*—which developed in an atmosphere of comparative peace compared to the turbulent conditions that marked the third century in Palestine. This proud new center of eastern Jewry revolved principally about the prosperous cities of Nehardea, Sura, and Pumbeditha which lay within the Tigris-Euphrates Valley with the Persian Gulf at the southern end. (All this territory today is in modern Iraq with Bagdad as its capital.)

Aside from being great commercial centers, what made these cities of such lasting importance was the fact that they were the seats of great academies. What the medieval universities were to Italy, what Cambridge and Oxford have been to England, such were Nehardea, Sura, and Pumbeditha to Jewry. In the halls of these academies Jewish learning was carried on with an intensity unparalled in any other age.

These academies soon began to claim the attention of the

---

[12] This, for example, can be seen not only in the life and work of Ezra who was a Babylonian Jew, but centuries later in the life and work of Hillel who likewise was the product of Babylonian Jewry.

world. Particularly so because Palestinian Jewry (held tightly within the talons of the Roman Empire) was dwindling to extinction whereas Babylonian Jewry, fortunately outside the Roman Empire, showed unmistakable signs of climbing to prominence and authority. Here and there attempts were made to regain for Palestine its earlier prestige, but the strong currents of history were not favorable to the Holy Land. Babylonian Jews had in a large measure foreseen what might happen to the dimming lights of learning in the historic center of their faith; and so they had sent their most promising students to attend the old academies. Notwithstanding the distance between the two countries there was constant intercommunication between the Babylonian and Palestinian sages. This active interchange resulted in a cross-fertilization which enabled Babylonian Jewry to be prepared to take over the leadership of Judaism when the lights went out in the land of Israel.

During the period of the growth of the *Gemara*—and for a long time afterward—Babylonian Jewry was studded with an increasing number of illustrious sages, scholars, and philosophers whose names are little known to the Christian world.[13] These men shed luster upon the particular academy with which they were connected and often attracted thousands of students. In their hands the mass of comment which evolved into the *Gemara* grew enormously.

Such a man, for example, was Abba Areka—a scholar of uncommon ability, wide culture, and possessed of a lofty spiritual nature. He was so great a leader that the people almost always called him *Rab* (meaning "Master"). Being a descendant of a distinguished Babylonian family he started life with splendid advantages which eventually led him into the presence of Rabbi Judah "the Prince," the redactor of the *Mishnah*. Having made the journey to Palestine, this young Babylonian soon became a member of the

---

[13] More than a thousand rabbis are mentioned by name in the *Gemara* (*see* p. 188). These men are collectively known as *Amoraim* to differentiate them from the founders of the *Mishnah* who are called *Tannaim*.

great Academy under Rabbi Judah. It is said that he acquired such an extraordinary knowledge of traditional lore
that he developed into a foremost disciple. At the height
of his superlative attainments, and while Rabbi Judah was
still living, Abba Areka returned to Babylonia where he
established an academy in the city of Sura on the Euphrates
River. At first it was a modest institution but it soon drew
hundreds of students of all ages who were attracted by
the charm and learning of its master. So successfully had
Abba Areka's academy been that it continued to exert a
profound influence on Jewish life for more than seven hundred years after his death.[14]

But Abba Areka was not the only Babylonian Jew to
study under the illustrious patriarch. There was Mar Samuel
—a luminous intellect—who was also an astronomer and a
physician. He too undertook the journey to Palestine, and
on his return to Babylonia became the head of the academy at Nehardea. As friends and colleagues Abba Areka
and Mar Samuel developed the one great aim of all *Gemara:*
the desire to penetrate the whole of human life with the
sense of law and right. The success of these two sages has
had an enduring significance upon Jewry not only because
their objective was lofty but also by reason of their saintly
lives. Their intellectual and spiritual expressions, as reflected
in the large mass of *Gemara* material involving their discussions and decisions, became an important formative element in the determination of the whole course of Talmudic
development.

In studying the nature of the *Gemara* it is important to
understand that its method owes its origin to Abba Areka.
The essential point of this method is that the Mishnaic text
of Rabbi Judah's code was taken as the foundation upon

---

[14] Abba Areka died in 247 A.D. but his academy continued to grow in
importance reaching its highest point under the direction of Rabbi Ashi
who presided over it for fifty-two years (375–427 A.D.). One of the most
distinguished heads of Sura was Saadia who died in 942 A.D. After Saadia
the great academy declined and was out of existence by the middle of the
eleventh century.

which the discussions, traditions, regulations, and the decisions of the *Gemara* were based. As Judaism came to express itself in the *Gemara* (a form suitable to the needs of
the time) there developed no abrupt break with former
generations of thinkers, only continuity. Thus the law
(*Halakah*) as it is everywhere spread throughout the
Gemara is derived from the *Mishnah*. Every statement of
the *Mishnah* was subjected to careful scrutiny, every opinion traced to its source, every apparent contradiction recon-
ciled, and every decision dissected until its principles were
understood. The sages of the *Gemara* were interested not
only in what the *Mishnah* said but also in what it implied.
So, over the centuries the cumulative mass of all this
Gemara-thinking expanded enormously. In time the *Gemara*
became so wedded to the *Mishnah* text that for all intents
and purposes it was regarded as one and the same thing.
That is why the term *Talmud* is used, a single word embracing both the *Mishnah* and the *Gemara*.

What is of interest to us is the fact that Abba Areka was
perhaps foremost among the sages who initiated this
Gemara process. His academy at Sura was its chief starting
point. Sura under the leadership of Abba Areka marked the
beginning of a process of which the *Talmud* is the conclusion. For this reason we can understand and appreciate why
the opinions of Abba Areka are copiously recorded in the
Gemara. For the same reason his many arguments and disputes with his colleague Mar Samuel constitute a significant part of *Gemara* history; for Abba Areka at Sura was
the supreme authority on religious law whereas Mar Samuel
at Nehardea was recognized as the authority and expert on
civil law.

*   *   *

Soon after Mar Samuel died the city of Nehardea was destroyed (260 A.D.) in a war between Rome and Persia. It
had been one of the earliest centers of Babylonian Judaism.
In all probability its origin went back to the settlement of

the very first Judean captives who were sent down there by Nebuchadnezzar in the sixth century B.C. With the destruction of Nehardea the activities of its academy were transferred to a neighboring town called Pumbeditha which soon took its place in importance and distinction by the side of the academy at Sura. It is one of the remarkable facts of Talmudic history that these two institutions continued to coexist as the acknowledged authorities of Judaism for more than seven hundred years after the death of their founders. In other words, long after the *Talmud* was completed both Sura and Pumbeditha continued their position of leadership for world Jewry in all matters of faith and practice.

The work begun by Abba Areka and Mar Samuel constitutes the beginning of the *Gemara*. After these two sages passed away their successors continued to add laws, rules, and regulations. These additions were developed as normal aspects of a growing and expanding society in much the same manner that the sum total of American law in 1955 is regarded as a much larger corpus of legal matter than it was in 1850. In other words American law in the hands of Abraham Lincoln as he practiced it before the circuit courts of Illinois in 1850 was a far more limited law than is now being used by any lawyer in the city of Springfield. The very nature of law is expansion because society itself is always in flux. One need not be a professional student of rabbinics to see that each succeeding generation kept on adding its wisdom to the *Talmud*—and sometimes its lack of wisdom. It is true that many of these *Gemara* additions have no connection whatsoever with the *Mishnah* and are concerned with matters unknown to its Founding Fathers— those sages whom tradition calls *Tannaim*. (By the same token is it not true that much of the American legislation in our day deals with subjects wholly undreamt of by the writers of the American Constitution?) By their activity the *Gemara* sages kept on adding their own store of tradition to the mighty process inherited from former generations so that in the end the literature of the *Gemara* came to embrace almost every subject of human interest.

However, it is not the expanded nature of the *Gemara* that is the problem for the reader. It is something quite different, namely: the dialectic subtleties of the discussions. The *Gemara* is full of disputations that are so highly involved that one is quickly lost in their labyrinthian coils. Frequently these coils keep on winding until they become entangled in casuistry of the most baffling type. Much of this kind of reasoning started in the early days of the *Gemara* but it mushroomed to huge proportions during the activities of Abaye (d. 339 A.D.) and Raba (d. 352 A.D.). These two sages, by reason of their long and intricate dialectical discussions, added enormously to the bulk of material that had accumulated since the days of Abba Areka and Mar Samuel.

The essence of any dialectical method of reasoning is that it does not derive its conclusions directly but achieves them by a roundabout process. This circuitous way can be seen, for example, in the *Gemara* illustration.[15] It starts out with the question: "What need is there for the *Mishnah* to give two pleas of the litigants?" etc. Then the *Gemara* goes into long, windy, and involved discussions (covering forty-eight pages in the authorized Soncino translation[16]) in which two things happen: (1) the *Mishnah* text is thoroughly dissected, and (2) its relation to other texts determined. With considerable coiling and winding the *Gemara* seeks to ascertain whether the *Mishnah* law on this point contradicts the decision of Symmachus. After several attempts at a solution it then comes to the conclusion that the *Mishnah* agrees in principle with Symmachus, and that the oath which the *Mishnah* prescribes for both parties is not a Biblical require-

---

15 *See* pp. 27-32.
16 The Soncino English translation of the entire *Talmud* is an authorized translation. It is the work of a group of eminent Jewish scholars, each an outstanding authority in his field. After two decades of publication the entire set of the *Talmud* is now complete with the issuance of the last volume which is the Index (London 1953).

ment but an idea instituted by the sages. Having arrived at this point the *Gemara* concludes that although the imposition of an oath is admittedly not a Biblical injunction nonetheless it is of vital importance otherwise any person might take hold of his neighbor's garment and insist that it belongs to him, in order to obtain possession of at least one half of it.

This dialectic method of the *Gemara* is called *pilpul*.[17] In its more simple and restrained form it is tolerable. But there are many sections of the *Gemara* where it is so involved that it appals the reader. Such prolix discussions are admittedly irksome. However, *pilpul* is essentially a detailed analysis of the *Mishnah* text. At times it lays great stress upon ingenuity—clever interpretation—which frequently gets into hairsplitting or what is known as "drawing the elephant through the eye of a needle."

Fundamentally, however, the pilpulistic method of legal discussion stands in contrast with the older method of tradition. Any jurist, for example, who was called a "Possessor of the Tradition" (*Baal Shemuot*) was so designated because he collected and arranged the legal decisions as they were handed down by tradition in simple Halakic sentences. He proceeded in a straight line to the significant point and ignored everything trivial, fanciful, or clever. He was not anxious to arrive at any surprising deductions. Enough for him were the time-honored authoritative traditions of the law embraced in the concept *Halakah l'Mosheh m'Sinai* (the law according to Moses from Mt. Sinia).[18] Not so the pilpulist. As the master of ingenious disputation and deduction the objective of the pilpulist was somewhat different: employing the dialectical method he was endeavoring to create something new out of what had already existed.

---

[17] The word *pilpul* means "pepper" or "spice" and therefore "sharpness" of mind. It also refers to sharpness of variance in discussions and disputes.
[18] Rab Joseph bar Hiyya (d. 333) who was head of the academy at Pumbeditha was called "Sinai" because—so it was said—all the laws of Judaism were as systematically arranged in his head as if he had heard them directly from the mouth of God at Sinai.

Only by ingenious inductions could the pilpulist become an "uprooter of mountains"—meaning that he was able to pull up a terrific amount of legal terrain and grind its contents to powder by the sheer force of his argumentation. Such a jurist was Rabbah bar Nachmani (270–330 A.D.). His keen dialectics won him the name of "Uprooter of Mountains" since he was exceptionally skilful in deducing new conclusions by separating individual passages of Scripture from their normal context. By using Nachmani's method the pilpulist had the advantage of being able to arrive at new conclusions, new concepts, new doctrines. His desire (aside from a show of acuteness) was to achieve flexibility. It was indeed a most roundabout manner of achieving a measure of legal independence in order to be able to render new decisions in those cases which had not been provided for in the now sacrosanct *Mishnah* text. Despite many false deductions, which had to be rejected, the method of *pilpul* had its good points for it gave its manipulators this advantage: they did not have to stand helpless before a massive mountain of immovable tradition.

The coilings and windings of the *Gemara* make it a work of uneven value. Some of the windings gather up material of very great importance while other windings seem wholly irrelevant. (Irrelevant, of course, to us in the twentieth century but certainly they were not irrelevant to those who for centuries lived close to its spirit.) Conditions of life in those far-off days were much different from ours; and that is why numerous questions, raised for discussion in the academies, seem to us awkward and antiquated. But if we are wise enough not to insist on looking at the *Talmud* through the lens of the twentieth century we will be able to appreciate its idiosyncrasies. Even its enormous size, its so-called mysterious architecture together with its coiling and windings will not dismay us; for we have intelligently arrived at the position where we can understand why each part of the *Talmud* deserves to be studied, especially by the student of religion. Then too there are other interests em-

bedded here deserving the attention of the historian, theologian, metaphysician, and most certainly the person who
is seeking knowledge on the evolution of law. For all these
reasons the entire *Talmud* is a vast mine rich in the de-
posits of many precious ores. Of course, one might easily
adopt a static conception of the *Talmud*. To do so, however,
would encourage many erroneous conclusions. This could
be especially harmful were our judgments limited by present day technological civilization. It must always be borne
in mind that the *Talmud* is the product of those centuries
close to the very end of antiquity, just before the beginning of medieval history. There are many appraisals of the
Talmud, couched in terms of medievalism, which are based
either upon excessive veneration or violent vituperation.
Most of these appraisals are quite false and do grave injustice to the lives and labors of those sages who achieved this
gigantic monument of the human intellect.

In its coilings and windings the *Talmud* may be compared to the *Congressional Record* of the United States
Government. Here, too, are to be found the relevant and
the irrelevant all jumbled together in a style somewhat
Talmudic! Anyone who is willing to sit down and read these
records covering a period of just ten years, from 1900–1910
would of necessity have to work his way through a mass
of unrelated matters thrown together in tremendous volume.
Here are to be found comments on a host of subjects too
staggering in number to itemize or detail. Yet, these were
the matters which were pressing considerations in the minds
of the representatives of the American people at that time.
Now, if we turn to the *Congressional Record* of the ten years
from 1940–1950 we are confronted by considerations which
seemingly come from another world. Consequently, by the
standards of 1950 much of what went on in Congress in
1900 seems indeed to be irrelevant.

The *Talmud* is the *Congressional Record* of the Jewish
people belonging to those centuries during which the Oral
Law was being discussed, debated, and developed down to

the period of its redaction in completed written form. And just as the *Congressional Record* of the U.S.A. embraces many nonlegal matters that entered into the discussions, so too the *Talmud*. This accounts for the discursiveness of that bulky literature as the Talmudic discussions keep roving from one subject to another. However, it is just this discursiveness which makes the *Talmud* interesting—and at times puzzling. Were it not for all this fascinating nonlegal matter (*Haggadah*) the *Talmud* would be a monotonous compilation of ancient laws. Such a nonlegal winding can be seen, for example, in the first chapter of tractate *Baba Bathra* which concerns itself about joint owners of property: how these owners may dissolve partnership and how they may divide the property. After laying down the law relative to the division of such things as courtyards, landed estates, gardens, an eating hall, a water tower, a bathhouse, a wine press, the *Mishnah* adds a chance remark as follows: "Sacred writings, however, may not be divided even if both agree."

Interestingly enough, this accidental remark of the *Mishnah* gives the sages of the *Gemara* a grand opportunity to talk about the Bible. And how they talk.[19] Practically everything that was known about the Bible in those days was caught up into the *Gemara*. As a result, we get valuable information about the books of the Old Testament, their origin, their authorship, and their dates of composition. The discussion on the Book of Job is priceless. Yet, mixed in with all of this highly valuable information about the Bible are matters of folklore when it is reported that Abraham "had a precious stone hung round his neck which brought immediate healing to any sick person who looked on it, and when Abraham our father departed from this world, the Holy One, Blessed be He, suspended it from the orb of the sun."

---

[19] In the Soncino English translation this discussion covers more than twenty pages.

Because three fourths of the *Talmud* is given over to jurisprudence it is natural that the most important interest of the *Talmud* should be in the realm of the law (*Halakah*). But Talmudic law, because it is based upon the Bible, is interpenetrated with ethics. It is this ethical content of the law which constitutes the uniqueness of the Hebrew contribution to jurisprudence; for the emphasis upon ethics turned all Jewish jurisprudence into religious jurisprudence. As in electricity the positive and negative currents are both needed to give the electric spark, so, too, in the *Talmud* both law and ethics are dependent upon each other to spark human living.

This passionate desire to ethicize all law can be seen to good advantage in the manner in which the *Talmud* handles the subject of retaliation, the law of damages for personal injuries. For example, in the Code of Hammurabi (which is a much older Semitic expression of legislation than the Bible) the instances in which the rule of "measure for measure" is applied go far beyond the Mosaic Code in primitive severity.[20] It is extremely doubtful if the law of "eye for eye" was ever applied literally in Jewish life. But the same, however, cannot be said of the earlier and more primitive stage of legal evolution during the reign of Hammurabi when the law of retaliation was taken in its most literal sense. Thus, according to the Code of Hammurabi, where a man strikes a pregnant freeborn woman as to cause her death through miscarriage, then the daughter of the assailant should be put to death. Or, in the case of the carelessness of the builder of a house: If the house falls and the owner's son is struck and killed in the ruins, then the builder's son should be put to death. Such extravagant application of the rule of "measure for measure" was made

---

[20] This Code, inscribed on a monument nearly eight feet high, was discovered in 1901–1902 on the site of ancient Susa (250 miles east of Babylon). Hammurabi was the king of Babylonia about the time of Abraham. The monument is now in the Louvre in Paris. It contains 3,600 lines in cuneiform writing in which the basic laws of Hammurabi's kingdom are set forth.

impossible among the Jews by the law of Deuteronomy 24.6 which states: "The fathers shall not be put to death for the children, nor shall the children be put to death for the fathers."

Much of early Mosaic law emerged out of a primitive Semitic background which included such peoples as the Babylonians, Canaanites, Amorites, and Phoenicians. In actual origin the Hebrews were a group belonging to the Aramean branch of the Semitic family. Long before the Hebrews appeared on the stage of history these Semitic peoples had achieved a certain legal development of their own which is reflected in the Code of Hammurabi. When the Biblical law of retaliation (as found in Exodus 21.24) is considered in the light of the over-all picture of primitive Semitic legal development it is not too difficult to understand "eye for eye" as a fossil element jutting out of a very ancient past—a past that is much older than the Jewish people.

The interpretative process took this primitive law of retaliation and changed its meaning. Long before the birth of Christianity the Pharisees had discarded its literalness from Judaism. It now remained for the *Talmud* (the mighty inheritor of the Pharisaic tradition) to handle it. We will therefore turn to Order DAMAGES (*Nezikin*) to tractate *Baba Kamma*. Here in chapter eight of this tractate we find the authoritative Jewish thinking relative to compensation for injuries. The *Mishnah* text starts off by enumerating under five headings how claims for damages of assault may be made: (1) for depreciation, (2) for pain, (3) for healing, (4) for loss of time, (5) for degradation. In connection with these five types of damages the sages of the *Gemara* discuss the meaning of retaliation in which they emphatically reject the literalness of "eye for eye." The argument of the *Gemara* is that true justice demands only monetary compensation. Here now are the words in which this thought is given:

GEMARA TEXT: Why pay compensation? Does the Divine Law not say "Eye for Eye"? Why not take this literally to mean putting out the eye of the offender? Let not this enter your mind, since it has been taught: You might think that where he put out his eye, the offender's eye should be put out, or where he cut off his arm, the offender's arm should be cut off, or again where he broke his leg, the offender's leg should be broken. Not so; for as it is laid down (Leviticus 24.18), "He who kills a beast shall make it good" (obviously because this verse pertaining to a beast stands in close juxtaposition to verse 17 pertaining to "man," the Talmudic thinkers used the theory of verse 18 to modify the harshness of verse 17. Therefore the *Talmud* at this point goes on to say)—Just as in the case of smiting [21] a beast compensation is to be paid, so also in the case of smiting a man compensation is to be paid.

To pay the injured person a monetary equivalent for the harm done was indeed a tremendous step forward in civilization. In studying the early stages of all systems of law, Jewish as well as non-Jewish, we meet a rough sense of justice which demands the infliction of the same loss and pain on the aggressor as he inflicted on his victim. What caused the Jews to replace this primitive justice with compensation? For one thing, the whole spirit of the Pentateuch was opposed to vengeance.[22] But most important was that cardinal tenet of Judaism which upheld the doctrine that every human being is created in the image of God. Life is from God and the body is from God; therefore, all retributive justice must take into account the basic elements of this ethic—"Justice, and only justice, you shall follow." [23] The double emphasis upon "justice" spurred the sages of the *Gemara* to delve deeply into each problem and treat it from every possible angle. That is why their discussions

---

[21] Taken from the Soncino English edition of the Talmud, tractate *Baba Kamma*, p. 474 ff. Some Bible translations use the word "smite" instead of "kill."

[22] "Vengeance is mine" (Deuteronomy 32.35) meaning that vengeance belongs to the Deity and must not be indulged in by man.

[23] Deuteronomy 16.20.

on "eye for eye" did not stop with the passage just quoted. Continuing with the problem one of the sages, Rabbi Dosthai ben Judah said:

GEMARA TEXT: [24] "Eye for Eye" means pecuniary compensation. You say pecuniary compensation, but perhaps it is not so, but actual retaliation (by putting out an eye) is meant? What then will you say where the eye of one was big and the eye of the other little, for how can I in this case apply the principle of eye for eye?

This shows sharp reasoning. Through such practical reasoning as this Judaism was to preserve its living actuality as an ethical monotheism, seeking justice in human relations in the name of God. Obviously it would be unjust to apply the rule of "eye for eye" in its literal sense in such cases where the eyes of the aggressor were larger or smaller than the eyes of the victim. Thus the inability to apply the Biblical rule justly was a clear indication that it needed amendment; and that amendment was elaborated in terms of a money payment for the eye that was forfeited.

In the true spirit of the *Gemara* still another angle on "eye for eye" is brought forward in the name of Rabbi Simon ben Yohai in order to show the impossibility of applying this Scriptural law literally:

GEMARA TEXT: What then will you say where a blind man put out the eye of another man, or where a cripple cut off the hand of another, or where a lame person broke the leg of another? How can I carry out in this case the literal principle of retaliation "eye for eye"?

❂   ❂   ❂

Of the six Orders of the Talmud—SEEDS, FESTIVALS, WOMEN, DAMAGES, SACRED THINGS, PURIFICATIONS—the one order that was given the greatest amount of attention was DAMAGES. Primarily because this Order was of immense practical value for daily life the sages, in their study halls and courts, were able to demonstrate religion in action. There are ten trac-

---

[24] P. 476 *Baba Kamma* (Soncino English Edition).

tates in DAMAGES, and each one is a splendid illustration of
the close connection of ethics with law. It makes no difference
whether the discussion is on compensation, robbery, violence,
bailments, sale or exchange, renting or leasing, trials, arbi-
trations, administration of oaths, capital punishment—or any
other subject be it civil or criminal—the Talmudic approach
was always the same, namely: Is this legislation grounded
in Scripture and centered in the will of God? The legal systems of other peoples were essentially the creation of the
state and drew their concepts from varying political interests such as the interests of royalty, castes, military dictator-
ships, or from types of governments. Not so the legal system
of the *Talmud*. The objective of the *Halakah* is righteousness between man and his fellow man. This is the essence
of the "social gospel" of Judaism. The ultimate authority
in human society is, therefore, not to be found in a king
or parliament or political party but in the close, constant,
and inseparable connection between ethics and law—and
only when both are able to stand the spiritual test of the
Torah, namely: Is this legislation grounded in Scripture
and centered in the will of God?

The *Talmud* enabled the Jew to live "under the law." To
live "under the law" meant to regulate one's life under concepts of what is right and what is wrong—that is, by concepts which could stand up in society after having successfully run the gauntlet of a Torah-true test. "Under the law"
never meant carrying around a heavy burden of stupid
regulations. Nor did it involve a motivation of fear in compliance with the law. The motivation had to stem from a
strong inner persuasion to do that which is inherently
right, rather than from fear of punishment. Centuries before
the growth of the *Talmud* the prophet Micah had put the
whole thing in simple words: "He has shown you, O man,
what is good; and what the Lord does require of you: but
to do justice, and to love kindness, and to walk humbly with
your God." [25]

---

[25] Micah 6.8.

The academies which framed and enacted the laws of the *Talmud* regarded their work as a continuation of the spirit of the old religious Sanhedrin at Jerusalem, just as the sages of the Sanhedrin regarded their work as a continuation of the labors of the Men of the Great Assembly. These bodies were more in the nature of research institutes rather than legislative congresses. Their procedure in all law-making was first to search the Scriptures—to investigate and study the Torah—and then to apply the results of such study to the needs of their generation. Because of its intimate connection with Sacred Writ the *Talmud* is always conscious of maintaining its status as the lineal descendant of the Old Testament. Like the Old Testament the *Talmud* takes on the ethical spirit which interpenetrates Biblical legislation. Its emphatic teaching is summed up in the folkloristic belief that when a man dies and appears before the Throne of Judgment the first question that is asked of him is not—Have you believed in God, or, have you prayed, or have you performed this or that ritual act but—"Have you dealt honorably and faithfully in all your dealings with your fellow man?" [26]

There is a well known story about Abba Areka, the founder of the academy at Sura, which further drives home this point. This story, which is based on an actual legal case, came before him and it reveals the lofty ethical spirit so greatly admired by the Talmudic sages; for it illustrates the manner in which the law was to be applied. Certain carriers of wine, whose business it was to transport barrels, brought suit against their employer. While engaged in the job of transportation, one of the barrels broke, spilling the wine. The employer in order to secure for himself payment for the damages took away the mantles of the carriers whereupon they summoned their employer before Abba Areka who ordered the employer to return the mantles to his workers. "Is this the law?" demanded the irate employer.

---

[26] *Talmud*, tractate *Shabbath* 31a. In connection with this belief one should reread Psalm 24.1-7.

"Do you call this justice?" Abba Areka answered "Yes."
And he upheld his position by quoting a Biblical exhorta-
tion—"So you will walk in the way of good men and keep
to the paths of the righteous." [27] The point is that although
the action of the employer in taking away the mantles of
the workers was sanctioned by the letter of the law (because the law gave the employer the right to make the carriers pay for the damage inasmuch as the damage had
evidently been an act of carelessness on the part of the
carriers) nevertheless Abba Areka, as judge, maintained
that there is such a thing as the "spirit" of the law which
overarches the letter of the law. Certainly, the employer
could base his rights on property damages but was there
not in this case a humane element pleading with the employer to forego his legal claim? Of course there was; for
was it not evident that these carriers were very poor men
who desperately needed their mantles?

◦   ◦   ◦

It was a task of tremendous magnitude to bring together
all the commentaries upon the various tractates of the
Mishnah. The mountainous mass of *Gemara* materials, embodying elaboration and expansion, had been accumulating
over the generations. All was now ready to be systematized
into one collection. Once the work was initiated it took
decades of sustained effort to whip it into shape. The man
who undertook this mammoth task was Rabbi Ashi, the
head of the academy at Sura.

Ashi became a unique figure in Talmudic history. In
many ways he has been compared to Rabbi Judah "the
Prince." Like that great patriarch he too was a wealthy
man, scion of a scholarly family. And just as Rabbi Judah
had been the head of an academy so now was Ashi. While
still a very young man this future chief editor of the *Talmud* became president of Sura. From the vantage point of

---

[27] Proverbs 2.20. The story about Abba Areka is taken from the *Talmud*,
tractate *Baba Metzia* 83a.

this exalted position, and with plenty of means at his disposal, he surrounded himself with a group of competent scholars whose task resembled the editorial board which had assembled long ago at the feet of Rabbi Judah "the Prince."

No one knows exactly the nature of the forces which urged these men to undertake the colossal task of redaction.[28] Whatever those influences were, Rabbi Ashi and his scholars must have felt that the time had now come when the authoritative preservation of the *Gemara* materials, already in existence, was more important than any further accretions. Therefore, everything that passed through Ashi's hands was very carefully sifted; and it took more than fifty years to do it! Those were the opulent years of Sura when Ashi was the head of its academy (375–427 A.D.) and in a position to carry through the work of redaction. To collect, arrange, and methodize all the legal and nonlegal traditions, which had been developed since the days of Abba Areka and Mar Samuel, required the skill of a sage who could grasp the unity of the *Gemara* underlying its complex diversity. With many parts of the *Gemara* coming from this age and that, now from one country and now from another, it is evident that a herculean task confronted the man who could bring all this together so that in the end the sum of all its parts would reveal a consistent pattern. True it is that Ashi's monumental compilation received a few later additions and amplifications; but his definitive work was never altered. In other words, the essential features of the *Talmud* have remained for ever fixed approximately as they came from Ashi's hands. Thus, from the academy at Sura, where Abba Areka had initiated the *Gemara*-process in the early part of the third century, Ashi now completed it in the fourth. For this reason it can be said that the *Talmud* is largely the product of Sura and its

---

[28] The most recent examination into the historical facts surrounding this editorial work can be found in Julius Kaplan's book *The Redaction of the Babylonian Talmud* (New York 1933).

scholars. But Ashi was more than a scholar. He contributed to the grandeur of Sura by rebuilding its famous academy and restoring the synagogue connected with it, personally superintending the work. Because of Ashi's eminence it was said of him that his position among his contemporaries was such that since the days of Rabbi Judah "the Prince" learning and social distinction "were never so united in one person as in Ashi." [29]

When Rabbi Ashi died in 427 A.D. the work of perfecting the *Talmud* was progressively advanced by his successors, particularly by those who followed him in the presidency of Sura. Talmudic methods, which had long undergone an intensive sharpening process in transmission, were used in the final redactional process. By "perfecting" the Talmud we mean rounding out the discussions, adding bits of legal knowledge or nonlegal interpretative matter but in no manner changing its essential features. The final touches were given by Rabina II whose death in 500 A.D. marks the end of the *Gemara* era.

It was indeed fortunate that the *Talmud* was completed and perfected in the seventy years between the death of Ashi and the passing of Rabina II. Ashi had had a strong premonition of the future, and he was not wrong. Social and economic conditions in Babylonia had been undergoing rapid changes and eastern Jewry was being deeply affected. Ugly clouds had appeared in the skies—what with corruption in the suzerain government, military defeats, and a wave of fanaticism brought on by pagan priests who temporarily gained control over the Zoroastrian religion—the state religion of Persia. A wave of intense persecution was unleashed against the Babylonian Jews. For a period of about forty years the academies suffered; many of their teachers were executed, students were hunted down and scattered, and studies discontinued because they were outlawed.

---

[29] Quoted from the *Talmud*, tractate *Sanhedrin* 36a.

However, with the appearance of Rabina II as head of Sura (488–500 A.D.), the Persian persecutions abated and a new era of tranquility came to the Jewish people as the great academies were slowly reopened and students again began to attend the sessions. Rabina II had made it his supreme objective to complete the compilation of the *Talmud* and close it to any further additions. In this work he collaborated with another sage Rab Jose who presided over the academy at Pumbeditha (475–520 A.D.).

THE HAGGADAH

To think of the sages of the *Mishnah* and the *Gemara* solely as jurists, men steeped only in the legal aspects of religion, would be a most lopsided appraisal. As authorities on Jewish life these men were deeply interested in all that tradition offered. Their concern was not limited to legal tradition but embraced medical traditions, historical traditions, folklore, ethics, biography, exegesis, linguistics, geography, astronomy, mathematics—indeed everything that pertained to life in those days. All these traditions are to be found in the *Talmud.* They are called *Haggadah*—a term used to differentiate everything of a nonlegal interest from the *Halakah.*

*   *   *

In trying to understand the nature of the *Haggadah* it must always be borne in mind that, like the *Halakah* (law), it, too, stems from the primary source of the Jewish Religion, namely: the Bible. Both *Halakah* and *Haggadah* came into existence as a result of the interpretative process which operated on the principle that there must be more in the Bible texts than appears on the surface. Within the *Talmud*

57

itself both *Halakah* and *Haggadah* (legal matters and non-legal subjects) are mixed together. This mixing of legal and nonlegal is an old Jewish practice. It can easily be seen, for example, in the Five Books of Moses (Pentateuch) where legislative matters and story materials are woven closely together. This method of handling materials is, to be sure, quite different from modern standards. At times it can be annoying to the average reader but once this archaic method is understood, the reader can adjust himself to it—and then the whole field of the *Talmud* becomes clearer.

In the academies of Palestine and Babylonia the *Haggadah* was a part of the same curriculum. Side by side with the study of the strict discipline of the law there were these other nonlegal, miscellaneous matters which delighted both scholars and students and the people at large. From this lighter side Jewish preachers drew inexhaustible materials for their sermons. Because the *Haggadah* was free from all the heavy apparatus of legal method and legal rule it had a very great popular appeal. Yet this appeal was never permitted to be carried to the extreme of minimizing the law or displacing it. So long as there was no infringement of the plain and established sense of Scripture the *Haggadah* was allowed free play. The supreme purpose of the *Haggadah* was to bring joy to man's heart in his efforts to live up to the requirements of the law in daily life. As interwoven strands within the *Talmud* both the *Halakah* and the *Haggadah* were considered inseparable.[1] Both issue forth into life from the same source and both aim at the same objective. Did a sage wish to derive sanction for a legal decision? Then, to be sure, he went to the text of Scripture to get his support. Did the same sage wish to press home a strong ethical lesson? Then, to be sure, he went to the text of Scripture so that, by a direct supporting

---

[1] The separation of the two was one of the main causes in the break between Judaism and Christianity. Christianity accepted the *Haggadah* but rejected the *Halakah*. This can be seen in the very nature of the New Testament which is Haggadic in character and almost wholly lacking in *Halakah*.

quotation from Holy Writ, he could effectively maintain: "As it is written," or, "As it is said." The same sages who developed the legal side of Judaism (*Halakah*) developed simultaneously the nonlegal side (*Haggadah*). In other words, the continuous reflection of these men upon the words of Scripture yielded two results: (1) legal interpretation which resulted in Talmudic legislation and (2) ethical interpretation which resulted in Talmudic edification. Or, to put the same thought in other words, it can be said that while *Halakah* interprets the whole of Scripture from the legal standpoint, the *Haggadah* interprets the whole of Scripture from the didactic standpoint.

* * *

Oftentimes the same man who was the leading jurist of his generation was also its most outstanding preacher. This double career was carried to a very high point of achievement in the life of Rabbi Meir who lived in Palestine in the second century.[2] Rabbi Meir is mentioned quite often in the *Talmud* in connection with the development of the *Halakah,* for he introduced the rule of testing the validity of a law on rational grounds rather than upon fanciful interpretations. To illustrate how necessary it is to use caution and restraint in the determination of a law Rabbi Meir trained his powers of dialectical skill to such a degree that the *Talmud* says: "He was able to give a hundred and fifty reasons to prove a thing legally clean, and as many more reasons to prove it unclean." [3]

Now this same Meir who was one of the most important sages of the law was an enormously popular public speaker. His appearances in the cities of Palestine particularly in his home town of Tiberias attracted large crowds who came to receive from him hope, understanding, and courage. Nor were they ever disappointed; for Meir based his discourses

---

[2] The word *Meir* means "One who enlightens." This name has many modern variants and spellings such as: Meyer, Maier, Mayer, Maher, etc.

[3] *Talmud,* tractate *Erubin* 13b.

on the stories of the Old Testament, its patriarchs, its prophets, its kings. He interpreted the Biblical narratives in terms of their practical application, thereby leading his hearers into the understanding of Scripture as a universal power that can be released to each individual in so far as his awareness to spiritual truth enables him to apply its wisdom to his daily living.

In the tractate *Sanhedrin* which is full of legal matters pertaining to courts and their procedures we come across a choice bit of *Haggadah* which is typical of Meir's output. Perhaps it was taken from one of his sermons dealing with the subject of the equality of man. The *Gemara* reports it as follows:

> Rabbi Meir used to say: The dust of the first man was gathered from all parts of the earth, for it is written—"Thine eyes beheld my unformed substance" (Psalm 139.16) and further it is written—"The eyes of the LORD which range through the whole earth" (Zechariah 4.10).[4]

This is indeed an interesting method of proving and upholding the teaching that man belongs to but one kind; that therefore we have the right to use the term mankind. Rabbi Meir's view coincides with the position taken by modern science which regards all men, irrespective of differences of races, as belonging to the same species, *homo sapiens*.

Now, if one were to ask whether Meir's view represents the authoritative position of Judaism on the subject of the equality of man, the answer would be yes. For it was not Meir alone but other sages, who, in their contribution to the development of *Haggadah*, gave out statements relative to the oneness of humanity. Both Hillel and Rabbi Akiba taught that the chief principle of the entire law is to be found in Leviticus 19.18—"You shall love your neighbor as yourself." But it was Ben Azzai who maintained that there existed in Scripture a still more important principle,

---

[4] *Talmud*, tractate *Sanhedrin* 38B. Meir knew Greek and Latin literature and used extensively stories which parallel Aesop's Fables.

embedded in the words of Genesis 5.1—"This is the book of the generations of Adam . . . God created man . . . in the likeness of God." According to Ben Azzai, the Bible teaches the dignity of all mankind (the generations of Adam) because all men are created in the likeness of God, meaning that while star, plant, and beast are creatures of God, man alone is his child.[5]

Out of such Haggadic treatment of Scripture the rabbis derived a variety of ideas about man and his conduct:

1. THE PICTURE ON THE COIN

Human beings mint coins bearing the likeness of a king. These pictures are stamped from one original. Now look at man himself and you will see that God (the King of kings) has stamped upon all the generations of man his pattern; for the original (Adam) was created in the likeness of God. But God's methods surpass the methods of a mint. Coins of a given issue are all identical. Yet, because God is God, all human beings differ. Although patterned after the image of the first man it is nonetheless true that no two men are exactly alike. As God created the world for Adam as an individual, therefore each individual is privileged to say: For my sake the entire world was created.

2. MAN INTERDEPENDENT UPON HIS FELLOW MAN

People in a boat at sea symbolize dependence upon each other. Using this illustration Rabbi Simeon ben Yohai gave the following bit of *Haggadah:* "A number of men were seated in a boat, and one of them took an augur and began boring a hole beneath him. His comrades exclaimed: What are you doing? He replied that it was no concern of theirs since he was boring a hole only beneath his own seat. They replied: Surely it is our concern, for the water will swamp the entire boat and all of us with it!"

3. IS ARMOR AN ADORNMENT?

In discussing the prohibition against carrying a burden on the Sabbath, the *Halakah* (legal rule) lays down the regula-

---

[5] Ben Azzai was both a pupil and colleague of Rabbi Akiba (50–135 A.D.). Meir was Akiba's most outstanding disciple.

tion that a man may carry on his person that which is generally considered an article of adornment or decoration. What then is armor? Is it an adornment or a burden? One jurist expressed his opinion in favor of permitting a man to wear his armor on the Sabbath on the ground that armor is an adornment. The majority decision however was against this view because the sages held that weapons of destruction do not constitute an adornment but rather a disgrace to humanity, basing the argument upon Scripture: "And they shall beat their swords into plowshares, and their spears into pruning hooks; nation shall not lift up sword against nation, neither shall they learn war any more" (Isaiah 2.4).

4. THE NATURE OF MATERIAL THINGS

Rabbi Meir used the fable of the fox to illustrate the idea that man ought not spend his years on earth exclusively in the pursuit of material possessions which are transitory—here today and gone tomorrow. On seeing some delicious fruit hanging from the trees in a garden the fox ran around the wall in the hope of finding an opening. The only available entrance into the garden was very narrow. The fox quickly discovered that he was too fat to creep through. He therefore undertook a three days fast until he was thin enough to get by. Once within the garden he gorged himself on its delicious fruit and thereby grew fat again. When the time came for him to slip out he couldn't squeeze through the narrow aperture. So he was compelled to fast another three days to become thin again. Consequently, when he crawled out he was just as thin as before. Outside the garden the fox gazed backward upon it and cried: O garden! O garden! What use have you been to me and what use are your fruits? Your place is indeed charming and delightful; your fruits are delicious and exquisite. But what have I now for all my labor and cunning? Am I not just as lean as I was before? Rabbi Meir compared the fox to man and the garden to the world. Naked does man come into this mundane plane and naked must he go out of it. Of all his worldly goods man carries nothing with him when he departs. Moreover, when a person enters the world his hands are clenched as though to say: "Everything is mine; I will inherit it all!" When man leaves the world the palms of his

hands lie wide open, as if to declare: "I have not acquired one
permanent material thing from the world." Since man does
not carry away any of his possessions, ought he not, therefore,
during the years allotted to him on earth, use his material
possessions for the spiritual, moral, and intellectual advance-
ment of his mind and heart?

5. THE BASIS OF DEMOCRACY

Why was Adam, the first man, created as a single individual? Because Scripture wishes to teach the supreme value of
every living soul irrespective of differences in race or religion.
He who saves one life it is accounted unto him as though he
had saved the whole world! Also Scripture wishes to teach
harmony, brotherhood, democracy. Once a person knows that
all men have descended from a common ancestor it becomes
almost impossible for him to go about boasting that he is descended from better stock than his fellow man.

6. THIS IS THE SERVICE

The emphasis is upon the word this—"and Moses said this"—
and Moses said, "this is the thing which the LORD commanded
you to do; and the glory of the LORD will appear to you"
(Leviticus 9.6). The *Haggadah* takes the word "this" homilet-
ically and arrives at the following meaning: God commands
each Israelite to perform the special, unique service of the high
priest. What the high priest does within the great sanctuary,
let the people do in the lesser sanctuary, which is the human
heart, the abiding place of the divine glory, for God says:
"I will dwell in their midst." So, then, as the priests offered
upon the great altar the life and force of sacrificial victims
so let each man offer upon the lesser altar the life and force
of his lustful soul which prompts him to sin. Upon this lesser
altar each man can purge his evil nature with the fire of the
love of God. This is the service. It is the one and unique
service of the one and unique God.

7. STATUS OF A NON-JEW

"Whence do we learn," asked Rabbi Meir, "that even a
heathen who studies Scripture (Torah) is on a par with the
high priest?" The question asked by Meir is designed to point
up the discussion that religion is not something limited to

special groups such as priests or Levites. To affirm his view Meir chose the passage of Leviticus 18.5.—"You shall therefore keep my statutes and my ordinances by doing which a man shall live." Rabbi Meir, knowing that the principles of the *Haggadah* maintain that every Bible word will upon further cultivation yield a most fruitful meaning, called attention to the universalistic wording of this passage. The text does not read—which if a priest or Levite or Israelite do—the text definitely says—"by doing which a *man* shall live."

❊   ❊   ❊

One of the most interesting aspects of *Haggadah* is the "historical" which brings together legends concerning great times, events, and illustrious personalities. No attempt was made by the Haggadists to be factually accurate. The aim of the historical *Haggadah* was the spiritual or moral lesson to be derived, not the presentation of the sober data of history. Inasmuch as all *Haggadah* is in the realm of folklore it ought to be understood at the outset that the rabbis were aware that their stories were partly legendary in character. Consequently, the historical *Haggadah* is full of anachronisms. Notwithstanding all this, genuine reports are to be found in the legendary embroidery of the historical *Haggadah;* but it takes the skill of a trained scholar to dissentangle the skeins of fact from fiction.

The purpose of the historical *Haggadah* is to extract out of history (Biblical as well as post-Biblical) edifying lessons. And just because edification was their objective the Haggadists gave free rein to their imagination.[6] Like the storytellers of olden Biblical days these Talmudic speakers made use of everything. In a true sense they were the direct

---

[6] The student of rabbinical literature should understand that not all *Haggadah* is to be found in the *Talmud.* Like a mighty river the *Haggadah* originates in the high mountains of Scripture; then it cascades through the *Talmud* only to broaden out into many books called the *Midrashim.* It makes no difference from what source a piece of *Haggadah* is quoted, whether from the Palestinian *Talmud* or the Babylonian *Talmud* or the *Midrashim,* it is all rabbinical. (For a list of important *Midrashim see* pp. 194, 195.)

continuation of those who quoted the ancient sagas of Israel and Judea. Witticisms and sayings current among the people were picked up by them and transformed, for these men had caught a glimpse into the eternal relationship of things. With unusual understanding the Haggadists never hesitated to draw both upon the familiar and the fanciful. Whereas the appeal of *Halakah* (law) was to the mind, the Haggadists labored mightily to make the appeal of the *Haggadah* reach the heart. The following specimens will illustrate how Biblical stories were ingeniously rewoven. It is this reweaving of Scripture narratives, centering around Biblical heroes as Abraham, Jacob, Moses, David, and Solomon, which transformed these characters into familiar and well beloved household figures, as the following specimens reveal:

1. ABRAHAM DESTROYS THE IDOLS

(Teaching the Judaic conception of the one and only God who is noncorporeal.)

This Haggadic tale begins with the life of Terah who is Abraham's father. Terah was in the business of idol making and selling. One day Terah left Abraham alone in the shop. Soon a woman came in and wanted to buy an idol to protect her family from thieves.

"Don't you have one?" asked Abraham in surprise.

"We had one, but it was stolen," she replied.

"How can you expect an idol to protect your family against thieves when it can't protect itself against them?"

"But I must worship something!" the woman insisted.

"How old are you?" Abraham asked.

"I'm sixty years old," she said.

"There's not an idol in my father's shop that is more than a week old. And if you want to see how powerful these idols are, just watch me—"

Abraham took an axe and started to smash the clay idols. The woman ran from the store in horror, but Abraham just went on smashing the idols until all but the largest one were destroyed. Then he put the axe in the hands of the large idol and waited for his father.

When Terah returned, he demanded: "Abraham, what have you done?"

"I have done nothing," said Abraham calmly. "A woman came in and offered some flour as a sacrifice to one of the idols. Whereupon that big one took the axe and destroyed all the others, as you can see."

"Abraham, you know these idols have no spirit in them. They cannot move nor can they fight."

"If they have no spirit, Father, what good are they?" asked Abraham.

2. JACOB WENT OUT FROM BEER-SHEBA

(To illustrate the value of a man to the city in which he lives.)

This bit of *Haggadah* is based upon Genesis 28.10. "And Jacob left Beer-sheba and went toward Haran." The rabbis raised the question why was it necessary to mention the town Beer-sheba? Would it not have been sufficient just to say that Jacob went towards Haran? Why does Scripture feel that it is necessary to preface his journey with the remark—"He left Beer-sheba"? What is the hidden reason? To teach us that when a righteous individual leaves a place his departure is a great loss. It is not the place that makes the man but rather the man that makes the place. When a righteous man lives in a city, he is its adornment, its glory, its true splendor. When the righteous man leaves his city all of its material grandeur cannot make up the loss.

3. JACOB AND THE STONE

(Troubles and worries—the hard stones of life—can be used to build an altar to God.)

Jacob in flight from Esau had to rest in the desert. At nightfall, says the Bible (Genesis 28.10-20), he gathered some stones in that eerie place for his repose. These stones were to serve him not only as a pillow but also for a shield. No sooner did Jacob gather these stones together when they set about quarreling between themselves. Each insisted that it alone should have the privilege of being Jacob's pillow. To still the bitter contention among the stones, God merged them all into one harmonious large stone. When Jacob awoke in the morn-

ing he took the newly merged stone and set it up for an altar
and poured oil upon the top of it. Then he called the name
of that place Beth-El, meaning the House of God.[7]

4. Why God Chose Moses

(To teach that faithfulness in small things leads to appoint-
ments for great things.)

Moses was grazing the sheep of his father-in-law in a
desolate place. He noticed that a young kid had strayed away,
so he went after it fearing that it might get lost or die of thirst.
Moses traced the steps of the kid to a ravine where the little
animal had found a well. Then he understood why the kid
had left the flock; and so he spoke to it tenderly: "My dear
little kid, I did not know that you ran away because you were
thirsty. Now you must be weary." When the little goat had
quenched its thirst Moses placed it upon his broad shoulders
and carried it back to the flock. When God saw what Moses
had done He said—"Because you have shown pity in leading
back one of a flock belonging to a man you shall lead my
flock, Israel."

5. Moses' Hands

(To teach the need of looking up to God, the source of all
true victory.)

Scripture says "Whenever Moses held up his hand, Israel
prevailed; and whenever he lowered his hand, Amalek prevailed" (Exodus 17.11). The *Haggadah* on this passage takes
as its background the bitter war between Israel and Amalek.
It will be recalled that Moses was leading his people to the
Promised Land. But the road towards it was not strewn with
flowers. There were many harsh experiences, perhaps none so
cruel as the antagonism of the Amalekites who offered no
friendship to the recently enfranchised Hebrews but only
strong military opposition. As commander in chief of his people Moses used his hands in signals. When he held up his

---

[7] This legend accounts for the Stone of Scone (sometimes called "Stone
of Destiny"). The coronation chair of England, located in Westminster
Abbey, rests upon it. It is supposed to be Jacob's Pillow, the identical
stone which was under Jacob's head when he slept in the desert.

hand Israel prevailed and when he lowered his hand Amalek prevailed. What does the Bible teach by telling us this? Did the mere raising of his hand enable Moses magically to make or break the battle? Only the simple-minded would believe that Moses needed only to wave his hand upward in the air for victory to come to the Hebrews. The holding up of his hands was symbolic of faith in God's power—"But Moses' hands grew heavy . . . and Aaron and Hur held up his hands, the one on one side, and the other on the other side; so his hands were steady until the going down of the sun" (Exodus 17.12). No matter how great the leader or how gifted the prophet it takes others to uphold his hands. No man can achieve victory by himself.

6. Sharing the Burden

(To illustrate that even so great a man as Moses was willing to share the burden of others.)

Scripture says (Exodus 17.12): "They took a stone and put it under him." Why a stone? Could not Moses have been given a cushion or a chair? Why does the Bible specifically state they put a stone under him? Actually, the Israelites wanted to give him a chair or a cushion but Moses refused saying: "My people are in trouble, I will bear my share of it with them; for he who bears his portion of the burden will live to enjoy the hour of consolation." Woe to one who thinks—"Ah, well, I will neglect my duty. Who can know whether I bear my part or not." Even the stones of the house, aye, the limbs of the trees shall testify against him, as it is written (Habakkuk 2.11): "For the stone will cry out from the wall, and the beam from the woodwork respond."

7. Things That Fly Away

(A plea for religion.)

When Moses came down from Mt. Sinai with the tablets of the Ten Commandments in his hands he saw his people dancing before the Golden Calf. Immediately the letters on the tablets flew away, and there remained only stones in Moses' hands. These stones became so heavy that he was forced to drop and break them. Is it not true that the worship of material things causes the letters (the knowledge of Religion) to fly away? And then what is left? Nothing but the stones of civilization which become heavy with pessimism, cynicism, and despair. Under such conditions civilization drops and is shattered. When the letters of tradition disappear in ignorance then religion too becomes a burden of stones rather than a joy for life. Each person should ask himself: Am I permitting the letters to fly away?

8. WHY FORTY YEARS IN THE DESERT?

(What happens when people are of little faith and place their own judgment over against God's promises.)

While marching in the desert towards Canaan Moses selected twelve men, one from each tribe, to reconnoiter the Promised Land. After forty days the twelve men returned and gave their report. They said that while the land was truly remarkable, rich and wondrous in the products of its orchards and farms ("a land flowing with milk and honey") nevertheless they found it fortified and its inhabitants powerful giants. Only two of the twelve spoke favorably—Joshua and Caleb; they gave a minority report. But the other ten spoke discouragingly. They said they felt like grasshoppers by comparison. When this report spread among the people the Hebrews cursed the day they had left Egypt. This attitude angered the Lord. "These people," said God to Moses, "are truly slaves; they are unworthy of the Promised Land. Yet, I will not turn them over to their enemies. If I did then it would be said that I was powerless to protect them. Instead, I shall punish them in the following manner: For every day that was spent cowardly reconnoitering the Land I shall cause the Israelites to wander a year in the desert. The transgression of the Golden Calf I have forgiven; but I cannot forgive them believing this report against my Word. Therefore I decree that the slaves who left Egypt shall not enter the Promised Land. This slave generation shall die in the desert. But it shall be otherwise with their children. I shall bring them into Canaan and cause them to inherit the land which I promised to Abraham, Isaac, and Jacob."

9. THE JEALOUSY OF KING SAUL

(To illustrate the difference in character between David and Saul.)

In the first interview between King Saul and David the King said—"You are not able to go against this Philistine to fight with him; for you are but a youth" (I Samuel 17.33). David replied, "Your servant used to keep sheep for his father; and when there came a lion or a bear, and took a lamb from the flock, I went after him and smote him . . . and this uncircumcised Philistine shall be one of them" (I Samuel 17.34 ff). When Saul asked him: "Who told you that you can kill Goliath?" David replied that "the LORD who delivered me from the paw of the lion and from the paw of the bear will deliver me from the hand of this Philistine." When King Saul heard these confident words of courage Scripture says—"Saul clothed David with his armor." But how could he? Was not King Saul taller than any man in his realm? When, however, Saul saw that his apparel fitted David a terrific inner jealousy raged within him. David, perceiving that Saul's face had turned white, said to the King—"I cannot go with these to meet Goliath, for I am not used to them." And so David put them off.

10. THE WISDOM OF SOLOMON

(Illustrating the King's ability to think quickly.)

The Queen of Sheba, who once visited Solomon, wished to ascertain in person whether his fame as the wisest of monarchs was true. She appeared before him in his palace holding in each hand a bouquet of flowers. And though one was natural and the other artificial, their resemblance to each other was so great that it was impossible to tell from a distance the difference between them. However, Solomon had to decide, for this was the test the Queen had arranged. Solomon's keen mind was now working fast. Observing a swarm of bees hovering outside the palace windows he ordered them opened. As soon as this was done the bees rushed in and at once fixed themselves on the natural flowers. The Queen of Sheba quickly learned that the wisdom of Solomon was genuine.

11. SOLOMON AND THE BOASTFUL BIRD

(A lesson in exaggeration.)

Solomon had the reputation of understanding the language of trees, animals, and birds. One day the King overheard a bird talking boastfully to its mate as she was sitting on the dome of the Temple. "If," he said, "I were to stamp my foot hard the whole Temple would collapse in a moment." Hearing this grandiloquent remark King Solomon called the male bird and, assuming an angry look, he asked how such an exaggerated thought could have crossed his mind. Trembling with fear the bird excused himself saying that he merely wished to tell his mate how strong he was. Solomon accepted both the bird's explanation and apology but cautioned him not to be so boastful in the future. That evening the bird returned to his wife who was anxiously awaiting him. When she asked what the great king wanted of him, he said: "King Solomon urgently implored me not to destroy his beautiful Temple."

12. ELIJAH IS GIVEN A LESSON

(Showing that even he who is most zealous for God must have a sense of balance.)

An angel appeared before Elijah at the entrance of the cave where he was hiding from the fury of Jezebel. The angel asked, "What are you doing here?" Elijah answered in disgust that the people of Israel were being ruled by Hebrews who turned out to be pagans eager to serve the idol Baal. "But," said the angel, "Why are you not with your people in their time of great need?" Elijah answered in terms which strongly condemned the people for their sins. Moreover he charged that their hardships were retribution and punishment for their misdeeds. Then the angel said to him, as it is written in Scripture (I Kings 19.11 ff), "Go forth and stand upon the mount before the LORD. And behold the LORD passed by, and a great and strong wind rent the mountains, and broke in pieces the rocks before the LORD; but the LORD was not in the wind; and after the wind an earthquake; but the LORD was not in the earthquake; and after the earthquake a fire; but the LORD was not in the fire; and after the fire a still small voice." Having witnessed these spectacular displays of nature Elijah stood

with his head bowed and his mantle covered his face. And
then God spoke to him: "I am as a father; the people are
my children. None may speak evil of the children without
shame being cast upon the father, even though the father may
know the children to be full of faults. Therefore, since you
have spoken against my children go and find Elisha, the son
of Shaphat, you shall anoint him to be prophet in your place.
Then return to my people." Elijah obeyed.

13. THE HORROR OF USURY

(To illustrate the Talmudic teaching against usury, based
upon Leviticus 25.36 and the words of Ezekiel 18.10-14.)

Nebuchadnezzar, the Babylonian king, feared that great
punishment would be meted out to him for having destroyed
Jerusalem. He consulted his pagan priests seeking their coun-
sel. They said to him: "O King, not by your strength was
Judea conquered but it fell because of the wickedness of the
Hebrews. Therefore avenge yourself for your humiliation.
Gather together all the Hebrew young men and slay them.
After that these people will not continue to boast that their
God humbled you." Acting upon the counsel of his Babylonian priests Nebuchadnezzar brought sixty thousand Hebrews to a desolate valley and had them all slain at his
command. When the prophet Ezekiel learnt of this massacre
he was given his famous vision in the Valley of Dry Bones
(Ezekiel 37.1-15). Appearing before the wicked king the
prophet Ezekiel said: "By the God of Israel these dead whom
thou didst slay will be revived. And I shall revive even those
who did not believe in the resurrection of the dead. And I
shall revive many Hebrews who in their misguided enthusiasm
for idolatry polluted our great Temple with pagan rites. I
shall revive the young men of Judea whose radiance on the
streets of Babylonia seemed to darken the sun in comparison,
those youths whom thou didst slay in jealousy." As Ezekiel
was speaking the dead arose and came to life. Only one
among the dead did not arise and live again: he had been a
usurer. For when a usurer dies, so great is the curse upon him,
he remains dead for ever! For does not Scripture say, "He
shall surely die; his blood shall be upon himself" (Ezekiel
18.13).

The foregoing illustrations of the *Haggadah*, based upon
Biblical history, lead most naturally into post-Biblical *Haggadah*. All *Haggadah* is essentially embroidered thought
embellished with practically everything in it—history, biography, folklore. No aspect of human interest is unrepresented here. The important thing to bear in mind is that the
Haggadah passes from myth to morality, from legend to
logic. For this reason the *Haggadah* was able to appropriate
selectively the best thought of the Jewish people and present it for popular edification. The next group of illustrations will demonstrate why the Jewish people felt that the
Haggadah contains light to direct them, food to support
them, and comfort to cheer them along life's way.

1. ALEXANDER AND THE SCALES

(To show that the greed of man is never satisfied.)

In his conquests of many lands King Alexander came to
Palestine. He sat down at a well to eat. The monarch had
with him some salted fish and when he rinsed them in the
water they acquired a fine flavor. "It seems to me," remarked
the Conqueror, "that this well must flow from the Garden of
Eden." Being an inquisitive man, Alexander determined to
follow the well upstream. He kept going until he reached
the entrance to Paradise. "Open the gate for me," he cried out.
From within the Garden came the reply: "This is the gate of
the LORD; the righteous shall enter through it" (Psalm 118.20).
Alexander kept pounding on the gate declaring that he was a
king and an important person. "At least," pleaded Alexander,
"give me something to show the world that I have been here."
His request was granted and a small fragment of a human
skull was thrown to him with the words, "Weigh it!" He took
the bone away and showed it to his wise men who brought
to him a pair of scales. Placing the bone in one pan the King
put some of his silver and gold against it in the other pan.
But the small bone outweighed them. This mystified the King
and he commanded that more silver and gold be added. Still
to no avail. At last Alexander added his heavy crown with
all its jewels and diadems. And yet the small bone outweighed
them all. Turning to his wise men he asked them to reveal

to him the meaning. "This," they explained, "is the eye socket
of the human skull; and the Eye of Man is never satisfied."
Alexander was now more perplexed than before. "How can
you prove that?" he asked. They answered him that the proof
was not difficult. All that the king had to do was to take a few
grains of dust and cover the eye socket with it and then see
for himself what happens. Alexander did so, and immediately
the pan of the scale holding the bone sank. It was in this manner that the great Macedonian learnt that the eye of man is
never satisfied. Indeed, the greed of the eye is stopped only
when it sinks to the grave and dust covers it.

2. How Justice Can Be Achieved

 (An elementary lesson in justice given to a powerful king.)

In his military campaigns through many lands Alexander
the Great came across a simple people who knew not the ways
of war, cruelty, or injustice. He lingered to learn their methods
of life. Two citizens appeared before their native ruler with
a lawsuit. "Your honor," said the first, "I bought a dilapidated
house from this man and while clearing it I found a treasure.
Now, inasmuch as I contracted to buy only the house I know
that the treasure that I found is not mine. I therefore insist
that the rightful owner be compelled by law to accept it."
To this argument of the plaintiff the defendant said: "I sold
the ruin to him with everything in it." The native ruler stroked
his beard in contemplation. Then turning to the plaintiff he
said: "Have you a son?" The plaintiff said he had. Then turning to the defendant he asked: "Have you a daughter?" The
defendant said yes. "The best solution to this lawsuit is very
simple," announced the ruler, "Let them marry one another
and enjoy the treasure together." Looking at King Alexander,
who showed utter astonishment at such a solution, the native
ruler asked:

"Why are you so amazed? Have I not given a correct judgment?"

"Of course you have," replied Alexander.

"In your country what would you have done with such a
case?"

"Both men," said Alexander, "would have been put to death
and the money confiscated for the royal treasury."

"Do you love gold that much?" exclaimed the native ruler in surprise.

3. THE JEWEL

(An example of utmost honesty in a business transaction.)

The great sage, Simeon ben Shetah, was a very poor man and a dealer in flax. One day his disciples came to him and said: "Oh master, allow us to buy you a donkey and you will not have to work so hard." They went and bought an ass from an Arab. Examining the beast they found a pearl round its neck. His disciples were overjoyed—"From now on you need work no more." When Simeon asked them why they entertained such an idea they told him the story of their lucky find. Simeon said to them: "Does its former owner know of it?" When they said "no," he commanded them to return the jewel. "Do you think that Simeon ben Shetah is a barbarian," cried the sage in righteous indignation. And he added: "I have bought the ass; I have not bought the jewel!"

The jewel was returned to the Arab who exclaimed, "Blessed be the God of Simeon ben Shetah," whereupon the sage said that he would prefer to hear the Arab say those words than to possess all the riches in the world.

4. THE KING AND THE WORKER

(Teaching the lesson that life is to be measured by deeds and not by time.)

The sages of the *Talmud* preached that the important thing is not how many years we add to life but rather how much life we added to our years. And so they told the story of a king who had a vineyard. On a certain day the king hired a number of laborers one of whom worked more carefully, more intelligently, and far more diligently than the others. This obvious demonstration of ability interested the king and so he took this laborer by the hand and, showing him royal friendship, walked with him through the gardens of the palace. They conversed on many subjects. At eventide all the laborers came to receive their wages. The king gave the one laborer whom he admired exactly the same amount he gave to the others.

But the others didn't like that; they were vexed and angered.

They said to the King: "Behold, we have worked the whole day whereas this one worked only a few hours."

Then said the King: "Why do you speak thus? Consider. This one, in a few hours, did more work for me than you who toiled the whole day long."

5. CARE OF THE BODY

(To show that the care of one's body should be a vital religious concern.)

At the close of one of his lectures in the academy Hillel the sage was followed by his disciples.

"O, Master, where are you going?"

'I am about to perform a pious deed," answered Hillel.

"And what may that be?" they inquired.

"To take a bath," said Hillel gleefully. "I am on my way to the bathhouse where I will wash and clean my body."

"Do you call that a pious deed?" asked his disciples in amazement.

"Yes, I do," replied Hillel. "If a man who is appointed to wash and polish the statues of kings receives not only payment for his work but is even regarded as among the great ones of the realm how much more important then is it that I keep my body, created in the divine image, clean. As it is written in Scripture: 'For God made man in his own image'" (Genesis 9.6).

6. AWARENESS

(To teach us that man has an important guest to entertain. Unfortunately many do not know who the guest is.)

Once when Hillel left his disciples they asked him where he was going.

"To do kindness to an important guest in my house," replied the sage.

"So," they said, "Do you have a guest in your house every day?"

"Yes, I do," said Hillel; and he proceeded to explain who the guest is. "Is not the Soul man's guest in his body every day?" And then the great sage added these significant words: "Today it is here and tomorrow it is gone."

7. FOR POSTERITY

(Though posterity has admittedly done nothing for you, still you must do something for posterity.)

A rabbi was once passing through a field where he saw a very old man planting an oak tree. "Why are you planting that tree?" said the rabbi. "You surely do not expect to live long enough to see the acorn growing up into an oak tree?"

"Ah," replied the old man, "My ancestors planted trees not for themselves but for us in order that we might enjoy their shade, use their lumber, or eat their fruit. I am doing likewise for those who will come after me."

8. A FATHER'S REFUSAL

(Teaching self-reliance.)

When the sage Akabya ben Mahalalel was on his death-bed his son asked: "Father, commend me to thy friends." His father refused: "No, my son, I shall not commend thee." The son was taken back by these words. "Father," he asked, "hast thou found aught unworthy in me?" The sage replied: "No, my son, I have found nothing unworthy. But remember this: thy deeds will bring thee near unto men, and thy deeds will drive thee from them."

9. THE RIP VAN WINKLE OF OLDEN DAYS

(The world undergoes such change that were a person able to fall asleep and emerge into some future generation he would not be happy.)

Honi, who lived in the days of Simeon ben Shetah, sat down to eat his meal of dry bread. He became drowsy and fell into a deep sleep. A huge rock protected him; and so Honi remained hidden from sight. He slept for seven full decades. When he awoke he saw a man picking fruit from a tree and eating it. He seemed to remember something about this tree and so he asked the man: "Who planted it?" When the man replied that his grandfather had planted it, Honi realized that he had been asleep for seventy years.

"Is Honi's son still alive," he inquired of the man.

"His son is no more but his grandson lives here."

"Do you know that I am the original Honi?" When he said these words the man laughed at him. Then Honi went to the study hall in the synagogue where the scholars of the community were studying the law and debating the various points of *Halakah* and *Haggadah*. He overheard the scholars saying: "These traditions are as clear as in the days of Honi who could always explain to the scholars any difficulty that arose."

"I am Honi," he broke in.

But they too did not believe him and turned their backs on him. Honi felt himself without a friend in the world and he prayed that he may die. His wish was granted. This gave rise to the popular saying: "Either fellowship or death."

10. HEAVENLY TREASURES

(Human life is greater than material treasures.)

King Monobaz, who was a convert to Judaism, ruled the state of Adiabene which was located within the territory of ancient Assyria. In a year of widespread famine he distributed royal treasures to the poor and needy. His ministers rebuked him saying: "Thy fathers amassed, but you squander. Thy fathers gathered treasures but you have dispersed both yours and theirs." Monobaz answered them: "My fathers gathered treasures for below while I have gathered treasures for above. They stored up treasures over which the hand of man can rule while I have stored up treasures in a place over which the hand of man cannot rule. My fathers gathered treasures in money while I have gathered treasures in souls. My fathers were interested in preserving material possessions while I am interested in preserving human lives. The treasures which my fathers laid by are for this world while mine are for eternity."

11. HOW THE FIRST FRUITS WERE BROUGHT TO JERUSALEM

(Telling how the first share of the crop was brought annually to the priests . . . a piece of post-Biblical *Haggadah* taken from the *Mishnah,* tractate *Bikkurim.*)

In what manner were the first fruits brought up? All the inhabitants of the towns of a district assembled in the principal city of the district; they spent the night in the market place of the city, and entered no house. Early in the morning the appointed officer would proclaim: "Arise, and let us go up to Zion, to the house of the Lord our God."

They that lived in the vicinity would bring fresh figs and

grapes; they that came from afar would bring dried figs and raisins. The bull went before them, its horns overlaid with gold, and a garland of olive leaves in its head. The flute played before them, until they drew near Jerusalem. When they drew near Jerusalem, they sent messengers before them, and adorned their first fruits. The governors, deputies, and treasurers came out to meet them; according to the rank of those that entered did they come out. All the craftsmen of Jerusalem stood up before them, and greeted them saying: "Our brethren, ye men of such and such a place, ye are welcome."

The flute played before them, until they reached the Temple mount. When they reached the Temple mount, each man (even King Agrippa) put his basket upon his shoulders. Then they went in as far as the Temple court. When they reached the Temple court, the Levites recited the song: "I will extol thee, O Lord, for thou hast raised me up, and hast not suffered mine enemies to rejoice over me."

The pigeons which were fastened to the baskets were offered as sacrifices, while those which they held in their hands were given to the priests.

The wealthy would bring their first fruits in baskets of silver or of gold, while the poor would bring them in wicker baskets made of peeled willow twigs. The baskets and the first fruits were given to the priests.

12. THE FALL OF THE TEMPLE

(A story designed to teach the divine origin of the Temple despite the frailty of its human management.)

The fall of the Temple was presaged by signs and wonders of an eerie nature. One day a heavy Temple gate swung open by itself. As the priests entered a sound like unto the beating of wings was heard, and a murmur as of a great host of voices saying, "Let us go hence."

When the priests saw that there was no hope of saving the Temple, they climbed out on the roof carrying with them the keys of Israel's great shrine. The people saw these priests throw the keys high up in the air and they heard them say: "We were not faithful stewards, and so we return the keys entrusted to us." Some add that a great Hand appeared out of the sky which grasped the keys whereupon the priests having returned the keys to Heaven leaped into the flames below the roof and perished.

*   *   *

Not everything in the *Haggadah* of the Talmud represents Jewish tradition at its best nor in its authoritative or definitive shape. There is much in the *Talmud* which is only the opinion of this or that rabbi responding to some passing circumstance or peculiar fashion or trend. Oftentimes we come across an outburst of temper or an intolerant expression, occasionally even a cruel or harsh remark. They are only a directing finger on a signpost giving the historian a clue to the times in which these things were spoken. All such *Haggadah* must be read and understood in the light of the different ages which produced them. Many opinions or views of this nature met with strong rabbinical opposition. For this reason it is exceedingly unfair to give quotations from the *Talmud* by lifting them out of their context or by omitting to state the nature of the circumstance which brought such thoughts to the surface. We ought no more look for consistency in the *Haggadah* of the *Talmud* than in a set of variegated opinions lifted from a single volume of the *Congressional Record* of the United States.

When it comes to Talmudic law (*Halakah*) one has a right to expect consistency. For *Halakah* is based upon a written document, the Pentateuch. But this does not hold in the realm of the *Haggadah* which is nonlegal. *Haggadah* gave the thinker free rein, he could express himself upon every conceivable subject from the sublime to the ridiculous. The views and opinions of approximately two thousand sages, jurists, orators, and philosophers are recorded in the *Talmud*. As the voices of these men come from widely separated ages there is frequent lack of harmony in the domain of their personal opinions. We should be careful not to think of these men as a single class, for they possessed different degrees of education, variations in outlook upon life; they

belonged to many different strata of society and lived under
different governments and different economic systems.

As an illustration of opposing thoughts expressed by these
men, it will be helpful to pass in review some contradictory
Talmudic ideas about woman. For example, no less a person than Mar Samuel taught that "listening to the voice of
a woman is a profanation." Another Talmudic sage, Rabbi
Sheshet, held that "the sight of woman's hair constitutes
a profanation." Upon examination we find that these statements were not just personal views, although personal experience had doubtless much to do with individual views.
Considering the important role that women held in Jewish
life from the days of Abraham, Isaac, and Jacob this reversal
of attitude as reflected in the statements just quoted helps
us to understand the nature of those currents of immorality
which had come into vogue during Talmudic times through
the spread of gnostic ideas.[8] Mar Samuel and Rabbi Sheshet were obviously endeavoring to protect Jewish home
life. This too seems to have been the motive of Rabbi Eliezer who deemed it inadvisable that women should spend
time in the lecture halls studying the law (although Ben
Azzai opposed Rabbi Eliezer's view and considered it incumbent upon each father to teach his daughter everything
pertaining to Scripture and the Oral Law).

Attitudes of appreciation and depreciation of woman
found their way into pithy expressions: Women are a law
unto themselves; women are fickle-minded; give me all evils
but not an evil wife; the best of women indulge in supersti-
tion; a bad wife is worse than death. On the good side we
find: Love thy wife as thyself and honor her more than self;
if thy wife be small bow down to take counsel of her; no
man without woman and no woman without man and
neither without God; he who has no wife lives without good,

---

[8] This point is discussed by Solomon Schechter in his paper entitled
"Woman in Temple and Synagogue" (*Studies in Judaism*, Vol. I). The
reader is also referred to Charles Kingsley's book *Hypatia* which gives
insight into the moral breakdown and licentiousness in certain periods of
Greek life as a result of woman's activity and leadership.

or help, or joy, or blessing; he who divorces his wife is unbeloved by God; it is woman alone through whom God's blessings are vouchsafed to a house.

The authority of Scripture prevented any age, no matter how greatly influenced by antifeminine ideas, from adopting attitudes which would violate Mosaic law. The Ten Commandments specifically enjoin: "Honor your father and your mother," thereby placing woman on a par with man. It is true that women were not considered competent witnesses in civil or criminal cases but this in no manner interfered with their position in their own household. That woman was not held in contempt can be seen from the pages of the Bible, particularly the Book of Proverbs which is full of expressions of reverence for the good woman and especially for one's own mother.[9] Women are frequently mentioned in the Bible and in the *Talmud*. As a matter of fact two books of Scripture are named after women: Esther and Ruth. In the *Talmud* there are stories of unusual women, such as Beruriah the wife of Rabbi Meir who distinguished herself by outstanding intellectual attainments. It was never intended by Jewish law that the sphere of the home, delegated to woman, should be considered an inferior program. "Male and female he created them," says the Torah, and that was considered sufficient safeguard for woman.[10] And inasmuch as the sages built their entire system of living upon the moral teachings of the Bible it was impossible for the *Talmud* (no matter how many personal observations were made by henpecked husbands) to take an authoritative view of woman beneath the plain sense of Scripture.

A number of interesting stories about women became very popular pieces of *Haggadah*:

----

[9] There is no tribute to motherhood in the sacred literature of any religion that surpasses Proverbs 31.10-31. Such a tribute could not have been written among a people who entertained a low estimate of woman. The position of woman was higher under Mosaic law than under any other system of antiquity.

[10] Genesis 1.27. *See also* Leviticus 19.3—"Every one of you shall revere his mother and his father."

1. WHY GOD MADE WOMAN FROM A RIB

(To extol modesty as woman's noblest virtue.)

This *Haggadah* is based upon Genesis 2.21 wherein the Biblical passage tells how the Lord God caused a deep sleep to fall upon Adam. While Adam slept a rib was taken from him out of which God fashioned Eve, the first woman. Why did God take a rib? Why was Eve not fashioned from some other part of Adam's body? God deliberated from which part of man to create woman. He said "I must not create her from the head that she should not carry herself haughtily; nor from the eye that she should not be too inquisitive; nor from the ear that she should not be an eavesdropper; nor from the mouth that she should not be too talkative nor from the hand that she should not be too acquisitive; nor from the foot that she should not be a gadabout. But I will fashion her from a hidden part of man's body that she should be modest."

2. THE WOMAN WHO KNEW WHAT WAS MOST PRECIOUS

(A lesson which teaches every woman how to be smart.)

There was a woman who lived ten years with her husband and had borne no child. They went to Rabbi Simeon ben Yohai and asked to be divorced. He told them that as their coming together was with a banquet so their separation ought to be with a banquet. They agreed and made for themselves a holiday and a banquet. During the banquet the husband drank more than enough. When his mind returned to him he said to her: "Look around in my house for what you think is most precious and take it with you as you leave for your father's house."

What did she do? When he had gone to sleep she beckoned to her servants and said to them, "Carry him on the mattress to my Father's house." They did just that. In the middle of the night the husband woke up.

"Whither have I been brought?" he asked.

"To the house of my father," she answered.

"What have I to do here?" he demanded.

"Did you not tell me last night to take that which was the most precious from your house and go with it to my father's house?" While he was reflecting upon these words, she added: "There is nothing in the world more precious to me than you."

They went back to Rabbi Simeon ben Yohai and he prayed for them. Later on they were blessed with a child.

3. THE GODLY WIFE

(Reinforcing the concept of the Godly wife by Biblical support.)

Rabbi Aha said: "If a man marries a Godly wife it is as though he had fulfilled the whole of Scripture from beginning to end. To him applies the verse (Psalm 128.3) "Your wife will be like a fruitful vine." Therefore the verses in Proverbs which extol the virtuous wife are arranged in complete alphabetical sequence.[11] It is solely for the merit of the righteous women in each generation that each generation is redeemed, as it is written: "He has remembered his steadfast love and faithfulness to the House of Israel" (Psalm 98.3). Why house? Could not Scripture have said "by reason of the children of Israel"? The answer is that "house" means wife.[12]

4. WOMAN'S POWER

(To illustrate the popular saying, "Woman determines man's behavior.")

A couple lived together for ten years and having no children, they said to each other "We are no profit to God" and so they were divorced. The man married an impious woman and she transformed him into a man of wickedness. The woman married a man of wickedness and she transformed him into a man of goodness.

❖   ❖   ❖

Interlaced with the discussions and debates of the rabbis, one finds scattered throughout Talmudic literature an attitude of rapturous love towards the law. This attitude is expressed so frequently as to form a special section of the

---

[11] The reference here is to Proverbs 31.10-31 where each verse in the Hebrew (but not in the English translation) starts off with a letter of the Hebrew alphabet in orderly sequence.

[12] This is an interpretative play upon words; for *house* is the regular rabbinic equivalent for *wife*.

Haggadah known as the "Sayings of the Fathers" (*Aboth*). Within this tractate are gathered the favorite maxims of approximately sixty sages who lived and labored in behalf of the law during a period of nearly five hundred years (300 B.C. to 200 A.D.). As this tractate is the most widely read portion of Talmudic literature its importance warrants giving the reader a full-scale view of its contents.[13]

However, stretching beyond the composition of the "Sayings of the Fathers" (which became a part of the finalized *Mishnah* in 217 A.D.) there developed another three hundred years of intellectual and spiritual activity until the *Talmud* was redacted by Rabina II in 500 A.D. During those three intervening centuries many rabbis added sublime thoughts to the *Haggadah* treasure of rhapsodical love for the law. As these lyrical gems mingle poetry with wisdom and spiritual insight it will be of value to present a few illustrations.

1. THE LAW IS ISRAEL'S BEAUTY

(To the sages the entire law, whether it dealt with petty things or important matters or whether it concerned itself with ritual or morality, was a glorious privilege to uphold.)

The Bible says "You are beautiful, my love" (Song of Solomon 1.15). The law is indeed beautiful, and its beauty is expressed through both its positive and negative commandments. It is beautiful in loving deeds, beautiful in your house with the heave offerings and the tithes, beautiful in the fields by the commands about gleaning, the Forgotten Sheaf and the Second Tithe; beautiful in the regulations about mixed seeds and fringes, about first fruits, and the fourth year planting; beautiful in the law of circumcision, beautiful in prayer, in the reading of the *Shema,* in the law of the doorposts (*Mezuzah*) and the phylacteries, in the law of the *Lulaf* and Citron; beautiful too in repentance and in good works; beautiful in this world and beautiful in the world to come.

---

[13] *See* pp. 161-180.

2. INSPIRATION FROM KING DAVID

(The rabbis frequently pictured King David as one of them spending hours in the daily study of the Torah.)

Beloved is the Torah for when King David asked God to give him something it was the law that he desired as it is written in Scripture "Thou art good and doest good" (Psalm 119.68), which properly interpreted means: "Thy goodness, O God, is exceedingly great towards me, and towards all those who come into the world. May thy goodness be ample towards me in that thou wilt teach me thy statutes." [14]

3. THE LAW IS LIKE A LIFESAVING ROPE

(The sages prove this by taking various verses from the Bible and stringing their thoughts together.)

It is written in the Book of Numbers (15.39) "not to follow after your own heart and your own eyes." The heart and the eyes are the panders for the body, for they lead the body to be unchaste. But it also says in the Book of Numbers (15.40) "So you shall remember and do all my commandments." Like a man who fell into the water: the steersman threw him a rope and cried aloud "Grasp the rope with your hand! Don't let go, for if you do you will lose your life!" So God has declared to the Israelites:

"You who held fast to the LORD your God are all alive this day" (Deuteronomy 4.4).

"Keep hold of instruction, do not let go; guard her, for she is your life!" (Proverbs 4.13).

"Be holy to your God!" (Numbers 15.40). As long as you execute the commandments of the law you are sanctified, but if you separate yourselves from them you are profaned.

4. THE LAW AS A SOURCE OF HEALING

(This thought is based upon Exodus 15.26 "I am the LORD your healer.")

God said to Moses, "Say to the children of Israel that the words of the law which I have given you are a source of healing for you and of life" for it is written in Scripture, "They

---

[14] Psalm 119.92 adds to this thought because David says there: "If thy law had not been my delight I should have perished in my affliction."

are life to him who finds them, and healing to all his flesh"
(Proverbs 4.22), and it also says in Scripture that the law
will be "healing to your flesh and refreshment to your bones"
(Proverbs 3.8).

5. THE CROWN OF THE LAW

(The greatest crown in life is the intellectual and spiritual
royalty that each person may confer upon himself.)

There are three crowns: the crown of the law, the crown
of the priesthood, and the crown of the kingdom. Aaron was
worthy of the crown of the priesthood and obtained it. David
was worthy of the crown of the kingdom and obtained it.
But the crown of the Torah (law) remains always available
so that no man shall have the pretext to say: "If the crown
of the priesthood and the crown of the kingdom were yet
available, I would have proved myself worthy of them and
have obtained them." For the crown of the Torah is available
for all. For God says: "Of him who proves himself worthy
of that particular crown I reckon it to him as if all the three
were yet available, and he had proved himself worthy of them
all. And of every one who does not prove himself worthy of
the crown of the law, I reckon it unto him as if all three
crowns were available but he had, unfortunately, proved himself unworthy of them."

6. THE SEARCH

(Finding the law is greater than finding any material treasure.)

It says in the Bible, "If you seek it like silver, and search
for it as for hidden treasures" (Proverbs 2.4). Rabbi Phinehas
said: If you seek after the words of the law as for hidden
treasures, God will not withhold from you your reward. If a
man loses some money or even a small coin in his house,
how many lamps and wicks does he not kindle till he finds it!
If for that which gives the life of an hour in this world, a man
kindles all these lamps and wicks, how much more should
you search, as for hidden treasure, after the words of the law
which gives life in this world and life in the world to come?

7. What a Father Did

(Illustrating the role of the enlightened parent.)

Nehorai said: I have put aside every occupation in the world to teach my son nothing but the law (Torah). For the benefits of it are enjoyable both in this world and in the world to come. It is not so with other occupations. If a man is sick or old or suffering, he cannot practice his occupation, and he dies of hunger. But the law keeps a man from all evil in his youth, and gives him hope and an assured outlook in his old age.

8. True Guardians

(A lesson on citizenship.)

Who are the true guardians of a city? Not the senators. And not the chief of the city guard. The true guardians are the teachers of the law and the teachers of the *Mishnah*.

9. Gold versus Glass

(Showing the value of the law.)

The words of the law are like golden vessels; the more you scour them and rub them the more they glisten and reflect the face of him who looks at them. So with the words of the Torah, whenever you repeat them they glisten and lighten the face, as it says in Scripture, "The commandment of the Lord is pure, enlightening the eyes" (Psalm 19.8). But if you neglect them they become like vessels of glass which are easily broken, as it says: "Gold and glass cannot equal it" (Job 28.17).

10. Love or Fear?

(The doctrine of obeying God out of love and not out of fear.)

It says in the Book of Psalms (119.113) "I hate double-minded men." Who are these people about whom the Psalmist speaks? They are those who ponder over the fear of God because of their sufferings, but not from love. David said: "I am not like them. It is not from compulsion or from fear but from love that I fulfil thy commands, O God! for does it not stand written in Scripture 'Thy law do I love'? Therefore, I hate what thou hatest; I love what thou lovest. An earthly ruler publishes his decrees and all obey them. They do so out of fear ouly. But I am not so. From love of the law I fulfil the law."

11. Not a Load but a Lift

(More about David's attitude. Of course it is not really David who is speaking but the sages who are giving their teaching by using his personality.)

David said, "Oh, how I love thy law" (Psalm 119.97). It is always with me. I have not neglected it at all. And because I have not neglected it, it has been to me not a burden but a song. Moreover, "Thy commandment . . . is ever with me" (Psalm 119.98) because I have not busied myself with other books but only with "thy law." "The law may be compared with a jar full of honey. If you pour water into it the honey trickles out. So, if you let other things enter your heart the words of the law go out."

12. King David's Harp

(A lesson to encourage people to study the law.)

There was a harp under David's head, and he arose and played upon it in the nights. Rabbi Levi said that the harp hung over his bed, and when midnight came, and the north wind blew on it, the harp played by itself. When David heard it he would arise and occupy himself with the law. Now when the Israelites heard the voice of David busying himself with the law, they said: "If King David studies the law, how much more must we!" And they did so.

13. The Supreme Doctrine

(To teach that it is man's duty to imitate God.)

What means the text: "You shall walk after the Lord your God" (Deuteronomy 13.4)? Is it possible for a man to walk after God of whom it is written "The Lord your God is a devouring fire" (Deuteronomy 4.24)? But the meaning is to follow the attributes of God: (a) As he clothed the naked (Genesis 3.21) so do you clothe the naked, (b) As he visited the old and the sick (Genesis 17.1) do you visit the old and the sick, (c) As he comforted the mourners (Genesis 25.11) so do you comfort those who mourn, (d) As he buried the dead (Deuteronomy 34.6) so do you bury the dead.

14. IN PARTNERSHIP WITH GOD

(To teach that faithful compliance with the law elevates man to copartnership with God.)

God says, "If you read the Torah (law) you do a *mitzvah* (noble act) for you help me to preserve the world, since if it were not for law the world would again become 'without form and void,' as it was before Creation."

15. HOW GOD IS LINKED TO THE LAW

(An illustration showing the linkage between God, Israel, and the law.)

Can there be a sale in which the seller sells himself along with the object he sells? God says, "I sold you my Torah, and with it I, as it were, sold myself." This transaction may be compared to a king who had only one daughter and another king sought her and married her. The father said, "My daughter is an only child. I cannot be parted from her. And yet to ask you not to take her away is also not possible for she is your wife. Do me, therefore, this kindness: whithersoever you go prepare for me a chamber that I may dwell with you, for I cannot forsake my daughter." So God says to Israel: "I have given you my Torah; I cannot be separated from her. Yet, I cannot say to you that you shall not take her. Therefore, in every place whither you go make me a house (synagogue) wherein I may dwell."

The love of the law, as expressed in Talmudic literature, is unique in the histories of mankind.[15] The reader need only search his own attitudes towards law, or review in his mind such knowledge as he may have of the attitudes of other races or nations to be convinced that nothing quite like the Talmudic view has ever been the possession of an entire people. The sages of Israel enjoy the distinction of having made the subject of law widespread and popular.

---

[15] Ben-Lakish (*see* p. 125) once said: "It is forbidden for a scholar to teach the *Halakah* in public unless he can present it in form as charming as when the bride is presented to her lover."

"This book of the law shall not depart out of your mouth, but you shall meditate on it day and night" (Joshua 1.8). The sages took this Biblical admonition with intense earnestness and zeal. Their love of the Torah penetrated deeply into all types of Jewish society. Discussions on the law, books about the law, schools for the study of the law, and popular lectures based upon every phase of legal thinking entered into the normal every day life of the people. Nothing like it exists in our modern society.

* * *

One of the purposes of the *Haggadah* was to help people understand God. Because *Haggadah* gave rein to the ingenuity of the interpreter in the use of metaphor, or pictorial accommodation, it became very important. The problem was how to bring the reality of God closer to the warmth of the human heart. This could not be done by adopting abstract metaphysical creeds or writing long and involved articles of faith. It was the "story" (*Haggadah*) based upon the Bible which supplied the need. The sages kept God close to the people by folkloristic transformation through the medium of the *Haggadah*. They brought God into the home and made him a member of the family.

In the specimen illustrations of this type of *Haggadah* one soon discovers that the rabbis possessed great ability to unfold to the fullest all the spiritual power hidden within Biblical texts. There is nothing legal here. No one is asked to pirouette with the scholars on the needle points of the law. One is required to be conscious only of the luminous so that the light coming from Scripture can be developed into a sustaining radiance. In spiritual insight and in the powers of spiritual conception the Talmudic sages were unquestionably superior to the pagan philosophers of Greece or Rome. The rabbis taught that God is "here" as well as "there" and by their stories they gave solid support to man's agelong quest for cosmic meaning. In typical rabbinical style these stories about God enlightened the eyes of the

Jew; they enabled him to behold all that essentially concerned his relationship to Deity; yet great care was taken not to guarantee an infallible answer.

1. GOD IS OFTEN CALLED "MAKOM"

(To teach that the word "Place" (*Makom*), by which God is frequently called in Talmudic literature, carries with it an important spiritual significance.)

Rabbi Ammi said: Why is God given the appellation of "place"? Because he is the place of the world, and the world is not his place. He fills the world, but the world does not contain him. Rabbi Abba ben Yudan said: The matter is like a warrior who rides upon a horse, and his weapons hang down on each side; the horse is an adjunct and secondary to the rider, but the rider is not an adjunct nor is he secondary to the horse.

2. THE GREATER GOD

(Showing a pagan woman the way to a better understanding.)

A heathen lady said to Rabbi Jose: "My god is greater than your God, for when your God appeared to Moses in the thorn bush, Moses hid his face, but when he saw my god, the snake, he fled before it" (Exodus 4.3). Rabbi Jose said: "When our God appeared to Moses in the thorn bush, there was no place to which Moses could have fled. Whither could he have fled? To the heaven? To the sea? To the land? For our God says, 'Do I not fill heaven and earth?' (Jeremiah 23.24). But from your god, the snake, a man has to run only a few steps to save himself."

3. GOD'S DWELLING PLACE

(God is near even though he is far.)

When God declared, "Make me a dwelling place," Moses pondered and said, "The glory of God fills the upper and the lower worlds, and yet he says to me, make me a dwelling place." How is this to be understood? Scripture supplies the answer: "You are the sons of the LORD your God . . . for I am a father to Israel" (Deuteronomy 14.1 and Jeremiah 31.9). It is an honor to children to be near their father, and an honor to a father to be near his children. Therefore, God's command to Moses is understandable. It means: make a house for the father that he may dwell near his children.

4. THE NATURE OF GOD

(A lesson on the nature of God built upon Jeremiah 23.24. "Do I not fill heaven and earth? says the LORD.")

A Samaritan asked Rabbi Meir: "Is it possible that he of whom it is written, 'Do I not fill heaven and earth' spoke to Moses from between the small space of the two staves of the ark?" [16] Rabbi Meir asked that the Samaritan bring him a mirror that magnifies. The Samaritan did so and saw himself enlarged. Rabbi Meir then asked that he bring a reducing mirror. The Samaritan now saw himself smaller. Addressing himself to the Samaritan, Rabbi Meir declared: "If you, who are a mortal made of flesh and blood, can change your appearance, how much more can he who is the divine Creator of the world? God's ability to fill heaven and earth is just as understandable as his ability to speak to Moses from between the two staves of the ark."

5. THE ONE GOD

(Despite many manifestations there is only the One. He is always the same God. In spite of varieties of representation there is no breach in divine unity.)

God said to Israel, "Because you have seen me in many likenesses, there are not therefore many gods. But it is ever the same God: I am the Lord your God." Rabbi Levi said: "God appeared to them like a mirror, in which many faces can be reflected: a thousand people look at it; it looks at all of them. So when God spoke to the Israelites, each one thought that God spoke individually to him. How do we know that this is so? Rabbi Levi deduced this idea ingeniously from Scripture because it says in the older Bibles "I am the Lord *thy* God"—the word "thy" is singular in grammatical form thereby indicating oneness. This is proof not only that God is one but that He appears to each person according to the individual's level of understanding. Obviously this is so,

---

[16] The staves mentioned here refer to those poles by means of which the ark of the Covenant was carried (*see* Exodus 25.10 ff.).

says Rabbi Levi, for Scripture does not use the plural grammatical form, "I am the Lord *your* God," but rather "I am the Lord *thy* God."

6. God's Many Names

(Each name teaches something about God.)

Rabbi Abba ben Memel explained: God said to Moses, "You desire to know my name. I am called according to my deeds. When I judge my creatures, I am called *Elohim;* when I wage war against the wicked, I am called *Sabaoth;* when I suspend judgment for a man's sins, I am called *El Shaddai* (God Almighty); but when I have compassion upon my world, I am called *Yahweh,* for *Yahweh* means the attribute of mercy, as it is said, 'Yahweh, Yahweh (the Lord, the Lord), a God merciful and gracious, slow to anger and abounding in steadfast love and faithfulness; keeping steadfast love for thousands, forgiving iniquity, and transgression and sin'" (Exodus 34.6-7).

7. How the Divine Power Is Weakened

(Lack of faith weakens God's power.)

Deuteronomy 32.18 declares: "You forgot the God who gave you birth." God says: "Each time I sought to do you good you weakened the divine Power: You stood by the Red Sea and said, 'This is my God and I will praise Him' (Exodus 15.2) and then you said, 'Let us choose a captain, and go back to Egypt' (Numbers 14.4). You stood at Mt. Sinai and said, 'All that the Lord has spoken to us we will do.' I sought to do you good but you turned to the Golden Calf and declared, 'This is your God, O Israel!' Lo, whenever I seek to do you good, you weaken the divine Power."

8. God's Relationship to Israel

(Teaching that Israelites have no need to fear.)

God said to Moses: "Am I not he whose sons you are and whose Father I am? You are my brethren and I am your brother; you are my companions and I am your companion; you are my beloved and I am yours. Have I caused you loss in any wise? I seek nothing from you . . . Is there any respect of persons with me? The reward for fulfilling each commandment is inherent in it whether the doer be Gentile or Israelite, man or woman, bondman or bondwoman." Hence they say that if a man enhances the glory of heaven, his own glory is enhanced with that of heaven. But whoso diminishes the glory of heaven while enhancing his own, will find his own diminished while the glory of heaven remains in its place.

9. WHAT GOD CAN DO

(To inform the Jew of God's methods.)

In a suit before a king, one man is prosecutor, and one man is counsel for the defence. The prosecutor cannot be counsel for the defence, nor can the counsel for the defence be the prosecutor. But with God it is otherwise. He can be both prosecutor and counsel for the defence. For example: (a) The same mouth which said, "Ah, sinful nation . . . offspring of evildoers" (Isaiah 1.4) said also, "Open the gates that the righteous nation . . . may enter in" (Isaiah 26.2). (b) The same mouth which said, "A people laden with iniquity" (Isaiah 1.4) said also, "Your people shall all be righteous" (Isaiah 60.21). (c) The same mouth which said, "Even though you make many prayers, I will not listen" (Isaiah 1.15), said, "Before they call I will answer" (Isaiah 65.24).

10. GOD AND AN IDOL COMPARED

(Both have the same attributes of being "far" and "near"— but what a difference!)

Rabbi Judah ben Simon said, "An idol is near and far. So too is God. How then are we to understand the difference?" The answer is: An idolater makes an idol and sets it up in his house. So the idol is near. When he cries unto the idol there is no answer to his human need, therefore the idol is far. But this is not true of God. From here to heaven is a very long journey which shows that God is far. But he is also very near, for if a man prays and meditates in his heart, God is near to answer his prayer.

11. SLAVE OR SON?

(Man's relationship to God depends upon man himself.)

Hearken to thy Father who is in Heaven. He deals with you as with an only son if you obey him. But if not, he deals with you as a slave. When you do his will, he is your father and you are his son. But if you do not his will then he is your owner, and opposed to your consent—you are his slave.

12. THE FATHERHOOD OF GOD

(To teach that the fatherhood of God is synonymous with his love.)

A king's son fell into evil ways. The king sent a tutor to him with the message, "Return, O my son." But the son sent to his father the reply: "With what can I return? I am ashamed to come before you." Then the father sent a note to him, saying: "Can a son be ashamed to return to his father? If you return, do you not return to your father?"

❂   ❂   ❂

From the examples of the various types and kinds of *Haggadah* brought together in this chapter, it can be seen that the whole realm of the *Haggadah* derives from the Old Testament. Some have compared the *Haggadah* to a stream issuing forth from an original source and then flowing steadily onwards until it pours its gathered waters into the vast "Sea of the *Talmud*." There are others who have thought of the *Haggadah* in terms of slumbering sparks which are awakened to life by the action of a hammer. "As the hammer splits the rocks into many splinters, causing numerous sparks to flash forth, so will a verse from the Bible yield many meanings." [17]

It does not make too much difference how we prefer to think of the *Haggadah* providing its method is understood, namely: the germination, from a single thought in the Bible, of new ideas which reveal an inner spiritual meaning not evident in the literal words of the text. *Haggadah* never aspired to the dignity of Scripture. But with the growth of Judaism the text of the Bible stood in need of supplementary expansion.

The sages wanted to express the larger intent of sacred

---

[17] *Talmud*, tractate *Sanhedrin* 34a. Compare Jeremiah 23.29 where it says: "Is not my word like . . . a hammer which breaks the rock in pieces?"

Scripture. They did this through the medium of interpretation which, to them, was not something different from the
Bible but rather the Bible itself—enlarged, expanded, and
fructified. For this reason they were never alarmed at a possible multiplicity of views. They found support for multiplicity in the final words of the Pentateuch—"in the sight
of all Israel." [18] Consequently, they concluded that these
words indicate that every Jew may see into the Torah
according to his own ability. Indeed, the greater number
of Haggadic interpretations the larger the area of infinite
mind. The Talmudic sages were aware, as we are aware,
that many a Bible text taken in its literal sense often means
little. However, when unveiled by interpretation, the same
text, which at first evokes no meaning at all, suddenly glows
with an inexpressibly profound significance. The Bible was
the realm into which the sages projected their thought and
from which they received in return large rewards. This constant interchange, often carried on with inconceivable sub-
tlety, gave the *Haggadah* an importance second only to the
Halakah.

---

[18] Deuteronomy 34.12.

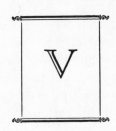

FOUNDERS OF THE TALMUD

INASMUCH AS THE *Talmud* is the creation of the rabbis it is only natural that many stories of their lives and labors should be found embedded in its pages.

By and large, the rabbis were men of humility and tolerance who supported themselves as farmers, small shopkeepers, or workers in various kinds of handicraft. Some were physicians who devoted their lives to the healing arts. Taken as a whole they were saintly sages practicing self-denial and charity in its widest sense, never at any time receiving compensation for their religious work. Without payment or material acknowledgment of any kind they taught the written and oral traditions of Judaism. Despite the somber cast of their background, which involved the destruction of their Palestinian homeland, they were essentially men of good cheer. The sunniness of their faith was remarkable considering that they lived under the rule of cruel foreign taskmasters who seemed to delight in wars and in every manner of outrageous persecution. Roman brutality, which subjected so many of Christianity's adherents to martyrdom, was no less ruthless in its wholesale murder of Jewish leaders. All the suffering endured by the early

Christian Church can be multiplied tenfold by the calculated fury in which the Romans battered down Jewish cities
and annihilated whole populations.

*   *   *

The martyrdom of Rabbi Hananiah ben Teradion illustrates how the Roman determination to uproot the teaching
of the Bible was met by the determination of the sages to
suffer death rather than yield their right of religious freedom. This story is told in tractate *Aboda Zara* (17b–18a) in
considerable detail. The little town of Siknin in Galilee had
been the residence of Rabbi Teradion. Here he directed
a school and administered the religious affairs of the community. So careful was he in handling the charitable funds
of Siknin that the *Talmud* has preserved a saying that no
one ought to contribute to any charity-treasury unless its
administration is like that of Teradion's.

Since the destruction of the Temple in the year 70 A.D.
the Jews had been anxious to throw off the Roman yoke,
but the more they labored to rid themselves of the Caesars
the more their country was subjected to insult, torture, and
pillage. In the year 117 A.D. Hadrian became the Roman
emperor, a ruler determined to strengthen his hold upon
Palestine by rebuilding Jerusalem as a pagan city which was
to have a pagan altar dedicated to Jupiter whose high priest
was Hadrian himself. Now it happened that in the year
130 A.D. Hadrian visited the Holy Land and announced his
determined policy of thorough-going paganization. To the
Jews this was no new experience. Their forefathers had confronted King Antiochus Epiphanes in the days of the Mac-
cabees. Still, the Romans possessed tremendous military
might, and the people of Palestine were not anxious for
open warfare if they could honorably avoid it. But this was
not to be, for Hadrian lost no time in issuing a decree
against circumcision. The offence goaded the people into rebellion under the leadership of Bar Kochba. For approximately five long years Bar Kochba and his people held

their own against the imperial armies while the desperate
fighting tore the land to shreds. Finally in the year 135 A.D.
the Romans emerged victorious. They had added to the
decree against circumcision a decree against the observance
of the Sabbath and festivals and a decree shutting down all
schools and academies; the teaching of the Bible was forbidden and the death penalty was to be meted out to any
sage who attempted to ordain rabbis.

It was during the height of the Roman implementation of
these edicts that Rabbi Hananiah ben Teradion stood his
ground. He was arrested at a public assembly while teaching the Bible with a scroll before him. Asked why he so
openly disregarded the imperial prohibition forbidding
such a practice, he replied: "I do as my God commands
me." The *Talmud* then says that they sentenced him to be
burnt at the stake. Seeing that he carried a scroll of the
Bible in his bosom, they took it and wrapped its parchment around his body. Then they set fire to it as they kept
heaping bundles of willow wood to keep the flames burning.
To prolong his sufferings wet wool was placed over his
heart. In this condition his daughter was forced to witness
the spectacle of her father being burnt alive. "Father," she
cried, "that I should have to see you thus." The sage answered, "If I were to be burnt alone it would have been
hard for me; but now that the scroll of the Bible is being
burnt with me, God who will avenge his own humiliation
will also avenge mine." Towards the end of his agony his
disciples said to him—"Rabbi, what do you see?" He told
them, "The parchment is being burnt but its letters are soar-
ing upwards."

Thus ended in martyrdom the career of a saintly teacher
whose prophetic words, lighted by the incandescence of his
spirit, have never ceased to give courage to those who have
been entrusted with the parchments of religious freedom.
Every age seems to get its share of cruelty and inhumanity,
perhaps none more brutal than the Hadrianic persecutions
which swept Palestine from 132–135 A.D. Yet, in all times

and in all places there have been choice spirits who, while seeing their sacred books burnt, have remembered the un- scorched letters of Rabbi Teradion's scroll winging their way upwards to an enduring infinity.

*　　*　　*

The outstanding supporter of Bar Kochba's rebellion against the Romans was not Rabbi Teradion but his brilliant con- temporary Rabbi Akiba ben Joseph who left his books, his home, and his academy to share the rigors of the campaign. Akiba was already a very old man when the Jews of Pales- tine decided that war was the only alternative to Hadrian's demands. Akiba himself had been to Rome as a member of an important delegation of rabbis in an effort to modify the ruthlessness of the imperial policy. When all efforts to bring about a relaxation of the edicts against Judaism failed, Rabbi Akiba became the spiritual leader of the Jew- ish people in backing Bar Kochba's rebellion. It was a war bitterly fought; the losses were tremendous on both sides. Rabbi Akiba was arrested and after a period of confinement he was condemned to die by torture. Ordinarily the Romans crucified their victims, the prisoner being nailed to a wooden cross where he would hang until dead. Rabbi Akiba was sentenced to be flayed alive with iron combs.

Of all the founders of the *Mishnah* Rabbi Akiba is re- garded as its most important sage. He is rightly called the father of rabbinical (Talmudic) Judaism for he accum- ulated and arranged the vast materials of the Oral Law in such proper, systematic, and methodical order that the work of those who came after him was made comparatively easy. A century after Akiba's death the redaction of the *Mishnah* took place under the editorial board of Rabbi Judah "the Prince." Had these editors not been able to draw upon the labors of Akiba's original Mishnaic collection, in all proba- bility the task could not have been carried through, at least not with such competence and skill. Akiba was the archi- tect of the *Mishnah*. Without his pioneer plans the entire

structure of the *Mishnah* would have been considerably different than what it turned out to be.

As a brilliant religio-ethical lawyer Rabbi Akiba added
greatly to the extension and interpretation of the *Halakah*.
So creative were his procedures that it was said of him that
he was able "to discover things that were even unknown
to Moses." [1] His genius in the field of the law (*Halakah*)
was one of the major formative factors in the determination
of the whole course of the *Talmud*. Because of his eminence
as a religio-ethical teacher of the law, and because of his
martyrdom, Talmudic literature has preserved a large number of stories (*Haggadah*) touching every phase of his life
beginning with his birth in about 50 A.D.

A study of Akiba bears striking resemblance to Abraham
Lincoln. Born of lowly people this man, who had been an
illiterate shepherd, lifted himself to enduring fame. Until
his fortieth year he could neither read nor write. The story
of his awakening occurred when Akiba pondered the significance of drops of water which dripped on a stone from
buckets near an old well. "If these drippings," mused Akiba,
"can by continuous action penetrate this solid stone, how
much more can the persistent word of God penetrate the
fleshy human heart if that word but be presented with
patient insistence."

The great romance within the *Talmud* is the love story of
Rachel, the daughter of a wealthy man, who married the
illiterate, tall Akiba against her father's wishes. At the insistence of Rachel, Akiba took to learning the alphabet;
and when he had mastered rudimentary things his wife
worked to send him to an academy. Rachel stood faithfully
by her plodding husband, sacrificing even her wealth of
hair—so the story goes—that it might bring money to finance
his education. Accordingly, Abika left Rachel and his children for a period of several years. But he was destined to

---

[1] Quoted from the *Pesikta* a Midrashic commentary (chapter *Parah*)
Edition Buber 39b. (As to Akiba's contribution in the field of legal interpretation *see* p. 192.)

return as a famous scholar. One day he came back escorted by many disciples who reverently followed their master to his old residence. On seeing a poorly clad woman about to embrace their distinguished sage, Akiba's students sought to restrain her. But Akiba exclaimed, "Let her alone; for what I am, and for what we are, to this noble woman our thanks are due. For her love, and through her love, I have by God's blessing become what you see." Akiba caught Rachel in his arms. The crowd, touched and humbled, left them together.

Notwithstanding the Roman decrees against teaching the Bible, Akiba continued to instruct the people in their religious duties. At the risk of his life he went about from town to town seeking to establish more schools while he spoke openly to large audiences. One day a man named Pappos ben Judah, who had been advising the Jews to submit to the Romans at all costs, asked Akiba if he did not fear the consequences of his actions.

"Would it not be better to give up teaching the law and thus save your life?"

"You speak like a fool, Pappos, even though many people think you are wise." Akiba was the incarnation of convincing and persuasive speech. "Let me tell you a parable," he said, "which has a bearing on the question you have asked."

Then Akiba, because he was so resourceful, so large of vision, and so consecrated to the Torah spoke these words:

"A fox one day was walking along the shore of a lake. He noticed that the little fish were scurrying to and fro in the water, in the greatest agitation. As he looked at them he had a strong desire to eat them. Addressing himself to the fish he asked: 'Why are you so frightened?' They told the fox that fishermen were spreading nets in the lake. 'We are endeavoring to flee from our enemies, and we are anxious to avoid the many nets and snares which they have prepared for us.' Reynard thought fast, 'I'll tell you what to do,' he said slyly, 'and it will be an easy way to secure your safety. Come ashore with me on yonder rocks and let us dwell

together as one people. Once you are on dry land we can
live together in tranquility in the same manner as our ancestors did before us.' The little fish laughed and replied:—
'O you foxy one! You talk like a fool even though many
think you are clever. What silly advice you are handing
out to us.' The fox was taken back by the fishes' appraisal
of his suggestion. 'But why?' he asked. 'The water is our
native element,' they replied. 'If we are in danger here how
much greater will be our risk if we leave it. If we are in
constant fear of our lives in the normal element in which
we live, do you suppose we can survive on dry land which is
an abnormal environment altogether repugnant to our nature and so contrary to our habits?' "

Then Rabbi Akiba concluded: "Even so it is with us, my
dear Pappos. The Jews may be compared to the little fish.
We live in the element of the Torah which is our sacred law.
This element is our support and our life. If we are beset
with dangers while we are in our own normal environment
what would happen to us if we came out of it and tried to
survive in a pagan Roman environment so repugnant to our
habits?" [2]

As the *Talmud* abounds in many pieces of *Haggadah*
which illustrate the philosophical outlook of the sages, it is
interesting to note how each generation of editors was
meticulously careful to preserve the stories touching the
spiritual attitudes of so notable a leader as Rabbi Akiba.
For example, there is the story of the lamp, the rooster and
the donkey, which elucidates the truth of Akiba's favorite
maxim of faith and optimism that "whatever God does, he
does for the best."

Akiba was once compelled by persecution to leave his

---

[2] This story taken from the *Talmud*, tractate *Berachoth* 61b. In another
place in the *Talmud* the question is asked why men are likened to fish
when, for example, the prophet Habakkuk (1.14) says—"Thou makest men
like the fish of the sea." The *Talmud* explains this by saying that as fish
immediately perish when they come to dry land, so do men immediately
perish when they separate themselves from the words of Torah (*Talmud*,
tractate *Aboda Zarah* 3b).

native land. In flight from the Romans he had with him only
his donkey for transportation, a rooster which served to
awaken him at dawn, and a lamp by which he could study.
As night was approaching, the tired wanderer came to a
village and asked for a lodging. To his astonishment he
found every door closed against him. Not one of the inhospitable inhabitants would give him a room. He was obliged
to go into a near-by forest. "It is very hard," said the sage
to himself, "to be compelled to seek shelter from rough
weather in the woods, but God's ways are right even though
we can't always understand them, and whatsoever he does
is ultimately for the best." Having affirmed his optimistic
faith under these trying circumstances, Akiba proceeded to
seat himself beneath a tree, light his lamp, and begin his
study of Scripture. He had scarcely read a chapter when
a violent storm arose and blew out his light. A bit later a
hungry lion came by and devoured his donkey. And not
long after that a wildcat ate the rooster. Akiba passed a
sleepless night. In the morning he trudged to the village to
see if he could purchase another donkey to continue his
journey. His surprise was astonishingly great when he found
not a single person alive. Apparently a band of robbers had
fallen upon the village in the night, slaughtered its inhabitants, and plundered their houses. "Now I know by experience," said Akiba, "that poor mortal men are often short-
sighted and blind. Frequently they regard those things as
evils which actually turn out to preserve them. Had not the
inhospitable people of that village driven me into the forest
I would have assuredly shared their fate. Had not the wind
extinguished my lamp, the robbers would have been drawn
to my place in the forest and have murdered me."

While the sages of the *Talmud* maintained the importance of faith, nonetheless they stressed the duty of man to
help himself. To neglect the duty of self-help upon the exaggerated idea that one can fold his hands in a do-nothing
attitude, while he casts all his problems upon God, was considered a violation of the religious spirit of Judaism. One

day as Rabbi Akiba was walking through the streets of Jerusalem, a sick man came up to him complaining about his ailment, asking the sage his advice. When Akiba told him of a remedy, another man reproached Akiba for not being truly religious. "If it is God's will that this sick man should have a certain disease, are you going to act against God's decision by removing the disease which has been decreed for him?" Rabbi Akiba asked the man the nature of his occupation. "I am a gardener as you may see by the tools which I carry in my hands," answered the man. "But why do you interfere with the earth which God has created?" asked Rabbi Akiba. The gardener thought for a moment, "If I were not to manure, prune, and water the trees, how could I expect them to produce their fruits?" "Even so it is with man," declared Rabbi Akiba as he pointed out that it no more constitutes a lack of faith in God to use medicines in order to cure a disease than it is a lack of faith in God to prune a tree. "Every man requires tender treatment and attention for his body in order to make it flourish and keep it in good condition."

Because he was a profoundly religious man, Akiba understood that absolute submission to the will of God can transform the apparent meaninglessness of suffering into an acknowledgment of God's providence. To explain the mystery of pain, Rabbi Akiba once discoursed on the subject of four types of sufferers. He drew a comparison of a king chastising his children. The first son on being chastised maintains silence, the second son rebels, the third supplicates for mercy, but the fourth son, the noblest and best, exclaims: "Father proceed with thy chastisement, as David said, 'Wash me thoroughly from my iniquity, and cleanse me from my sin.'" [3] For Akiba these words were a confession of faith. Not that he could rationalize suffering or explain it away. But there was for him a unique spiritual splendor in the great conflict with suffering. In the philos-

---

[3] Psalm 51:2. This discourse of Rabbi Akiba is found in *Talmud*, tractate *Semachoth*.

ophy of Akiba, the very hardness of man's lot, the brevity of his years, the infinite moral struggle of his days and hours, his sorrows, losses—even the battles he wages and loses—have the purpose of strengthening the soul. This for him was the meaning of the great passage in Deuteronomy 6.5, "You shall love the LORD your God with all your heart, and with all your soul, and with all your might." These words were actually upon his lips when the Roman executioners were tearing his flesh with combs of iron. When this kind of faith dominates the soul, even death adds dignity to man.

No Talmudic sage lived in the immediacy of his relation to God more vividly than Rabbi Akiba. That is why Akiba coined the phrase: "Whatever God does is done for the best." Of course, this view is very old. It found expression in the Bible in that magnificent statement in the Book of Job 1.21: "The LORD gave, and the LORD has taken away; blessed be the name of the LORD." One of the major differences between Judaism and paganism was on this very point of suffering. "Be not like the idolators," said Akiba, "when all goes well with them, they honor their idols; but if misfortune comes, they curse their gods. Not so the Israelites. If God sends them happiness they bless Him, and if God afflicts them with sorrow they bless Him." No man of Akiba's generation had the right to speak more authoritatively about suffering than he, for no man knew suffering in all its ways more than this rabbi. Yet, he never wavered, never lost faith. When his end came in martyrdom, he faced it with sublime insensibility to pain. In the account of Akiba's death preserved in the Palestinian version of the *Talmud*, it is said that Tineius Rufus, the Roman governor, was personally present at the execution and when he saw the sage recite the *Shema* with a smile on his lips he asked Akiba: "Are you a sorcerer that you laugh at your sufferings?" Akiba replied: "I am no sorcerer nor am I insensible to my suffering, nor is it my wish to mock you with my smile. But I rejoice at the opportunity you have given me to love my God with all my soul. I have shown my love for God with my heart and my possessions. But this day is unique, for I have an opportunity to show my love of God by yielding to Him my soul. I am therefore happy that I have attained this moment."

❊   ❊   ❊

Among the youthful scholars who were ordained by Rabbi Akiba, in defiance of Emperor Hadrian's decree, there was a young man from Asia Minor who became in a very true sense Akiba's successor. His name was Meir.[4] In all probability Meir fled to Babylonia after the death of Akiba and the collapse of the Bar Kochba rebellion. However, he returned to Palestine when Rome announced that Antoninus Pius had succeeded to the imperial throne upon the death of Hadrian. With the coming of a new emperor the harsh edicts against Judaism were relaxed and a new era was ushered in. Rabbi Meir was among those who re-established recognized authority in Judaism by assisting in the reorganization of the academy and high court (Beth Din) in a small Palestinian town in Galilee known as Usha. At Usha the youthful Meir, who had married the brilliant daughter of Rabbi Teradion, became one of the pillars of Jewish tradition.

Meir, even more than Akiba, distinguished himself as a religio-ethical lawyer. Over three hundred laws in the Mishnah are connected in some manner with his name. So important were his legal opinions that the sages who came after him accepted a large number of anonymous laws as belonging to his school. Meir loved law not only for its ethical content but for its intellectual exercise. He delighted in bringing up for discussion hypothetical cases full of complications in order to sharpen the acumen of his disciples. Yet withal he was a man of wit and humor, an irresist-

---

[4] Nothing is known of Meir's family. His real name is not certain. (See p. 59.)

ible orator with unique powers to attract large audiences interested in popular discourses.

Meir's popular lectures were given Friday evenings after the Sabbath meal. On one occasion the distinguished sage delivered an exceedingly long but interesting sermon which kept his audience in the academy far late into the night. Among the women in the audience there was one who had the misfortune to have a hot-tempered husband. As soon as the lecture was over she hastened home only to find the house plunged in darkness. "Where have you been?" Her husband stormed the question in her ears. "Perhaps you are aware," said the wife defensively, "that I, like others, appreciate the sermons of the wise Rabbi." "So!" he shouted in a rage, "It's Rabbi Meir." The wife gladly acknowledged her intellectual interest. "Well," said the irate husband, "You shall not step over the threshold of my house until you spit in the face of Rabbi Meir."

The poor woman knew full well that she was at the mercy of her husband. At first she thought that his ridiculous order, spoken in the white heat of anger, would soon be forgotten as a passing whim. But unfortunately the husband was adamant. Her situation, being locked out of her house, became desperate and the news of it spread throughout the city. Neighbors finally persuaded the woman to visit Rabbi Meir and seek his advise. Reluctantly she went to him and was happy to find the sage eager to help her. Regardless of his own dignity Rabbi Meir was most anxious that peaceful marital relations be restored. He pretended to have sore eyes. "I have an ailing eye," announced Rabbi Meir, "and my doctor assures me that if I can get a woman to spit in it seven times it would be healed." Whereupon he summoned the woman to spit in his eye seven times. "But wouldn't just once suffice?" she asked timorously. She hesitated to do as the rabbi commanded but when he insisted she was persuaded. "Now go home and tell your husband that not once but seven times you spat in Rabbi Meir's face." To his disciples, who were horrified at witnessing the ordeal, Rabbi

Meir explained that the spiritual good in re-establishing peace between husband and wife amply justified his temporary loss of dignity.

By and large, the wives of the sages enabled their husbands to fulfil the highest ideals of their rabbinical careers. One need only mention Rachel, the wife of Rabbi Akiba, whose steadfast love enabled the once illiterate shepherd to achieve so notable a place in Talmudic Judaism. Of a different type was Beruriah, the wife of Rabbi Meir. She was trained from childhood in an atmosphere of scholarship. Her father, Rabbi Teradion, was one of the most eminent sages of that generation. Consequently, Beruriah is the only woman whose place in the *Talmud* receives recognition not alone because she was the wife of a great man but because she possessed merit as a scholar of distinction in her own right. Learned legalists listened to her opinions on matters of the *Halakah* and eagerly sought her advice and counsel on a variety of subjects related to the law.

Beruriah's influence upon Rabbi Meir was a significant factor in his career. He respected her keen mind which could unravel complicated legal problems and at the same time grieve with tender-hearted womanliness upon the sins, miseries, and misfortunes of people. Her husband once complained bitterly about some Jews living in the neighborhood who were indulging in pagan practices in open violation of Jewish law. Their attitude plagued Rabbi Meir to a point where he cursed them in vexation and prayed that they should die. Beruriah overheard her husband's prayer and called him to account for its wrong emphasis. "What is in your mind?" she asked with great spiritual concern. "Do you pray for the death of these people because it is written in Scripture, 'Let sinners be consumed from the earth' (Psalm 104.35)? Well, if that's your authority, permit me to tell you that it is also possible to read the same text in such a manner that it condemns sins to perish, but not sinners. Isn't it better anyhow to wish that sinners should repent than to pray for their destruction?" [5] When her husband admitted she was right then Beruriah continued: "Look, if you please, at the other part of that same verse. Does it not say 'and let the wicked be no more'? And does this not logically imply that when sins cease then the wicked will be no more? Rather, my dear husband, should you pray that these people who are violating the law should repent and consequently be no more wicked." The *Talmud* says that Rabbi Meir, convinced of the correctness of Beruriah's interpretation, offered prayer on behalf of the people who vexed him—and they repented.

It happened once on a Sabbath that Rabbi Meir had been in the synagogue and in the academy all day instructing the people. During his absence from his house his two sons, both promising young lads, suddenly died. The *Talmud* does not mention the cause of their death, but it could well have been a case of food poisoning. Beruriah placed the bodies of her sons on the bed and covered them with a sheet. Without saying a word to any one she awaited Rabbi Meir's return to the house. He immediately asked where his sons were. "I looked around the school and I did not see them." Beruriah brought him a goblet for the ceremonial of praising the Lord at the end of the Sabbath day. Rabbi Meir recited the blessing, drank the wine, and asked again about the boys. "They will not be afar off," she said, and she placed food before him that he might eat. No sooner was the meal over than she asked him a question: "Some time ago some precious jewels were entrusted to my safekeeping. Now the owner has come to claim them again. Must I give them back to him?" Rabbi Meir looked at Beruriah gravely. "I am surprised," he said, "that my wife should even think it necessary to ask such a question. The answer is obvious. You wouldn't hesitate, would you, to restore to the owner

---

[5] Unless a person is a student of the Hebrew Bible, the point that Beruriah was making cannot be fully appreciated. The nub of the whole thing is that the same consonants may be vocalized to read sins instead of sinners.

what is rightfully his?" Beruriah replied by saying that while she knew what was right, yet in this case she did not want to return the jewels to the owner until she had acquainted him with the matter. Thereupon she led him tenderly to the upper room where their children lay dead. "My sons! my sons!" cried the father in anguish. "My sons the light of my eyes!" The mother turned her head and wept bitterly. At length she took her husband by the hand, and said, "Did you not teach me that we must not be reluctant to return that which was entrusted to our keeping? These are the jewels which God gave us to guard and today he claimed them." As they held each other they recited the words of Job (1.21): "The LORD gave, and the LORD has taken away; blessed be the name of the LORD."

The important work that Rabbi Akiba had achieved in writing down the Oral Law was carried forward by Rabbi Meir. We have already seen that it was not only the bulk of the Oral Law which required its commitment to written form but other factors too, such as the rise of Christianity and perhaps more importantly the Hadrianic persecutions. Meir, in continuing the labors of Akiba, contributed enormously to the rise of the *Mishnah*. When the task of issuing a single authoritative *Mishnah* was finally undertaken by Rabbi Judah "the Prince" the editorial board had in front of them not only the Mishnaic work of Akiba but also the Mishnaic work of Meir. In developing the law, Rabbi Meir was most anxious to have his disciples achieve a rationalistic approach. He discouraged any blind acceptance of the words of the sages of former generations no matter how overhung with tradition. Meir believed in reason as one of God's great gifts to man; and Meir wanted his disciples to use that gift. "Look not to the vessel," he would say, "but to its contents. There are new vessels (young rabbis) which are full of old wine; and there are many old vessels (the acknowledged leaders) which contain not even new wine."

Because he was at home in Greek and Latin literatures, Rabbi Meir was able to fill his lectures with stories drawn

from wide fields of human experience. He captivated his
audiences with fables, parables, maxims, and unusual interpretations of Scripture. Known as the Jewish Aesop, it
was said that he possessed a collection of three hundred
fables. Three of them are quoted in the *Talmud.*

Rabbi Meir died somewhere in Asia Minor where he had
gone after his conflict on legal and personal matters with
the Patriarch Simeon III, son of Gamaliel II. Although the
Patriarch had raised Rabbi Meir to the dignity of *hakam*
(wise man) in which office he was charged with the duty
of preparing the subjects which were to come before the
high court, nonetheless the growing power of the patriarchate finally displeased Meir and he left Palestine never again
to return. Among the eulogies which enshrine the name of
Meir none was more eloquent than the words of his contemporary, Rabbi Jose, who said that "Meir was a great
man and a saint, and was humble withal."

*   *   *

The *Talmud* itself carries the tradition that on the day on
which Rabbi Akiba died in martyrdom, Rabbi Judah "the
Prince" was born. He who was to become the redactor of
the *Mishnah,* and immortalize his name among the thousands of Judaism's great scholars, came to be called by the
simple title "the Rabbi"—that is, the rabbi par excellence.
His spiritual title "the Rabbi" was to shine more resplend-
ently than his political title "the Prince" for in truth his
princely status was recognized by Rome. Upon the death of
his father in 165 A.D. Rabbi Judah I "the Prince" became
patriarch of all the Jewish people throughout the world. He
was now in a very true sense the nearest thing to a Jewish
pope at a time when the Roman Catholic papacy was in its
most embryonic form.

Though Judah "the Prince" was patriarch and chief rabbi
of his generation, and though he was a man of great wealth,
he was among the humblest of all the sages. So great was
his personal piety that the *Talmud* frequently refers to him

as "the Holy." Yet his holiness did not bear the monastic stamp. He was very much a part of the normal everyday life of his people, his family, his children, his law court, and his disciples at the academy. Instead of making religion a burden he used all his powers to repeal several prohibitions of the sabbatical year which were still effective in his day. "I am prepared to do anything reasonable that any man may ask me to do," he once declared as the policy of his rule. These were not idle words. When a man was brought for trial before him on the grounds that he did not observe the regulations of the sabbatical year, Rabbi Judah carefully listened to the accusation and then said: "What else could you expect the poor man to do when he was hungry?" [6] In a similar vein he acted to reduce the burden of tithing while at the same time he brought the high influence of his office to eliminate an excessive number of fast days on the theory that the population should not be overburdened no matter how eager certain religionists were to develop greater piety.

In the year 175 A.D. the Emperor Marcus Aurelius visited Palestine. As Judah I had already been on friendly terms with Rome there is every reason to believe that the many anecdotes found in the *Talmud* (and Midrashic literture) about his visits and discussions with an emperor could have taken place with Marcus Aurelius. Both were unusual personalities, both were moralists, philosophers, and profoundly interested in spiritual forces. However, these "emperor-rabbi" stories are so embellished with legendary accounts that it is often very difficult to separate fact from fancy. Nevertheless, *Haggadah* of this nature became a vital part of the Talmudic biography of Judah "the Prince." Above all, these stories are valuable because of their high ethical teaching.

---

[6] Palestinian *Talmud,* tractate *Taanith.* It is interesting to note that beginning with Hillel's liberalization of the sabbatical year (*see* p. 184) his descendants strove to maintain their founder's tradition in reducing the difficulties surrounding that law.

Sometimes the Emperor would meet the Patriarch in a secret underground passage which led from the royal palace to the Rabbi's residence. But there are other reports that tell about legendary interviews which took place at sumptuous banquets which these men gave in honor of each other.[7] When they wanted to express very important views they had recourse to a species of sign language. As the Emperor needed good counsel he frequently turned to the Rabbi for advice on important matters of state, or in the case of a contemplated military campaign against an enemy. Once a royal emissary brought to Rabbi Judah a direct question from the Emperor as to what should be done with the matter of improving the financial conditions of the Empire. The message said: "The treasury is empty. Tell me what to do." The Patriarch led the emissary into his garden, and without saying a word the sage pulled up some of his large radishes and replaced them with young plants. When the emissary asked the Patriarch for a direct reply to the Emperor's question he was told that none was necessary. Upon returning to the palace the emissary reported that Rabbi Judah gave no answer to the question. "Did he," asked the Emperor, "do anything in your presence?" The emissary related what he had seen. The Emperor quickly understood the hint. He discharged some big officials and appointed others in their place. In a short time the royal treasury was again filled with gold.

The Emperor often engaged Rabbi Judah in religious and philosophical discussions, for it was his desire to investigate Judaism with the intention of becoming a convert. In one of his talks with the Patriarch the Emperor asked a pointed question about life after death. He wanted to know if it would not be possible for the wicked to plead that their sins were committed by their bodies; and seeing now that they were souls without bodies could they not justifiably argue that God ought not hold them guilty or subject them to

---

[7] Midrashic literature even preserves a detailed description of the menus! (See *Genesis Rabba* 11.4 and *Esther Rabba* 1.3.)

divine punishment? In presenting this question to Rabbi Judah, the Emperor was challenging the Jewish conception of punishment. The body could say—"It is the soul that transgresses; for just as soon as it leaves me upon death I am as inert as stone." And the soul could reason likewise and blame the body by saying that since death separated her from the body she is now able to hover like a bird in the pure air, free from all the gross passions of flesh. Thus by blaming each other the body and soul could manage to get God to relieve them from divine punishment. Rabbi Judah said that this was not true and he undertook to explain the correct interrelationship between body and soul by telling the following story: The owner of a garden hired two watchmen to guard the fruit trees one of whom was blind and the other lame. The lame one, seeing the luscious fruit hanging on the trees, desired to eat. He then entered into an arrangment with the blind man which enabled him to stand on the back of his unseeing companion while he plucked the fruit. Later the owner arrived and he wanted to know who ate all the fruit. The blind man said: "You cannot blame me for you know I can't see." The lame one followed suit and said: "You can't blame me for I am unable to walk." But the owner quickly grasped what had transpired and he ordered the lame man to mount the back of the blind man and he judged them as one. "Similarly," said the Patriarch, "God will judge the body and soul as one."

Many decisions of a legal and religious nature are recorded in the *Talmud* as having been rendered by Rabbi Judah and his high court (*Beth Din*) which was composed of the leading sages of that period. As important as these decisions were, the one great achievement which has immortalized this Patriarch is the final redaction of the *Mishnah*. Because of Judah's eminence the *Mishnah* contains many of his own sentences which are introduced by the words: "Rabbi says." Any one who is at all familiar with Mishnaic literature is appreciative of the huge task of compilation and redaction which had to be undertaken before the finalized *Mishnah* was given to the world. Judah followed the arrangement of his predecessors, notably Rabbi Akiba and Rabbi Meir. But large masses of materials had to be rejected. Not all the traditional oral laws which had come down through the centuries were regarded as sufficiently authoritative or important enough to be retained. Therefore in appraising the work of Rabbi Judah one cannot help being impressed as much by what he excluded from the *Mishnah* as by what he included.[8]

With the approval of Rome, Rabbi Judah had been invested as Patriarch (*Nasi,* Prince) of all Jewry when he was about thirty years old. The seat of his residence for many decades had been in a town called Bet She'arim in Galilee. Now that he was coming towards the end of his long career he was living in Sepphoris, a village high up in the mountains, because his health had been failing. He had already passed his eightieth year when the finalized *Mishnah* was placed in his hands. All his life he had devoted himself to the study of the Written and Oral Law. It must have given him immense satisfaction to know that he had lived to see the great work at last completed. Very well could he recite his favorite prayer, the prayer he had himself composed, knowing that its petitions had been amply answered: "May it be thy will, my God and the God of my fathers, to deliver me this day and every day from arrogant men and from arrogance; from a bad man and from a bad neighbor; from any mishap, and from the adversary that destroys; from a hard judgment and from a hard opponent whether he be a son of the Covenant (Jew) or not a son of the Covenant (Gentile)." As an official of the Roman state, and as a personal friend of the Emperor, Rabbi Judah's movements were always accompanied by Roman guards who would have protected him personally from the insults of arrogant men. Yet he prayed each day to be de-

---

[8] The materials which Rabbi Judah rejected from his *Mishnah* can be studied in extraneous collections called the *Tosefta.* They may also be found in the *baraitot.* For an explanation of these terms *see* pp. 196, 197.

livered not only from arrogance in others but from the same
fault in himself.

So long had Rabbi Judah reigned as Patriarch that there
grew up a tradition that no one would be allowed to announce his death; for it was hard to believe that there would
ever come a time when such an exalted figure would have
to close its earthly career. "Rabbi" had united in his person
all the qualifications of external and internal authority. It
was said of him that not since Moses did the Jews have so
great a leader in whom spiritual knowledge and worldly
rank were so gloriously united. But if the people themselves
refused to believe that death would ever claim him, Judah
knew otherwise. Realizing that he would soon pass into
eternity he asked to see his two sons. To the oldest (Gamaliel III) he gave the charge of the patriarchate and to
the younger (Simeon) he recited the rules of the office of
hakam, the same office that Rabbi Meir had occupied with
such distinction under the Patriarch Gamaliel II. And then
the aged leader held up his ten fingers and whispered:
"I have not enjoyed more of the luxuries of this world than
these ten fingers could have brought me by daily labor with
them." He wanted those who were to inherit his leadership
to know that as he had denied himself the pleasures pro-
curable by great wealth so would they be expected to walk
uprightly before the Lord.

Judah's death is recorded in Talmudic literature. No one
had the heart to announce his passing. One story tells about
his housekeeper who ascended the roof and prayed: "The
immortals desire Rabbi to be with them, and the mortals
desire Rabbi to be with them. May it be thy will, O God,
that the immortals overpower the mortals." The housekeeper then took a jug and hurled it down from the roof
to the ground. At that moment his disciples knew that the
soul of the rabbi had left its earthly abode.

"Go," said the disciples to Bar Kappara, "and investigate." He went into the residence and found that Judah
"the Prince" was dead. Returning to the disciples he broke

the news in a parable (for there was a tradition that no one would be permitted to announce the Patriarch's passing in any ordinary fashion).

"Is he then dead?" they exclaimed in agony.

"You have said it, not I," was Bar Kappara's reply.

Immediately they all rent their garments.

❖ ❖ ❖

The successors of Rabbi Judah "the Prince"—the men who followed him as patriarchs—were not of his caliber. They were leaders, but certainly lesser men who neither possessed Rabbi Judah's intellectual stature nor his talents for rulership. Oftentimes the sages chafed at their patriarchal presumptions. Of Gamaliel III, Judah's oldest son and successor, scarcely anything of his life previous to his elevation has been recorded; and scarcely anything exists to tell us about his later activities even when he took over the reins from his illustrious father.[9] However, there were sages in Palestine during that period who were exceptionally gifted men. One of them was Johanan bar Nappaha (born at Sepphoris 199 A.D.—died at Tiberias 279 A.D.).

It was fortunate for Johanan that he was brought up in Sepphoris. Now Sepphoris was never at any time a big town but it was the residence of the patriarch. The high court of world Jewry was there. And so was Rabbi Judah's academy which was crowned by his editorial board, those scholars who were working on the *Mishnah*. As Johanan grew older he attended the lectures given by Rabbi Judah "the Prince" sitting seventeen rows behind Abba Areka, that tall student from Babylonia. But Johanan did not remain at the academy too long because the patriarch's discussions on the law were far over his youthful head. However, in the short time he attended the academy he had significantly impressed the aged patriarch; for it was said that

---

[9] Three sayings of Gamaliel III are incorporated in tractate *Aboth* ("Sayings of the Fathers"). *See* p. 163.

great things might some day be expected from Johanan because "Rabbi" himself had so predicted it.

Johanan's parents died while he was still a child. He came into a small inheritance which consisted of some arable land, a vineyard and an olive orchard. For a while Johanan managed to live on the meager income of these properties. So great was his love for learning, so intense his desire to become a leader, that he finally sold his holdings one after another to advance his education. Many years later, after he had achieved fame, he was walking one day with Rabbi Hiyya ben Abba outside the city of Tiberias towards the direction of Sepphoris. They came to a field—so says an old record [10]—and Rabbi Johanan remarked: "This field was mine and I sold it to enable me to study the law." They came to a vineyard and then to an olive orchard. Johanan reiterated his remarks each time. Suddenly there were tears in Rabbi Hiyya's eyes. "Why do you weep?" asked Johanan. His friend said, "Because you have left nothing for your old age." Then Johanan replied, "Do you think it was a foolish thing for me to have done? I merely sold what was created in six days to acquire what was given in forty days; for does it not say in Scripture (Exodus 34.28) that Moses was on the mount with the Lord forty days and forty nights to obtain the law?"

The significant aspect of Johanan's career is that it began after the completion of the Mishnah. This fact places Johanan among the first of those sages to be called Amoraim.[11] With the completion of the Mishnah, and the death of Rabbi Judah "the Prince," the city of Sepphoris declined as a center of Jewish activity in favor of Tiberias situated in the most beautiful section of Galilee on the western shore of Lake Gennesaret. When Johanan left Sepphoris to become head of the academy at Tiberias there was no longer any

---

[10] *Leviticus Rabba*, Emor 30.1.

[11] On the difference between those sages who labored after the completion of the Mishnah (*Amoraim*) from those who flourished before it was issued (*Tannaim*) see pp. 38, 41.

question as to the importance of Tiberias. Even the seat
of the patriarchate was shifted from Sepphoris to the city
where Johanan was now teaching the law. While Johanan
was building the importance of Tiberias in Palestine, another teacher—that tall young man from Babylonia, Abba
Areka—was building the importance of the academy at Sura.
As Johanan in Palestine was basing the further development of the law upon the *Mishnah,* Abba Areka was doing
the same thing in Babylonia. As Johanan was developing
a Palestinian type of *Gemara* in Tiberias so was Abba Areka
developing a Babylonian type of *Gemara* in the city of Sura.
Thus it was that both in Palestine and Babylonia simultaneously the *Mishnah* was now the authoritative voice
of Jewry, made so by two young men who had studied at
the feet of Rabbi Judah "the Prince." From the labors of
Johanan and his successors there developed the Palestinian
Talmud; and from the labors of Abba Areka and his successors there developed the much more massive Babylonian
Talmud.

Johanan was in every way an extraordinary man whose
life and labors rose above commonplace generalizations
about Talmudic Rabbis. Even in his appearance he was
unusual for he was a handsome man of striking appearance and completely beardless. The esthetic side of life
greatly appealed to him. Unlike those who think that God
is served by ugliness, Johanan insisted that there was no
harm to religion if people wished to decorate the walls of
their houses and add a touch of beauty to daily drabness.
Johanan was interested in clothes, always insisting on careful dress. "Out of reverence for the law (Torah)," he once
remarked, "it is a shame for a scholar to go about in patched
shoes, and it ought to be a sin punishable by death for a
scholar to go about in a spotted garment."

In the *Talmud* one rarely comes across a gushing note
as to the personal appearance of this or that sage. Yet, of
Johanan's "good looks" the following effusive account gives
some idea of how he impressed the people: "If one would

have some conception of the beauty of Johanan he must take a newly wrought silver goblet from the hands of the silversmith and fill it with ruddy garnets; then he should crown its brim with a wreath of red roses and place it between light and shadow. Its unusual reflection of light will represent something of the glory of Johanan's dazzling beauty."

Through the efforts of Johanan the city of Tiberias became the undisputed center of Palestinian Jewry. There were important academies in other Palestinian towns, such as in Caesarea and Lydda; but none could compare to the eminence of Johanan's. In the fertile soil of Tiberias the great roots of tradition, Scripture, *Mishnah, Midrash, Halakah,* and *Haggadah,* grew very deep. The history of Tiberias from the days of Johanan until the end of the patriarchate (425 A.D.) shows that scores of prominent sages flourished there. In this atmosphere the Palestinian *Talmud* was developed. Each treatise of the *Mishnah* was taken up and carefully studied. All discussions, commentaries, and elaborations (called *Gemara*) were collected. Unfortunately the scholars of Tiberias were prevented from completing their work. War, persecution, and economic upsets hampered their efforts. That is why the Palestinian *Talmud* never developed to the size, the significance, or the influence of the Babylonian *Talmud*. It remained in a fragmentary condition. Roman authorities practically taxed Palestinian Jewry out of existence. Johanan complained bitterly about it. "Such is the way of an evil kingdom when it proposes to seize people's property," he explained in loud tones of denunciation. "It appoints one to be an overseer and another a tax collector. By these devices it takes away the possessions of the people."

Because the name of Johanan is closely associated with the Palestinian *Talmud* there grew up a tradition that he had edited it. Actually, this could not be true for Johanan died in 279 A.D., whereas the Palestinian *Talmud* quotes the views of important sages who lived in the Holy Land as late as the latter part of the fourth century. While Johanan did not edit the Palestinian *Talmud* it is nonetheless true that his work comprises the most important aspect of it. This is due to several significant reasons: (1) the fact that Johanan became assistant to the patriarch whose residence was now in Tiberias, (2) the fact that he had studied under Rabbi Judah "the Prince," (3) the weight of his own personality which carried with it great moral persuasion so that he was regarded as the most prominent Palestinian Jewish figure of the third century, and (4) the fact that his decisions were backed up by the power of the patriarchate which was the only type of Jewish authority recognized by Rome.

Closely associated with Johanan was that other dominant personality of Palestinian Jewry, Rabbi Simeon ben Lakish, who had been a professional athlete and gladiator until Johanan changed the course of his life. Ben Lakish chanced to be walking one day on the banks of the River Jordan clad in armor when he saw a woman bathing in its waters. Overcome by a strong desire to possess her he took off his regalia and plunged into the river. But the figure he saw bathing was not a woman. It was the beardless Johanan. "Such beauty as you possess," remarked the athlete sheepishly, "should belong to a woman." Johanan, who never lost an opportunity to recruit young men for the rabbinate, said to ben Lakish, "If you will turn your talents to education, I will give you my sister for a wife. If you think that I am beautiful you should see her." The understanding words of Johanan so impressed the gladiator that he agreed to give up his life of professional athletics to devote himself to the law.

The incident, in all probability, is legendary, but it was too good a story to be discarded for it established in the minds of the people that ben Lakish, the man of great bodily strength, was now the brother-in-law of the illustrious Johanan, even though he had been a professional athlete. Within a few years he became so proficient a scholar that next to Johanan there was no doubt but that ben Lakish was an eminent sage. It was even held that in certain departments of the law ben Lakish was superior to Johanan. "He who sees ben Lakish expounding in the academy will imagine that he sees a man uprooting mountains and crushing them one against each other," so says a passage in the *Talmud*. But the highest tribute ever paid the man who had once been a gladiator came from Johanan, "Whenever ben Lakish is absent from the academy, I feel as if I lacked my right hand." Well could he say this for ben Lakish frequently challenged the reasoning of Johanan. His skill in debate developed to a point of such penetrating keenness that Johanan was frequently compelled to change his previous legal opinions.

Both *Talmuds*—the Palestinian and the Babylonian—contain numerous references to the legal views of Johanan and ben Lakish for they achieved recognition among the foremost rabbinical sages of all time. Above the record of their debates and discussions, the redactors of Talmudic literature have not forgotten to preserve for posterity some of their choice *Haggadah*. Among the things that Johanan used to say the following are memorable:

"Deception with words is even worse than deception in money matters."

"The slave is the same child of God that I am."

"When people devote themselves to the study of Scripture and to charity, their evil natures are under their control. But if not, then they are under the control of their evil natures."

"The observances of six types of commandments reward men in this world while the principal of the good deed is rewarded in the world to come. These commandments are: (1) hospitality to strangers, (2) visiting the sick, (3) careful prayer, (4) rising early to go to the academy, (5) raising children to the knowledge of Scripture, and (6) judging every one according to his good deeds."

Of Simeon ben Lakish much of a Haggadic nature has

been preserved. For example, he was the first to declare that the Book of Job is fiction and that all the events which befell Job were purely imaginary. In the opinion of ben Lakish the nonhistorical character of Job did not in any manner minimize the profound lessons of that book, for its purpose is to give people certain moral and philosophical insights into the problem of human suffering without teaching that Job as a person actually lived. Ben Lakish maintained what Biblical scholars today acknowledge, namely: that the Book of Job is poetic composition.

Among the many things that ben Lakish used to say, the following utterances reveal the lofty intensity of his nature:

"Truth is the seal of God."

"No man commits a sin unless struck by momentary insanity."

"Improve yourself first before you attempt to improve others."

"When a man lends his neighbor a sum of money to help him rehabilitate himself, he does that man a kinder deed than if he had given him the money in charity. It is better still if one could invest that money in a partnership, for this makes the poor man feel that he neither has to borrow nor to take charity."

"A scholar should be as modest as a bride and like her he must also guard his conduct that no shadow of immorality fall upon it."

"Two scholars who encourage each other are beloved of God."

"When a court has to pass sentence it must consider small matters of the same importance as great ones."

"He who is merciful when he should be harsh, will in the end be harsh when he should be merciful."

"Do not live in the neighborhood of an ignorant man who is pious."

"The world exists only by virtue of the breath which comes from the mouths of school children. The instruction

of the young should not be interrupted even by the building
of a sanctuary."

*   *   *

The intellectual and spiritual activities of Johanan and ben
Lakish, as they were being carried forward in Palestine,
were matched by the parallel activities of Abba Areka and
Mar Samuel in Babylonia.[12] Abba Areka was able to bring
a copy of the finalized Mishnah back to Babylonia with him
when he completed his studies under Rabbi Judah "the
Prince." On his return to Babylonia he established an
academy at Sura which quickly attracted hundreds of students. With the amazing success of Sura it was evident to
the Jews of the world that there were now two important
centers of the law—Johanan's academy in the west and
Abba Areka's in the east—and that in the event Rome annihilated one, the other would survive.

Babylonia was in the fortunate position of being outside
the Roman empire. The Jews who lived in Babylonia were
free from Roman persecutions, Roman taxations, and all
the dissolving influences which threatened the existence of
Jews in Palestine. The Babylonian Jewish community had
long been in a flourishing condition and was well able to
offer asylum to those Palestinians who were escaping the
oppression of the Caesars. So important was the return of
Abba Areka to Babylonia that the year (219 A.D.) became
memorable as the year in which a new era had been in-
augurated. Up to the time that Abba Areka returned with
the Mishnah in his hands, the Jews of Babylonia, like all
Jews living outside of Palestine, were wholly dependent
upon the patriarch and his high court located in Palestine.
Decisions in regard to religious questions had to be settled
there. Seeing that the Mishnah had been issued as an authoritative code (in which a definitive settlement of all past
disputes had been reached and stood recorded) it no longer
became necessary to refer everything to Palestine. Now that

---

[12] The reader will help his understanding of Abba Areka by reading
pp. 38-43.

the hurdle of the Oral Law had been overcome by its re-
duction to written form (*Mishnah*), by the greatest of all the
patriarchs, it enabled any authorized scholar anywhere to
busy himself with the law. Abba Areka was such an authorized scholar; and while it is true that Judah "the Prince"
did not give him full ordination, he bestowed upon Abba
Areka sufficient authority so that he could be called *Rab*.[13]
This meant that a decision arrived at by Abba Areka would
be as binding as any issued from a Palestinian authority.
This marked the beginning of independence on the part
of Babylonian Jewry. Complete independence was achieved
a century later when the economic collapse of Palestine
made Babylonia the center of authority for world Jewry.

In choosing to establish a wholly new academy Abba
Areka was motivated by high ideals. Had he wished he
could have been elected head of other institutions in Babylonia, but he turned them down, including the rectorship
of the famous college at Nehardea. No one was aware of
the new age confronting Jewry more than he. Perhaps he
sensed that with the death of Rabbi Judah "the Prince"
and the completion of the *Mishnah* that Palestinian scholarship would exhaust itself within a few generations. That is
why he set out to induce men of ability to study the law
under him so that they could qualify to serve as judges
(regulating judicial procedure by basing their work upon
the finalized *Mishnah*) and could become moral and spiritual leaders of the people.[14] The passion of a pioneer stirred
deeply within Abba Areka and he decided to become the
founder of a great academy at Sura.

The city of Sura was indeed a challenge for this rabbi
who had returned to Babylonia with fanfare and acclaim

---

[13] Babylonian scholars had to content themselves with the lesser title of
rab. Judah "the Prince" would not confer upon them the title "rabbi";
for he wanted to make sure that religious leadership would for ever be
dependent upon a central authority in the Holy Land. The Patriarch
therefore decided to limit full ordination only to those who gave assurance
that they would not leave Palestine.

[14] More than one hundred of his disciples are mentioned by name in the
Talmud.

as a great religio-ethical lawyer. The people of Sura were largely uneducated, rude, and uncouth in their speech. Low moral standards were in evidence both in family life and in business. One could easily imagine this to be the last place where a man of Abba Areka's talents would wish to stake out his claim. Nonetheless he chose Sura. Not because it was promising but because it constituted a summons to fight the good fight. For Abba Areka was essentially a crusader. Notwithstanding the claims of his work at Sura he was constantly on the go, traveling from city to city throughout Babylonia, preaching, teaching, settling disputes, organizing courts, schools, and synagogues. He was constantly urging people to a sounder spiritual and moral life and to a stricter observance of the rituals of Judaism. He saw in the whole system of rituals a means whereby people could discipline themselves. For example, when it came to the observance of the dietary laws, Abba Areka insisted that these regulations be understood as a means of consecration. He therefore placed their observance on moral grounds. "What difference does it make to God," he used to ask in his lectures, "whether one slaughters the animal by cutting the neck in front or in back? Or, what does it matter to God whether one eats ritually pure (kosher) food or impure things? None whatsoever. This shows that these laws embedded in the Bible were given only for the purpose of testing men."

With the passing of the years the city of Sura stood transformed by the efforts of this one sage. Not only did Abba Areka improve the moral tone of the townspeople, but he had portions of the city rebuilt to express the new life now surging within its walls. Like Johanan in Palestine Abba Areka loved beauty in dress, architecture, embroidery, jewelry, and in the planting of gardens. Slowly the city of Sura came to be rebuilt in beautiful style with its synagogue the highest structure in the city, for it was Abba Areka's firm conviction that "a city which builds the roofs of its houses higher than the roof of its synagogue is doomed to destruction." As the city of Sura became known, and as its religio-

legal prestige grew, its influence upon Jewry was felt far
beyond the borders of Babylonia. Johanan in Tiberias recognized that and wrote to Abba Areka addressing him: "To
our teacher in Babylonia." On one occasion Johanan, who was
unquestionably that generation's highest authority within
Judaism, said that Abba Areka was the only person to whom
he would willingly yield and subordinate himself.

During a long and highly successful career Abba Areka
instituted numerous reforms and improved the moral attitude of the people towards many social abuses.[15] Of the
varied spheres of his interests none received more whole-
hearted attention than the problem of women's rights. In
an age when women were subjected to archaic laws which
put them at a disadvantage economically and socially, Abba
Areka came forward to champion their lot. It was his aim
to revise obsolete legislation so that women would enjoy
equality with men. From time immemorial the husband
had the right to divorce his wife at his own pleasure. (The
manner in which Abraham dismissed Hagar as recorded in
Genesis 21.9-14 illustrates the exercise of this authority.)
With the development of Hebrew life there grew up over
the centuries a desire to restrict the husband. As far back
as the period of the first century before the destruction of
the Temple, the great sage Shammai had interpreted the
text of Deuteronomy 24.1 in such a manner as to reach the
conclusion that the husband could not divorce his wife
except for cause, and that cause must be sexual immorality.
But Shammai was far ahead of his day.[16] The School of
Hillel, so liberal and understanding in other matters, opposed Shammai and held to the old Biblical position that
the husband need not assign any reason whatever in order
to obtain a divorce. The concept of the "indecency" was so
interpreted that the slightest cause could serve as grounds

---

[15] For example, his interest in employer-employee relationships is reflected in the story told on pp. 52, 53.

[16] Jesus, who came a generation after Shammai, apparently held Shammai's views concerning divorce. (See Matthew 19.3-9.)

to break the bond of marriage. It was enough for a man to desire a more beautiful woman than his wife for him to be able to divorce her.

> When a man takes a wife, and marries her, if then she finds no favor in his eyes, because he has found some indecency in her, and he writes her a bill of divorcement, and puts it in her hand, and sends her out of his house . . .[17]

One of the important tractates of the *Mishnah* is entitled "Divorces" (*Gittin*). Here are gathered together all the oral laws which, over the centuries, modified the Biblical right of the husband. By the time these laws were put down in the finalized *Mishnah* it was plainly evident that new moral attitudes had whittled away the husband's Biblical right. The husband now found himself considerably restricted. The changes introduced by the sages had gone a long way in bringing the abuses of divorce under control. They imposed such formalities in giving the divorce and such a detailed examination of witnesses that they succeeded in making divorce difficult, thereby improving the position of the wife. The laws of the *Mishnah,* which Abba Areka had studied in the academy of Rabbi Judah "the Prince," went so far as to make it possible for the wife under certain circumstances to ask the court to force her husband to give her a divorce. Under those circumstances the husband was compelled by the court to give the wife a divorce.

All the legal aids for women, listed in the *Mishnah,* did not go far enough for Abba Areka. It irritated his sense of social righteousness when he saw a woman chained to a bad husband with no chance to break those chains because her own peculiar set of conditions did not happen to come under any of the categories enumerated in the *Mishnah.* Abba Areka therefore undertook to add a number of causes for divorce to improve still further the rights of women.

---

[17] Deuteronomy 24.1. The complete dominance of the husband was almost universal in ancient times. The wife was regarded as the purchased property of the husband. It was the same among the ancient Arabs and Romans. See article on "Divorce" in *Encyclopaedia Britannica.*

But it was not enough in Abba Areka's judgment to pass better divorce laws. It was necessary to reduce the possibility of divorce by achieving better marriage relations. In order to prevent the mishap of divorce Abba Areka urged that "a man must not marry off his daughter when she is so young that she cannot tell whom she would like to marry." In addition he forbade the marriage of (1) a young girl to an old man, (2) the marriage of a boy who was obviously immature, and who did not fully understand what he was doing. As the master of the city of Sura, Abba Areka would have people flogged who disobeyed him. It is said that he flogged any one who married a woman simply through intercourse. He sternly disapproved of street marriages, meaning that he forbade a man merely on seeing a woman in the street to marry her without a prior agreement as to her rights under the wedding contract. He would rage against any man who went about town declaring that the divorce given his wife was invalid.

Important as were his contributions in the field of law and social reform, Abba Areka did much for the liturgy of the synagogue. He labored with his disciples at Sura to enrich the Jewish prayer book and to fix many of its forms. Certain lofty prayers of the solemn New Year's service (*Rosh Hashana*) were written, arranged, and developed in large part by him, or by those who worked with him. For Abba Areka was a man of prayer. His faith in its power was enormous. Yet, he seldom prayed for any personal benefits. He constantly practiced the discipline of private meditation knowing that sin fractures man's vision of life. It was his rule, the first thing each morning, to cleanse his thoughts: "If one knows that his thoughts are troubled he should not pray." It was characteristic of Abba Areka that rather than ask God for future favors, he would thank him in expressions of gratitude for what already had been done. He maintained that the privilege of praising the Deity was in itself a cause for thanks. Abba Areka suggested, therefore, that all Jews should say: "We thank thee, O God, for having led us out of Egypt; delivered us out of bondage; and hast permitted us to render thanks unto thy great Name."

In one of his arrangements for the New Year's service, Abba Areka fixed the form of a prayer known as *Alenu,* so called from its initial word which means "it is incumbent upon us" or "it is our duty." Over the centuries the Jewish people attached such importance and solemnity to the *Alenu* that it was lifted from the New Year's service to become the concluding prayer of each daily service. No matter where Jews live, no matter whether they worship in synagogues or in the privacy of their homes, they conclude their formal prayers with the *Alenu.* Because of its importance as an assertion of the kingship of God throughout the universe, the *Alenu* became the accepted conclusion for every Jewish service. *Alenu* stresses man's duty to adore God. It declares the nothingness of paganism and idolatry and ends with the sublime hope that all men will some day abandon every form of evil, and worship God alone in purity of mind and heart.

Abba Areka died after twenty-eight years of leadership at Sura (219–247 A.D.). He was deeply mourned by the Jews of the world, but especially by Babylonian Jews whose institutions of learning he had lifted to a leading position within Judaism. He had dealt with hundreds of religious questions and settled problems of conduct in marriage, business affairs, court procedures, and synagogue ritual. Above all he is remembered as a founder of the *Gemara,* that great commentary on the *Mishnah* which his disciples and followers at Sura developed, thereby carrying the name and influence of Abba Areka down the long corridors of the centuries.

❖   ❖   ❖

"The man is departed of whom I stood in awe," said Mar Samuel in a final tribute to the life of Abba Areka. Mar Samuel's career had run parallel to the life and labors of his

older contemporary. While Abba Areka had presided at
Sura, Mar Samuel had been the chief judge at Nehardea
and the head of the ancient academy in that city. Like Abba
Areka he had gone to Palestine to study at the feet of Rabbi
Judah "the Prince" and on his return to Babylonia he too
brought back a copy of the finalized *Mishnah*. The academy
at Nehardea had long been the leading institution of the law
among the Jews of Babylonia until Abba Areka carved out
the pre-eminence of Sura. It will be recalled that the rectorship of Nehardea had first been offered to Abba Areka but
he turned it down with the suggestion that Mar Samuel, his
younger colleague, be given the post.

Long before Mar Samuel had gone to Palestine to study
under Rabbi Judah "the Prince" he had achieved recognition as a physician and astronomer. The acquisition of medicine and astronomy, such as they were known in his day,
in no wise prevented him from pursuing his religious studies.
The *Talmud* outlines the background of his early education
giving the names of his tutors. From the time that he was
a lad his father, who was one of the leading silk merchants
of Nehardea, encouraged the boy in his quest for Biblical
lore and the attainment of proficiency in all departments
of *Halakah* and *Haggadah*. Thus, from early youth, Mar
Samuel combined knowledge of the sciences with religion.
It was this combination which highlighted his career with
unusual distinction.

In the field of medicine Mar Samuel was important for
Jewry. Many of his medical maxims and dietetic rules found
their way into the *Talmud*. Through dissection, practiced on
the cadavers of executed slaves, he became a master of anatomy. The ailments of women engrossed his attention. Because he stressed the need to avoid all unhygienic conditions, his wise counsel did much to make generations of
Jews conscious of uncleanliness as a source of disease. Actually, Mar Samuel was very close to the modern germ theory
for he opposed energetically the view, then current even
in intelligent circles, that most diseases were due to the

evil eye. Mar Samuel sought the origin of disease in various noxious influences such as in air pollution, bad water, and wrong climatic effects.

Above all, Mar Samuel seems to have specialized in the treatment of the eye, having developed a certain kind of salve which was widely used in Babylonia. It is interesting to read in the *Talmud* that when he journeyed to Palestine to study the law, Rabbi Judah "the Prince" designated him to be his personal physician, and in this capacity he skilfully treated the eyes of the old sage. Perhaps Mar Samuel thought that his medical services to Rabbi Judah would induce the aged Patriarch to ordain him as a rabbi. But he too, like Abba Areka, was refused for similar reasons. And that is why Samuel was never called rabbi, only *Mar*, which means "a wise master."

However, the patriarch's refusal to ordain scholars who lived outside of Palestine did not prevent either Mar Samuel or Abba Areka from achieving eminence. For example, no Jew in the entire world could match Mar Samuel's knowledge of astronomy. The Persian King, Sapor I, who was the ruler of Babylonia in those days, became his friend, as did Ablat, the heathen astronomer. It was said of Mar Samuel that he knew the courses of the stars in the skies better than he knew the streets of Nehardea. In his academy all students were taught the practical phases of astronomy particularly as they applied to the calendar. This was an important innovation among rabbinical scholars. For centuries the determination of the calendar (new moon, festivals, holy days) had been the exclusive province of the Sanhedrin. In each case the determination required that witnesses had to be examined before the Sanhedrin would allow messengers to go out of the city of Jerusalem to communicate to the people the arrival of any holiday. It was a cumbersome method which was continued even after the destruction of the Temple in 70 A.D. The right to determine the calendar passed from the old Sanhedrin to the patriarchs. Now for the first time within Judaism this right was made obsolete by the accuracy of Mar Samuel's astronomical tables. It was a serious blow to the prestige of the patriarchate and was one of the reasons why it eventually lost its influence and declined.

Together with the dynamic activities of Abba Areka the labors of Mar Samuel lifted Babylonian Jewry to heights of importance greater than had ever been achieved by any Jewish community outside of Palestine. The academies of the Babylonian Jews became a breakwater against the floods of barbarian peoples and their pagan ignorance. These academies created for the Jews codes of justice, guides for health, prayers for the synagogues, elementary educational programs for small communities, research in the fields of Bible and Biblical lore. During the lives of Abba Areka and Mar Samuel the academies of Sura and Nehardea led the way in the development of the *Gemara*. Abba Areka became the authority in the field of religious law while Mar Samuel was acknowledged the supreme authority in civil jurisprudence.[18]

Such bits of biographical information that we are able to gather from the *Talmud* indicate that Mar Samuel was a modest man, gentle in the exercise of his powers, and unselfish in his acts. It was one of his favorite sayings that a man ought never "exclude himself from the community but rather seek his welfare in that society." In his solicitude for helpless orphans he imposed upon every court the task of acting as father for them. He stored grain until prices had risen in order to sell it to the poor at the low prices of the harvest time. In passing judgment, or in his efforts to arrive at a correct decision, he never obstinately insisted on his own opinion. At all times he advocated a high morality. "It is forbidden," he declared, "to deceive any man be he Jew or heathen." His concept of the universal brotherhood of man flowed from his belief in the

---

[18] *See* pp. 39, 40 for a discussion of Samuel. *Also* p. 148 for an explanation of his legal principle "The law of the government (even though non-Jewish) is the law."

fatherhood of God. "Before the throne of the Creator there is no difference between Jews and pagans, since there are many noble and virtuous people among the Gentiles."

Approximately a decade after Abba Areka died, Mar Samuel passed away in Nehardea (257 A.D.). Shortly after his death the city of Nehardea was sacked and completely destroyed (260 A.D.) in a bitter war between Persia and Rome. Sad as was the loss of this ancient seat of learning, the act of destruction was no new experience for Jews. Each generation seemed to understand that it lay within the very nature of Judaism to rise phoenix-like from the ashes of violence. With Mar Samuel gone and Nehardea destroyed, a disciple, by the name of Judah bar Ezekiel, established an academy at Pumbeditha, which wisely took over where Nehardea had left off.

❁　　❁　　❁

Scores of exceptionally gifted rabbis fill the pages of the *Gemara* period which stretches from the work of Abba Areka and Mar Samuel in the third century to the final redaction of the *Talmud* under Rabina II at the beginning of the sixth century. Insight into the lives of a few of these representative men will always prove helpful in understanding the great literature they created.[19] Rich and poor were among them as they rose to eminence by sheer ability. It was not enough for this or that rabbi to have had political influence. Basically he had to possess merit in himself and in his teachings in order to stand the test of inclusion within the *Talmud*.

Quite a few areas of thought passionately held by the sages no longer have any relevance for modern Jews. For example, the subject of angels which occupies a significant place within the *Talmud* has been completely dropped from twentieth century Judaism. Michael, Gabriel, Raphael, and

---

[19] For a detailed account of the lives of the founders of the Babylonian *Talmud* (*Gemara* period) the reader is referred to Gershom Bader's book, *Jewish Spiritual Heroes*, Vol. III (New York, 1940).

a host of other angels, seem to have spread their wings and flown over to Christianity where their fanciful activities were enshrined in the medieval art of the churches. Demons too have been dropped as a vestigial remnant of crude primitive beliefs. Satan, Lilith, Samael, Ashmodai are names no longer even familiar to modern Jews.

The concept of a personal Messiah has shared the same fate. Along with angels and demons it has gone into the limbo of discarded ideas. Although the *Talmud* is heavily laden with the concept of the "Messiah," twentieth century Judaism has dropped that subject too; but not because Christianity took over the idea by declaring Jesus of Nazareth to be the Messiah. Up to modern times most Jews held to some form of Messianic belief. This belief was never too well defined either in the Old Testament, in the Apocrypha, or in the *Talmud*. It always occupied a highly speculative, nebulous position and persisted within the minds of the Jewish people as a psychological escape, the Messiah being the "redeemer" who would usher in a kind of Utopian age in which all Jews could be redeemed from their troubles and live in peace. This Jewish concept of the Messiah was indeed a far cry from the Christian view. Moreover, nowhere in the *Talmud* is there the slightest indication that the Messiah would ever be a superhuman Son of God in the sense in which this doctrine was developed in New Testament literature.

Such as it was, the idea of a Messiah met rejection from many Talmudic scholars. Rabbi Akiba, during the Hadrianic persecutions (132–135 A.D.), stoutly maintained that the Jewish soldier Bar Kochba was the Messiah. Millions believed it. But not men like Rabbi Johanan ben Torta who told Rabbi Akiba quite bluntly that he was harboring a misleading idea. "Sooner," said Johanan ben Torta, "will grass grow out of your cheekbones than that the Messiah will appear." Mar Samuel discounted all extravagant Messianic claims and promises. The Patriarch Hillel II (320–365 A.D.) inveighed against the concept as both useless and harmful. He said that Jews ought not waste their time expecting a Messiah because all the so-called prophecies about such a person had reference to the age of King Hezekiah of Biblical days and had nothing to do with the Jews of later times.

As modern Jews no longer believe in the coming of a personal Messiah, all Messianic discussions and speculations found in Talmudic literature are considered of interest only to the historian.

VI

WHAT THE TALMUD MEANS TODAY

WITH THE COMPLETION OF THE *Talmud* one wonders why
so monumental a work was not given formal ratification. It is true that a group of scholars called *saboraim*
dominated the intellectual and spiritual life of Babylonian
Jewry for about two centuries after Ashi and Rabina II had
redacted the *Talmud*. It is true that these *saboraim* were
engaged in perfecting the *Talmud* by arranging its discussions more carefully and at times even adding comments
of their own. Yet the *saboraim* made no change whatsoever
in the text finalized by Rabina II. Some historians are in-
clined to believe that perhaps the *saboraim* are the ones
who did the major job of putting the *Talmud* in its present
written form. There may be an element of partial truth in
these views; but unfortunately the historical data relative
to the activity of the *saboraim* are in such utter confusion
that it would be extremely difficult to make any dogmatic
assertion. Perhaps the role of these *saboraim* is much more
significant than it is usually believed to be. Be that as it
may, the important question still remains: why was the
Talmud when completed by Rabina II (or by the *saboraim*
after him) not given some kind of formal ratification?

In the light of the Jewish theory called the "Chain of Tradition" this question is not too difficult to answer. The "Chain of Tradition" regards the sages of each generation as individual transmitters in a chain of witnesses reaching back to Moses, the first link. Once this theory is understood it enables us to grasp the profound meaning of that well known Talmudic statement: "Everything that an acute student of the law will teach in the distant future has already been proclaimed on Mt. Sinai." [1] If we did not know about the theory of the Chain of Tradition this claim would indeed sound ridiculous. The Jewish spirit, so liberal in its very essence, regarded the constant unfolding of the law not as something disconnected or apart from the original revelation at Sinai, but rather a gradual evolution and development of that which already had been given. Within the mind of the Jew the law (Torah) possessed an inexhaustible potential, a vast treasury of inheritance constantly being made available to the needs of each successive generation. Such an attitude prevented Talmudic law from becoming static, for Talmudic law was regarded as a part of the original Divine Revelation which could never be exhausted. [2] Therefore every fresh interpretation, though in appearance seemingly new, was not new at all but very old even though just recently discovered. For this reason the entire history of the *Talmud* shows a guarded effort against sealing Jewish law in a closed book. A formal ratification of the *Talmud* was therefore unnecessary: (1) because the original ratification of the Torah at Mt. Sinai was in itself sufficient; (2) because such sufficiency embraced the right of interpretation which never permitted the veneration of the written Torah to impede progress; (3) because the

---

[1] Palestinian *Talmud*, tractate *Peah* ch. 2 col. 17a. Compare this statement with another similar pronouncement from *Midrash Rabba* ch. 28 sec. 4. "Every truth that a prophet will proclaim in any generation he already received from Mt. Sinai, even though he was not personally present at that revelation."

[2] The forces which created the *Talmud* were in the main liberal forces and are not to be identified with the forces which subsequently attempted to mummify it.

Talmud, which is the Oral Law reduced to written form, was always regarded as an essential part of the original revelation.

There is no air of finality in the *Talmud.* Subsequent legal codes, basing themselves upon the *Talmud,* were designed to give the impression of finality. But not the *Talmud* itself. One finds in the *Talmud* not finality but continuity. Yet the *Talmud* is unquestionably Judaism's most authoritative formulation.

❖   ❖   ❖

The decline of Babylonian Jewry began about the ninth century. There were many reasons for this: persecution, war, political changes, and perhaps a breakdown of older methods of agriculture. Put together all these reasons spelled emigration of population to other parts of the world, particularly to Europe. As the east was declining the west was beginning to flourish. Already one hears of vigorous new activity in the cities of Spain, Italy, France, and in Germany along the Rhine.[3]

And now there set in a process of a progressive loosening of the bonds which had long tied the Jewish settlements of Europe to the seats of authority in Babylonia. What was now happening, of course, was a repeat performance of the transfer of authority when centuries earlier Babylonian Jewry had first attained spiritual independence from Palestine and then managed to lift itself into a position of supremacy. Once having been worked out, this pattern of transfer was destined to repeat itself again and again in the long course of medieval Jewish history up to and including modern times. In the struggle that was now taking place between the east and the west all the elements of the transfer can be seen: (1) the movement of population away from old centers, (2) persecution, (3) war, (4) changes in the

---

[3] The first important Jewish academy in the west was established about 950 A.D. in Cordova (Spain) by Moses ben Hanoch. Jewish communities in North Africa were also beginning to flourish at this time.

economic aspects of the old order, (5) the shutting off of
popular revenues which always led to the decline and eventual shut down of the academy, (6) the strong challenge
stemming from newer lands and more vigorous communities.

The pathos of the decline of the great Babylonian academies is nowhere more clearly set forth than in the letter
written by Nehemiah ben Kohen Zedek (who was the head
of Pumbeditha from 960–968 A.D.) and addressed to a western community: "We do not know why you have left us
forgotten and despised. Have you become tired of us that
you do not even answer our letters? Or do you perhaps
doubt the legitimacy of our office . . . or our scholarship
and piety?" A few years later another head of Pumbeditha,
Sherira Gaon, wrote in similar vein pleading with the newer
Jewish communities of the west to support the Babylonian
schools—"For how can the body be healthy," asked Sherira,
"if the head be sick?" Ground by the upper and nether
millstones—the distintegration of the east and the growing
power of the west—the renowned academies of Sura and
Pumbeditha were gradually worn down and became mere
ghosts of their former greatness. By the middle of the eleventh century they had ceased to be. Thus after eight hundred years of continuous leadership the authority of Judaism was transferred to the academies of Europe.

Safe in the lands of the west the Jewish sages of Europe
established schools for the continuing study of the *Mishnah*
and the *Gemara* in essentially the same spirit that dominated their eastern predecessors. Actually, these men of the
west were supplementing a feat that had been carried out
by the Babylonians when Palestine declined. And just as
the sages of Sura and Pumbeditha had long ago furnished
Jewry with the answer on "How to be a Jew" so these newer
sages (confronted with the problems of Europe) were prepared to give Jewry a supplementary answer applicable to
the medieval age that was now upon them. If, over the long
course of the centuries, Judaism has been able to survive
up to our modern times then the credit for maintaining its

identity must be attributed to the profound effect that the study of the *Mishnah* and the *Gemara* exerted upon the Jew.

❉   ❉   ❉

Despite the dispersion of the Jewish people throughout the globe, Judaism came to possess an over-all unity which was made possible by the *Talmud*. In the development of the *Halakah*—which lives immortal within the folios of the *Mishnah* and the *Gemara*—the sages created one vast umbrella of religio-ethical law. Of course, there were some Jews like the Karaites who did not wish to live under that umbrella, and so they rejected the *Talmud*.[4] Like the Sadducees of old the Karaites regarded only the written Torah (Scripture) as valid. Their rejection of the Oral Law as embodied in the *Talmud* consequently forced the Karaites into the position of trying to live solely by the antique legislation embedded within the Bible. It was inevitable therefore that Karaism should become a throwback. Its static conception of the Bible prevented its adherents from embracing the concept of progress as set forth in the Oral Law. For this reason the Karaites became merely a footnote in the history of Judaism.[5]

Towards the end of the fifth century—by the time the *Talmud* was completed under Rabina II—the Jewish people exhibited an unusual degree of uniformity in belief, practice, and spiritual outlook. Consequently even today when the world speaks of Judaism it means only one thing, namely: Talmudic Judaism. It is this continuity of religious conviction, crystallized into definite rules of conduct, which has come down to our modern age. The way of life which the *Talmud* so minutely prescribed for the Jewish people welded them into one folk, no matter how widely scattered over the earth's surface. This result could never have been

---

[4] The founder of the Karaite sect was a Babylonian Jew, Anan ben David, who came into prominence in the year 760 A.D.

[5] Karaite Jews always constituted very small communities. They lasted into the twentieth century but are now almost wholly extinct.

achieved had Jewish law been purely secular. Because the
Halakah is essentially spiritual, it endowed the Jewish people with a power to unite and to survive that is unique in
the history of mankind.

Various prejudices combine to distort the average person's conception of the *Talmud* so that this great literature
looms as a formidable record of dry bones. As a result of
this kind of thinking the world has disastrously under-
valued Jewish law. Instead of trying to understand the
legalism of the *Talmud* it brushes the record aside as a monument of misplaced energy. Yet, a brief appraisal of Talmudic law, free from prejudice, might show that there is
much in it that could be considered relevant to the needs
of modern society. The compelling force of great principles
needs to be reasserted in a day when people think that the
road they travel now, the road which seems so new and
difficult in the atomic age, is essentially a road without
signposts. These people are mistaken, for this road has been
traveled before—by the feet of the sages.

* * *

The purpose of Jewish law was to establish proof of man's
kinship with God. Even while engaged in coiling legal arguments the jurists of the *Talmud* never forgot that they were
the heirs of the Hebrew prophets. God being omnipresent,
so they reasoned, then it must follow that every phase of
human existence is interpenetrated by the Divine Mind
with its moral summons. Nothing, therefore, in the life of
man was considered by these jurists to be outside the domain of ethics. This is the meaning of what Rabbi Bar Kappara expounded when he asked: "Which is a brief Scriptural
passage upon which all the principles of the law depend?"
Bar Kappara answered the question by quoting Proverbs
3.6: "In all your ways acknowledge him, and he will direct
your paths."

The *Talmud* provided for progress in that it magnified
human participation in the development and authorization

of the law. After all, what is the object of legal authority? Is it to prepare men for manhood or to keep them in perpetual childhood? For this reason the sages laid down the principle, "The words of the written Torah are fruitful and multiply," meaning that without minimizing the Pentateuch as the revealed word of God, nevertheless there is such a thing as the human interpretation and expansion of the Divine message. Often a Biblical text is quoted in the *Talmud* not as proof for a law but as providing an indication or indirect support for it. Indeed, a large amount of Talmudic law has no Biblical foundation whatsoever. Nonetheless the *Talmud* maintains that morality can be expressed in the spirit of the Bible. It is one of the essential principles of the *Talmud* that as man's moral ideas advance the law can be so adjusted as to meet new situations. While it is true that the exterior aspect of the legal discussion in the *Talmud* is unattractive to the modern mind, nonetheless the interior spirit of it ought not to be relegated to the limbo of forgotten things.

It is fundamental to the understanding of the legal system of the *Talmud* that God is the source of law and not the state. This was derived from the clear teaching of the Old Testament which nowhere presents this doctrine more clearly. than Deuteronomy 17.14, 18, 19:

> "When you come to the land which the LORD your God gives you, and you possess it, and dwell in it, and then say, 'I will set a king over me, like all the nations that are round about me' . . . And when he sits on the throne of his kingdom, he shall write for himself in a book a copy of this law from that which is in charge of the Levitical priests; and it shall be with him, and he shall read in it all the days of his life, that he may learn to fear the LORD his God, by keeping all the words of this law and these statutes and doing them."

That which gave Talmudic law its amazing universality and its durability is the fact that its authority was believed to be rooted in universal moral law, and the still more important fact that the moral law derives its authority from God who gives it its abiding worth. Because they held this view the Jewish people regarded themselves as a unique people. The Palestinian author Josephus, who was writing to Greek and Roman readers in the first century A.D., said: "Our legislator Moses ordained our government to be what, by a strained expression, may be called a theocracy, by ascribing the authority and power to God." [6] From its earliest tribal beginnings the Jewish people regarded the direct rule of God over their community as their most important uniting bond. With them it was a much stronger bond than the sense of a common origin. Also, it was much stronger than any combination of secular interests. Even the wars which they fought as a primitive people were regarded as the Wars of *Yahweh*. [7]

Numerous peoples of antiquity had varying systems approaching theocracy but in reality they were not theocracy but what may more rightly be called hierocracy, the rule of priests. It is significant to note that the Hebrew prophets thundered against their own kings and priests in a manner unmatched by the prophets of any other people. This prophetic expression of the Old Testament could not have taken place if the basis of Judaism had been anything other than ethical theocracy. "Let not the wise man glory in his wisdom," proclaimed Jeremiah, "let not the mighty man glory in his might, let not the rich man glory in his riches; but let him who glories glory in this, that he understands and knows me, that I am the LORD, who practice kindness, justice, and righteousness in the earth; for in these things I delight, says the LORD." [8]

A large part of the struggle between the Sadducees and Pharisees revolved around the conflicting views of a theo-

---

[6] Josephus: *Contra Apion* 2.17. The word *theocracy* was in all probability coined by Josephus. It correctly expresses the Hebrew idea.

[7] Judges 5.4-5, 23.

[8] Jeremiah 9.23, 24. The prophet Isaiah summed it up saying: "The LORD of Hosts is exalted in justice, and the Holy God shows himself holy in righteousness" (Isaiah 5.16).

cratic state or a hierocratic state. The Sadducees upheld the hierocratic concept, the rule of the priests. They looked upon the Pentateuch as their monopoly because the Pentateuch confers upon the Priests an authority unlike that given to any other class in ancient Israel. But this priestly authority was being constantly challenged by the growth of the Oral Law. With the destruction of Jerusalem in 70 A.D. the Sadducees were wiped out which left Pharisaic Judaism in complete control.

It was the very essence of Pharisaism that the law is the exclusive manifestation of the theocratic concept. This enabled the Pharisees (and subsequently the Talmudic sages) to get along very well without priests and kings. Only the law was needed. Even prophecy, as expressed by the great classical prophets of Scripture, was terminated as no longer necessary or essential. The development of the law (Torah) as the progressive word of God was by itself considered sufficient for all time and all places. Therefore, down to its minutest details, the *Talmud* indicates that all legislation— civil, criminal, political, social—is essentially the revelation of God flowing from this one supreme source, Holy Scripture.

In the *Talmud* (as indeed in all Jewish law) religion, ethics, and jurisprudence so commingle as to be organically one. The rabbis, in their wildest proposals or in their most coiling arguments, would not have separated ethics from law. That would have been utterly inconceivable for them. Indeed, the outstanding characteristic of the whole system of Jewish jurisprudence is its conscious emphasis that in law mankind is to seek and find the manifestation of God. The true meaning of law is to be found in its ethical content. This is not always evident at first but becomes evident when it is understood that moral principle is the inner meaning of law. Once this is comprehended the next step is to realize that the assurance and meaning of ethics is found in God since he stands for righteousness. Consequently, the ethical content of the law is no self-delusion.

According to the Talmudic sages the law (Torah) was given in a desert in order to teach mankind that its revelation was without the assistance of any human government. The same explanation was used by the rabbis to teach the universality of the law because the desert is a wide open place, a no man's land, where all who so desire might come and receive its benefits. It was not intended to be limited to any country or any age. In accepting the law the Jews were not to think that God created it for them. There is an interesting *Haggadah* tradition which illustrates this point. It tells the story of how God went with the law to the various peoples on earth and invited them to accept it. The pagan kings and the peoples rejected the law. Then God turned to the Jewish people and invited them to accept it. But they too wished to evade the responsibility whereupon God imposed the law upon them under threat. "He inverted Mt. Sinai over them like a huge vessel and declared: 'If you accept the law (Torah) well and good; if not you will be buried under this mountain.'" [9]

*   *   *

In an age of widespread illiteracy, Talmudic learning conferred upon the Jewish masses a high degree of education. Once having studied the divine meaning of the law, the Jew could not look upon the pagan state in the manner of its illiterate subjects. Not that Talmudic law denied the value of the state. The state had its place but it was up to every God-fearing person to understand correctly just what that place was. The attitude of Judaism towards the state is nowhere more succinctly summarized than in the words of that learned judge Mar Samuel (died 254 A.D.) whose dictum, "The law of the land is the law" (*dina d'malchuta dina*) became the permanent expression of Jewry on this important issue.[10] But Samuel's dictum was nothing new.

---

[9] *Talmud,* tractate *Shabbat* 88a.
[10] *Talmud,* tractate *Baba Kamma* 113b. Jesus attitude towards the state was the Pharisaic-Talmudic attitude which he summarized in the words:

Hundreds of years before him the prophet Jeremiah sent a letter to the first exiles in Babylonian captivity in which he admonished them: "Seek the welfare of the city where I have sent you into exile, and pray to the LORD on its behalf." [11]

Talmudic law, as expressed by Mar Samuel's principle, commands every Jew to obey the law of the country in which he lives. He is to be a good citizen, pay taxes, help his country in times of war, and promote its welfare in peace. Mar Samuel's principle carries with it the understanding that the law of the country wherein the Jew lives is binding upon him even when it is in conflict (in a civil sense) with his own system of Talmudic law. However, in purely ritual or religious matters Judaism must always reserve to itself the right to self-determination. "I take an oath against you," says a representative passage in the *Tanchuma,* "not to rebel against the (Roman) government even if its decrees against you should be most oppressive; for you have to keep the king's commands. But if you are bidden to deny God and give up the Torah, then obey no more." [12]

Nowhere in the *Talmud* is any form of government sponsored. Actually, it never made any difference to the sages what kind of government held the administrative power as long as its conduct was morally right and compatible with elementary standards of decency. Most naturally the *Talmud* clings tenaciously to the sovereignty of God; but this did not mean that the laws of various governments were not to be tolerated. Tolerance and obedience were to be encouraged as long as the laws of the state did not conflict with the essentials of religion. The Talmudic sages, for example, did not object to the form of the Roman government; their grievance was against its cruelty, barbarism,

---

"Render to Caesar the things that are Caesar's and to God the things that are God's" (Matthew 22.21).

[11] Jeremiah 29.7.

[12] *Tanchuma,* Noah 10. *Tanchuma* is the name given to one of the oldest Midrashic collections consisting of homilies and Haggadic interpretations of the Pentateuch.

and corrupt standards. Just where to draw the line between the things of God and the things of Caesar never proved too easy a task for the scholars of the *Talmud*. Nor is it any less so for modern man who is still busy drawing his own conception of the jagged line dividing the two spheres. However, nothing emerges from a study of the *Talmud* which is clearer than the insistence that spiritual values are above the claims of temporal power.

This Talmudic flexibility towards forms of government had another side to it, flexibility in attitude towards other religions, races, and cultures. While authoritative Judaism always held to the Biblical doctrine of the "Election of Israel," meaning the concept of the Chosen People, this doctrine of the election of the Jew did not imply the rejection of the non-Jew. Despite a few anti-Gentile expressions which come from periods of intense persecution, or uttered under provocation in the heat of some embittered experience, it can be said that the *Talmud* is remarkably kind and charitable towards all non-Jews. Here and there within the bulk of this vast literature is to be found an occasional coarse remark or a statement of hostility arising out of some suspicion of pagan ill-will. But these individual harsh utterances certainly do not represent the authoritative position of the *Talmud*. Centuries before the phrase "religious tolerance" became known to western civilization the Talmudic rabbis had repeatedly emphasized that Judaism was bound to the Biblical teaching of the fatherhood of God; and because all men are God's children they are entitled to the rule of justice and mercy irrespective of racial, religious, or national boundaries. This flexible attitude towards the heathen (stranger) is even reflected in Biblical times when the animosity against non-Hebrews is assumed to have been prevalent. It is true that the Old Testament writings display a passionate intolerance toward those who practiced various forms of idolatry and immorality. Ancient Jewish law expected the Gentile to forego the worship of idols (Leviticus 20.2 and Ezekiel 14.7) and the practice of sorcery, incest, and other abominations (Leviticus 18.26). There were, to be sure, certain restrictions in the matter of the reception of strangers, especially in the case of those ancient enemies, the Edomites and the Egyptians. But these laws did not prevent Biblical legislation from declaring that God loved the stranger: "For the LORD your God is God of gods and Lord of lords, the great, the mighty, and the terrible God who is not partial and takes no bribe. He executes justice for the fatherless and the widow, and loves the sojourner, giving him food and clothing. Love the sojourner therefore; for you were sojourners in the land of Egypt." [13]

Time, which corrects the errata on the pages of human wretchedness, always helped the sages of the *Talmud* to carry the ideals of the Bible through periods of national catastrophe and distress into eras which were more serene and tolerant. After all, Jews could not overlook that the Old Testament commands consideration for the non-Jew in thirty-six places. "You shall love your neighbor as yourself" (Leviticus 19.18) was regarded as the fundamental doctrine of Judaism second only to the belief in God. The Talmudic rabbis were in the habit of saying that since the paths of the Torah were designed by the divine lawgiver to lead to peace, the Jewish people should do acts of kindness, consideration, and grace unto those not of the faith. God says: "Both the Gentiles and the Israelites are my handiwork. How can I then let the former perish on account of the latter?" [14]

Although the sages were teachers belonging to different ages, and though they frequently spoke with different accents, yet all were unanimous that Judaism should regard every person irrespective of his race or religion as a child of the one universal God. "Have we not all one father? Has

---

[13] Deuteronomy 10.17-19. It is interesting to note that one of the most beautiful books of the Old Testament was named after a pagan woman, Ruth.

[14] *Talmud*, tractate *Sanhedrin* 39b. For a very scholarly treatment of the Talmudic attitude on the non-Jew the reader is referred to the article on "Gentiles" in the *Jewish Encyclopedia*.

not one God created us?" are the words of the ancient prophet (Malachi 2.10) which refute the charge that Judaism limits the love of man to his own Jewish neighbors. In addition to the statement of Malachi the charge of racial narrow-mindedness is further contradicted by Leviticus 19.34 and Deuteronomy 10.19. Even if the rabbis of the *Talmud* had wished to indulge in anti-Gentile legislation their belief in Scripture as the revealed Word of God would have effectively checked them. He who hates any man—so runs the rabbinic teaching—hates God in whose likeness man was created. In no uncertain language the *Talmud* lays down the law that it is incumbent on the Jew to make no distinction in charitable assistance. The Jew is to help non-Jewish poor, heal non-Jewish sick, and bury non-Jewish dead with the same devotion he gives to his own.[15]

*   *   *

The liberalism which pervades the *Talmud* was due to the fluid conception of the Oral Law. The very nature of the Oral Law provided for the dynamic element of change and stood in marked contrast to the written law (Torah) which gave assurance of stationary strength. Oral Law implies fluidity, an ongoing process that can never be brought to a conclusion. Such a progressive conception of the operation of law led to geniality and tolerance which the sages possessed in good measure. Whenever their legal debates went far afield or whenever they sensed the tendency of the law to become a burden they invoked the text of Deuteronomy 30.12: "The law is not in heaven." This bit of Scripture was interpreted by them to mean that God intended the law to be applied in a sensible and down-to-earth manner. "Were the law given as a fixed, rigid, and immutable code," said Yannai a Palestinian sage of the second century, "there would be no reason to hold court and pass out judgment."[16]

---

[15] *Talmud*, tractate *Gittin* 51a, tractate *Nedarim* 38b, tractate *Tamid* 28a.
[16] Palestinian *Talmud*, tractate *Sanhedrin* 4.2.

Paradoxical as it seems, the sages could dispute with each other most vehementaly and yet be broad enough to admit the value of an opposite opinion. "Abba Areka must have spoken in his sleep when he said such a thing," is the terse comment of one of the rabbis who could not agree with so eminent a thinker as Abba Areka and did not hesitate to say so.[17] Because the right of individual thinking was cherished, scholars were able to see deeper into complex problems. So searchingly does the *Talmud* lay bare the anatomy of a legal problem that when these "doctors of the law" are through dissecting a given legal case one is often left somewhat groggy from the experience of following their arguments. That is why the *Talmud* does not always reach unanimous agreements.

Often the law in dispute is left in an undetermined state, to be solved by some future generation of leaders, simply because the Talmudic rabbis were not able to arrive at a majority decision. In those cases where the conflicting opinions are allowed to stand it is because the sages realized full well that neither opinion contained the whole truth, each being in need of the views expressed by the opposite opinion. In such an atmosphere dogmatism could not flourish. "And why do they record the opinions of Shammai and Hillel when these do not prevail?" asks the *Mishnah;* and it answers the question by saying that these conflicting views are recorded so that no man shall insist on his opinions— "To teach the generations to come that none shall persist in his opinions; for even the fathers of the world did not persist in their opinions." [18]

When differences arose between the sages, it was the majority view that became the recognized and authoritative manner of determining the law. In this connection the *Talmud* tells the story of a heated discussion between Rabbi Eliezer and his colleagues. Its purpose is to illustrate that the soundness of a man's position, in a disputed legal case,

---

[17] *Talmud,* tractate *Baba Kamma* 65a.
[18] *Mishnah,* tractate *Eduyoth* 1.4.

cannot depend upon miracles, or upon recourse to anything supernatural. Only the carefully reasoned decision of the majority must prevail. The exact words of the *Talmud* are interesting; for embedded in the quasi-legendary account is the principle that miracles do not constitute legal proof.

GEMARA TEXT: On that day Rabbi Eliezer brought forward every imaginable argument but the sages would not accept them. Finally he said, "If the rule is as I teach it, let this carob tree prove it!" Thereupon the carob tree moved back two hundred cubits out of its place. But the sages said, "A carob tree cannot prove anything." So Eliezer said, "If the rule is as I teach it, let the stream of water in this channel prove it!" Whereupon the stream of water turned and flowed backwards. But the sages said to him: "The waters of a channel cannot prove anything." Then Eliezer said, "If the law is as I teach it, let the walls of the school decide." And the walls of the school leaned over as to fall. But Rabbi Joshua (Eliezer's opponent) reprimanded the walls, saying, "When scholars are engaged in a legal dispute, what business is that of yours?" Out of respect for Rabbi Joshua the walls did not tumble; but out of respect for Rabbi Eliezer they did not stand up straight again; and so they are still there, leaning over. Then a heavenly voice was heard, saying: "Why do you dispute with Rabbi Eliezer? The law has always been what he teaches it to be." But Rabbi Joshua, rising to his feet, exclaimed, "It is not in heaven" (Deuteronomy 30.12). What did he mean by these words? He meant that the law is no longer in heaven, it had already been given at Mount Sinai, once for all time, and we need no longer pay heed to a heavenly echo. For in the Torah, given at Sinai, it is written: "The opinion of the majority shall prevail." Then the prophet Elijah (who is always appearing to rabbis) appeared to Rabbi Nathan. The Rabbi asked the prophet: "What was God doing at that moment when the value of miracles, as proof in a legal case, was being denied?" The prophet replied, "God laughed with joy saying: 'My children have conquered me, my children have conquered me.'" [19]

---

[19] *Talmud*, tractate *Baba Mezia* 59b. The words "the opinion of the majority shall prevail" do not actually occur in the Bible but were deduced, by rabbinic interpretation, from Exodus 23.2.

One of the purposes of the law was to arrive at uniformity amid the shifting and perplexing changes of human existence. Law is an attempt at orderliness, a desire for a reasoned way of doing things and a definite aim at the normal. As such it is the very opposite of a miracle which by definition seeks to introduce into human affairs elements that transcend the normal order. Biblical miracles, of course, have always stood in quite a different category in the minds of religious people. But even here the sages laid stress on those miracles which could be explained naturally. The *Talmud* is full of popular stories, folklore and fanciful tales, but their effect upon determining the law was never important. The work of the sages was characterized by a conscious endeavor at rationalization. Certainly Talmudic rationalization could not be furthered by appealing to the argument of miracles. There is no logic in a miracle, nothing to sharpen anybody's wits or confer mental acuteness. Belief in miracles tends to create an atmosphere of dogmatic credulity, the very thing the sages wished to avoid. Therefore, Rabbi Joshua's rejection of the miracles marshaled by Rabbi Eliezer ben Hyrcanus sustained the argument that the law was on the side of the carefully reasoned conclusions of the majority. Refusal to recognize the principle of adherence to majority decision eventually led to the necessity of banning Rabbi Eliezer from the lawmaking academy. His colleagues voted against him.

* * *

There is sadness in the heart of the historian when he must record the end of any great epoch of creativity. The age of the *Talmud* came to a close after the editorial work of Rabina II (d. 500 A.D.). It was not an abrupt ending but sharp enough to indicate to the leaders of Jewry that an altogether different period of history was now exerting its influence upon them. The liberalism, the geniality, and the tolerance which had characterized the thinking of the old-time sages was in eclipse. As the years rolled on the Babylonian community was confronted with social and economic problems far more vexing than had ever faced the creators of the *Gemara.* With all their changes there developed a changed attitude towards the sixty-three tractates that make up the *Talmud.* The fluidity which had so long characterized the labor of the sages in behalf of the Oral Law came to a halt.

The redaction of the *Talmud* was necessary and inescapable but it nailed down the Oral Law into an unalterable written form that soon became sacrosanct. For a thousand years or more the Oral Law had resisted capture; but now that it had been successfully booked attempts were made to seal its infallibility. Post-Talmudic rabbis generally felt that it was improper to hold an opinion different from that of a *Tana* (a sage of the *Mishnah*) or from that of an *Amora* (a sage of the *Gemara*). While the old-time sages allowed themselves some very sharp criticisms against their contemporaries and predecessors, this critical attitude was no longer regarded favorably. All Talmudic opinions were now held to be holy. In those instances where the opinions of the sages were in obvious conflict it was deemed best to work out some kind of harmonization. Not to believe in the correctness and literal truth of every word in the *Talmud* was branded as heresy. Sherira, for example, one of the last heads of Pumbeditha (died 968 A.D.) claimed that he who is brazen enough to dispute one word of the sages is a rebel against God and his law, for all the words of the sages are words of the living God.

Having elevated the writings of the *Mishnah* and *Gemara* to a status of authority almost equal to that of the Bible, there was only one important thing left for the rabbis to do with the sixty-three tractates of the *Talmud,* and that was to extract from its folios a sufficient body of laws to make a code for all Jewry. The purpose of the codes was to answer the question: What is the precise requirement of the law? And while it is true that the codes covered the life of the Jew with a network of small complicated rules they aimed at fixing universal standards for religious practice. But even greater than that aim was the basic desire to promote legal righteousness in the entire household of Israel.

The story of the various codes, and how the post-Talmudic rabbis developed them out of the *Halakah* (law) embedded in the *Talmud*, is a most interesting chapter in the history of jurisprudence. Unfortunately, the study of these codes does not come within the scope of this volume. Yet there is one element—perhaps the most important element of the codes—which ought not to be overlooked as we listen to the last dying gasp of Babylonian Jewry. This element may be expressed by the word, "authority." For these codes, which sprang into existence following the redaction of the *Talmud*, succeeded in presenting to the Jews of the world a unique over-all authority based upon the interpretative work of the sages. It was this authority stemming from the interpretations of the *Talmud* (both in the field of *Halakah* and *Haggadah*) which held the Jewish people together over the centuries with remarkable powers of resistance and cohesion. The authority of the codes was based upon the authority of the laws within the *Talmud*.

What is so astonishing about these Talmudic laws is that they were able to function over the centuries without the power of a state to enforce them. The great Catholic bishop St. Augustine, living in the fifth century, wrote with profound admiration on the ability of these laws to preserve the Jewish people: "The Jews although vanquished by the Romans, have not been destroyed. All the nations subjugated by the Romans adopted the laws of the Romans; this nation has been vanquished and nevertheless retained its law. And inasmuch as its law pertains to the worship of God they have preserved their ancestral customs and ritual." [20] Not only did these Talmudic laws function without the power of a state, they functioned without the power of a priesthood or a central church organization.

---

[20] St. Augustine: *Sermo* 374.2.

How was this possible?

It will be remembered that the Jews lost their state in
70 A.D., and at the same time their priesthood and their
Temple. But instead of defeating Judaism these changes
actually made the religion stronger, the reason being that
the authority of Jewish life which had been divided between state and priesthood was now centralized in but one
thing—the law (both in its written and oral form). Unlike
the state nobody could destroy the Torah. After all, the
Torah was something which existed in people's minds and
hearts where no enemy could possibly enter. In the same
category stood the synagogue. Unlike the one and only
Temple at Jerusalem no enemy could possibly destroy the
many thousands of synagogues spread throughout the
world. It was a comparatively simple thing for the Romans
to have demolished the Temple thereby bringing the entire
sacrificial system to an end. But no amount of Roman
persecution could burn all the copies of the Bible which existed throughout the world; and no amount of Roman domination could obliterate the Jewish religion seeing that it no
longer depended upon animal sacrifice. A knowledge of the
law (Torah) was the one and only thing which Judaism
required for survival. Thus the inwardness of the Torah
created for the Jews an immunity against the ravages of
social, religious, political, and economic antagonisms.

How did the law come to be invested with power to
achieve so phenomenal a result?

We have already mentioned the concept of revelation.
The strength of the written law (Torah) was undoubtedly
rooted in the firm belief that it was revealed to mankind
by God himself. But other religions of antiquity likewise
had their own private conceptions of revelation in which
they too regarded their own laws as of divine origin. One
need only look at the Hammurabi monument in the Louvre
in Paris to see how the ancient Babylonians depicted their
king, Hammurabi receiving a code of laws from the sun-
god. But what all the religions of antiquity lacked and what

Judaism alone possessed was the power of interpreting its divine revelation so that it could have a human flexibility and relevance for each generation. It was not just revelation alone that enabled the Jews to survive; it was revelation plus interpretation. The combination was unique. Something new had entered human affairs.

This combination was discovered by the Jews during the Babylonian Exile shortly after Nebuchadnezzar had taken captive the men of Judea and forced them to live on alien soil. It was this combination which enabled the Jewish people to survive for it gave them a deep spiritual understanding which rescued their religion from all manner of dilemmas and seeming contradictions. Those anonymous leaders of the Exile—they who developed the idea of the Oral Law—were in search of truth. They were not out after truth in the abstract, after the manner of the Greek philosophers. These leaders were in search of truth that would enable them to adjust the lives of their people to the affairs of the world no matter what the text, who the author, or how grotesque the inconsistency.

The richness and inwardness of Judaism, as it began to be cradled in the Exile, was due to the generous use of interpretation and reinterpretation. What is scriptural interpretation but a sincere search for the will of God, a ceaseless yearning of the human heart for a deeper relevance? Because the Torah was regarded as the necessary link between God and man, these exiled Jews came to the conclusion that it was not therefore something for ever fixed and closed but rather a revelation that could give progressive answers to newer situations. "Once God has spoken; twice have I heard." [21] The "once" is revelation and the "twice" represents interpretation.

We have already seen how each generation poured its mental and emotional strength into the texts of the Old Testament and came up with fresh interpretations which

---

[21] Psalm 62.11.

were welcomed as additional sources of spiritual enrich-
ment. Such fruits of the spirit were the result of human effort, and it was human participation that made the authority of Scripture a living authority. Granted that God gave
man revelation (Torah, the divine law), he also gave man
reason, and reasoning powers are capable of expansion and
progress. It is obvious that without reason man cannot
appreciate or understand the Torah. So, of necessity, the
two have a close interrelationship. That is why the Jews
rejoiced in the concept of the Chosen People. Among other
things it meant most importantly that they were the human
agency through which the authority of Scripture could express itself to mankind.[22] The central fact is that the development of the Oral Law, by which we mean the interpretations of the sages, became a great link in the chain
of spiritual awareness which is stated so succinctly in the
opening sentence of tractate *Aboth:* "Moses received the
law (Torah) on Mt. Sinai and handed it down to Joshua;
Joshua to the elders; the elders to the prophets; and the
prophets handed it down to the men of the Great Assembly."

Here then is the answer we are seeking to the question
of Talmudic authority. It is the answer given in the language in which the sages themselves repeated it over the
centuries. Here too we catch a glimpse of the enduring
nature of that authority which, in each generation, was
capable of transmitting the past into the present and driving
it onward towards the future. As Talmudic authority grew
from age to age it became more luminous, more significant,
more impressive; for men saw in that authority not only a
continuity with the past but an assignment for the future.

---

[22] Deuteronomy 29.29. The transmission of the Divine Law was given
into human hands. "The things that are revealed belong to us and our
children."

UNDERSTANDING THE TALMUD

Part Two

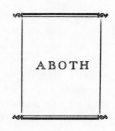

ABOTH

SAYINGS OF THE FATHERS

I

1. Moses received the law on Sinai and handed it down to Joshua; Joshua to the elders; the elders to the prophets; and the prophets handed it down to the men of the Great Assembly. They said three things: Be deliberate in judgment, raise up many disciples, and make a fence round the law.

2. Simeon the Just was one of the last survivors of the Great Assembly. He used to say: By three things is the world sustained: by the law, by the (Temple) service, and by deeds of loving-kindness.

3. Antigonus of Soko received the law from Simeon the Just. He used to say: Be not like servants who minister unto their master for the sake of receiving a reward, but be like servants who serve their master not upon the condition of receiving a reward; and let the fear of Heaven be upon you.

4. Jose ben Joezer of Zeredah and Jose ben Johanan of Jerusalem received the law from them. Jose ben Joezer of Zeredah said: Let thy house be a meetinghouse for the sages and sit amid the dust of their feet and drink in their words with thirst.

NOTE: Of the sixty-three tractates of the *Mishnah* ABOTH is best known and most often quoted. It is the outstanding classic of Rabbinical literature. Interestingly enough ABOTH was set down in the Order DAMAGES where it appears as the ninth tractate (*see* p. 15). It is the oldest collection of the ethical maxims of the sages and represents the full blossom of Pharisaic teaching.

5. Jose ben Johanan of Jerusalem said: Let thy house be wide open and let the poor be members of thy household; and engage not in much gossip with women. This applies even to one's own wife; how much more then to the wife of one's neighbor. Hence the sages have said: He that talks too much with women brings evil upon himself and neglects the study of the law and will in the end inherit *Gehenna.*

6. Joshua ben Perahyah and Nittai the Arbelite received the law from them. Joshua ben Perahyah said: Provide thyself with a teacher and get thee a companion (fellow disciple); and judge every man in the scale of merit.

7. Nittai the Arbelite said: Keep thee far from an evil neighbor and associate not with the wicked; and abandon not belief in retribution.

8. Judah ben Tabbai and Simeon ben Shetah received the law from them. Judah ben Tabbai said: Make not thyself like them that would influence the judges. When parties to a lawsuit are standing before thee let them be in thine eyes as wicked men, but when they have departed from before thee let them be in thine eyes as innocent, the verdict having been acquiesced in by them.

9. Simeon ben Shetah said: Examine the witnesses diligently and be cautious in thy words lest through them they learn to falsify.

10. Shemaiah and Abtalion received the law from them. Shemaiah said: Love work; hate domination; and seek not undue intimacy with the ruling power.

11. Abtalion said: Ye sages, give heed to your words lest ye incur the penalty of exile and ye be exiled to a place where the waters of learning are impure and the disciples that come after you drink of them and die; and the Heavenly Name is consequently profaned.

12. Hillel and Shammai received the law from them. Hillel said: Be of the disciples of Aaron, loving peace and pursuing peace, loving thy fellow creatures and bringing them nigh to the Torah.

13. Hillel used to say: He who aggrandizes his name, loses his name. He who does not increase his knowledge, decreases it. He who learns not, forfeits his life. He who makes unworthy use of the crown (of the Torah) shall pass away.

14. Hillel used to say: If I am not for myself who will be for me? Yet, if I am for myself only, what am I? And if not now, when?

15. Shammai said: Make your study of the law a fixed habit.

Say little and do much, and receive all men with a cheerful countenance.

16. Rabban Gamaliel said: Provide yourself with a teacher and remove yourself from doubt, and accustom not yourself to give tithes by guesswork.

17. Simeon his son said: All my days have I grown up among the wise and I have found naught better for a man than silence. Not the expounding of the law is the chief thing but the doing of it. Whoso multiples words causes sin.

18. Rabban Simeon ben Gamaliel said: By three things is the world sustained: by truth, by judgment, and by peace, as it is written in Scripture: "Speak the truth to one another, render . . . judgments that are true and make for peace" (Zechariah 8.16).

II

1. Rabbi Judah "the Prince" said: Which is the right course that a man should choose for himself? That which is an honor to him and elicits honor from his fellow men. Be as scrupulous about a light precept as of a weighty one, for thou knowest not the reward alloted for each precept. Balance the material loss incurred by the fulfilment of a precept against the spiritual gain and the material gain accruing from a transgression against the spiritual loss it involves. Reflect upon three things and you will not come within the power of sin: Know what is above you —a seeing eye, a hearing ear, and all your deeds recorded in a book.

2. Rabban Gamaliel the son of Rabbi Judah the Patriarch said: Excellent is study of the law when combined with a worldly occupation, for toil in them both puts sin out of mind. All study of the law which is not supplemented by work must in the last analysis prove futile and may lead to sin. Let all who occupy themselves with communal affairs do so for Heaven's sake; for then the merit of their fathers sustains them and their righteousness endures for ever. And as for you, God will then say: I count you worthy of great reward as if you had wrought it all yourselves.

3. Be you guarded in your relations with the ruling power; for they who exercise it draw no man nigh to themselves except for their own interests. They appear as friends when it is to their advantage, but they stand not by a man in his time of stress.

4. He used to say: Do his will as if it was your will that he may do your will as if it was his will. Make your will of no effect before his will that he may make the will of others of no effect before your will.

5. Hillel said: Separate not yourself from the congregation; and trust not in yourself until the day of your death. Judge not your fellow until you are come unto his place. Say not of a thing which cannot be understood that it will be understood in the end. Say not: When I have leisure I will study; perchance you may never have the leisure.

6. Hillel used to say: A brutish man dreads not sin; an ignorant man cannot be pious, nor can the diffident man learn, or the impatient man teach. He who engages excessively in business cannot become wise. In a place where there are no men strive you to be a man.

7. Moreover he saw a skull floating on the surface of the water and he said unto it: Because you did drown others they drowned you; and at the last they that drowned you shall be drowned.

8. He used to say: The more flesh the more worms; the more possessions the more anxiety; the more women the more witchcraft; the more maidservants the more lewdness; the more menservants the more thieving. But the more study of the law the more life; the more schooling the more wisdom; the more counsel the more understanding; the more righteousness the more peace. If a man has acquired a good name he has gained something which enriches his manhood; but if he has acquired words of the Torah he has attained unto life eternal.

9. Rabban Johanan ben Zakkai received the law from Hillel and from Shammai. He used to say: If you have learnt much in the law claim not for yourself moral excellence, for to this end were you created.

10. Rabban Johanan ben Zakkai had five disciples and these are they: Eliezer ben Hyrcanus, Joshua ben Hananiah, Jose the Priest, Simeon ben Nathaniel, and Elazar ben Arak.

11. He used to recount their praise: Eliezer ben Hyrcanus is a plastered cistern which loses not a drop; Joshua ben Hananiah —happy is she that gave birth to him; Jose the Priest is a saintly man; Simeon ben Nathaniel is fearful of sin; Elazar ben Arak is an ever-flowing spring.

12. He used to say: If all the sages of Israel were in one scale of the balance and Eliezer ben Hyrcanus in the other, he would outweigh them all. Abba Saul, however, said in his name: If all the sages of Israel, together with Eliezer ben Hyrcanus were in one scale of the balance, Elazar ben Arak would outweigh them all.

13. Rabban Johanan ben Zakkai said to them: Go forth and see which is the good a man shall cherish most. Rabbi Eliezer

said, a good eye. Rabbi Joshua said, a good companion. Rabbi Jose said, a good neighbor. Rabbi Simeon said, the gift of foresight. Rabbi Elazar said, a good heart. He said to them: I prefer the words of Elazar ben Arak more than your words, for in his words your words are included.

14. He said to them: Go forth and see which is the evil way which a man should shun. Rabbi Eliezer said, an evil eye. Rabbi Joshua said, an evil companion. Rabbi Jose said, an evil neighbor. Rabbi Simeon said, he that borrows and does not repay. He that borrows from a man is as one that borrows from God, for it is written (Psalm 37.21) "The wicked borrows and cannot pay back, but the righteous is generous and gives." Rabbi Elazar said, an evil heart. He said to them: I prefer the words of Elazar ben Arak more than your words, for in his words your words are included.

15. They each said three things. Rabbi Eliezer said: Let the honor of your fellowman be as dear to you as your own. Be not easily moved to anger. Repent one day before your death. Warm yourself before the fire of the sages, but be heedful of their glowing coals lest you be burned, for their bite is the bite of a jackal and their sting the sting of a scorpion and their hiss the hiss of a serpent, and all their words are like coals of fire.

16. Rabbi Joshua said: The evil eye, the evil inclination and hatred of his fellow creatures put a man out of the world.

17. Rabbi Jose said: Let the property of your fellow man be as dear to you as your own. Qualify yourself for the study of the law, for the knowledge of it is not yours by inheritance. Let all your deeds be done for the sake of Heaven.

18. Rabbi Simeon said: Be heedful in the reciting of the *Shema* and in prayer. When you pray do not make your prayer a form of routine but a plea for mercies and supplications before God, for it is written, "For he is gracious and merciful, slow to anger, and abounding in steadfast love, and repents of evil" (Joel 2.13). Be not wicked in your own sight.

19. Rabbi Elazar said: Be eager to study the law. Know what answer to give to an unbeliever. Know before whom you toil and who is your employer who shall pay you the reward of your labor.

20. Rabbi Tarfon said: The day is short, the task is great, the laborers are slothful, the wage is abundant and the master is urgent.

21. He used to say: It is not incumbent upon you to finish the task. Yet, you are not free to desist from it. If you have studied much in the law much reward will be given you, for

faithful is your employer who shall pay you the reward of your
labor. And know that the reward for the righteous will be in
the time to come.

III

1. Akabya ben Mahalalel said: Reflect upon three things and
you will not fall into sin. Know from whence you are come and
whither you are going and before whom you are destined to
give account and reckoning. From whence have you come?—
from a putrid drop. Whither are you going?—to the place of
dust, worm, and maggot. Before whom are you about to give
account and reckoning?—before the supreme King of kings, the
Holy One, blessed be he.

2. Rabbi Chanina, an assistant of the high priest said: Pray
for the welfare of the government, since but for fear of it men
would swallow each other alive.

3. Rabbi Hananiah ben Teradion said: If two sit together
and no words of the law are interchanged between them, theirs
is the session of the scornful, as it is written (Psalm 1.1) "Nor
sits in the seat of the scoffers." But when two sit together and
words of the Torah pass between them, the Divine Presence
rests between them, as it is written (Malachi 3.16) "Then those
who feared the LORD spoke with one another; the LORD heeded
and heard them, and a book of remembrance was written before
him, of those who feared the LORD and thought on his name."
Scripture speaks here of "two." Whence do we learn that if
even one sits and occupies himself in the law, the Holy One,
blessed be he, appoints him a reward? Because it is written
(Lamentations 3.28) "Let him sit alone in silence when he has
laid it on him."

4. Rabbi Simeon said: If three have eaten at one table and
have not spoken over it words of the law (Torah), it is as
though they had eaten of the sacrifices of the dead, for it is
written (Isaiah 28:8) "For all tables are full of vomit, no place [1]
is without filthiness." But if three have eaten at one table and
have spoken over it words of the law, it is as if they had eaten
from the table of God, for it is written (Ezekiel 41.22) "He
said to me, 'This is the table which is before the LORD.'"

5. Rabbi Chaniah ben Hakinai said: He who keeps awake
at night and goes on his way alone and turns his heart to idle
thoughts endangers his life.

---

[1] The Hebrew word *Makom* means "place" and is frequently used for
God. (*See* p. 92.) Rabbi Simeon ben Yochai gives this passage from
Isaiah a rabbinical twist.

6. Rabbi Nehunya ben Ha-Kanah said: Whoso takes upon himself the yoke of the law, from him shall be taken away the yoke of government and the yoke of worldly care; but whoso throws off the yoke of the law, upon him shall be laid the yoke of government and the yoke of worldly care.

7. Rabbi Halafta ben Dosa of Kefar Hanania used to say: If ten men sit together and occupy themselves with the Torah (law), the Divine Presence rests among them as is suggested by the verse (Psalm 82.1) "God has taken his place in the divine council." And whence do we learn that this applies even to five? Because it is written in Scripture (Amos 9.6) "And found his vault upon the earth." And how do we learn that this applies even to three? Because it is written (Psalm 82.1) "In the midst of the gods he holds judgment." And whence can it be shown that the same applies even to two? Because it is written (Malachi 3.16) "Then those who feared the LORD spoke with one another; the LORD heeded and heard them." And whence even of one? Because it is written (Exodus 20.24) "In every place where I cause my name to be remembered I will come to you and bless you."

8. Rabbi Eleazar of Bartotha said: Render unto God what is his, for you and all that you have are his, as David expressed himself (I Chronicles 29.14): "For all things come from thee, and of thine own have we given thee."

9. Rabbi Jacob said: If a man is walking by the way and studying and then breaks off his study and says: "How fine is this tree?" or "How fine is this ploughed field?" Scripture regards him as though he was guilty against his own soul.

10. Rabbi Dosethai ben Yannai said in the name of Rabbi Meir: He that forgets one word of his study, Scripture regards him as though he was guilty against his own soul; for it is written (Deuteronomy 4.9) "Only take heed, and keep your soul diligently, lest you forget the things which your eyes have seen." Could this apply even if a man's study was too hard for him? Scripture says: "And lest they depart from your heart all the days of your life" (Deuteronomy 4.9). Thus a person is not guilty unless he deliberately puts those lessons away from his heart.

11. Rabbi Hanina ben Dosa said: He in whom the fear of sin takes precedence of wisdom, his wisdom will endure; but he in whom wisdom takes precedence of his fear of sin, his wisdom will not endure.

12. He used to say: He whose works exceed his wisdom, his

wisdom endures; but he whose wisdom exceeds his works, his wisdom will not endure.

13. He used to say: He in whom the spirit of mankind finds no delight, in him the spirit of God finds no pleasure.

14. Rabbi Dosa ben Harkinas said: Sleeping away the morning, carousing at noonday, childish babbling and sitting in the meetinghouses of the vulgar wastes a man's life.

15. Rabbi Eleazar of Modiim said: If a man profanes things that are sacred, and despises the set feasts and puts his fellow to shame publicly, and makes void the covenant of Abraham our father, and discloses meanings in the law which are not according to the *Halakah,* even though a knowledge of the law and good works are his, he has no share in the world to come.

16. Rabbi Ishmael says: Be submissive to an elder and courteous to the young. Receive every man with good cheer.

17. Rabbi Akiba said: Jesting and frivolity lead a man towards lewdness. Tradition is a safeguarding fence around the law (Torah). Tithes are a fence to wealth. Vows a fence to abstinence. Silence is a fence to wisdom.

18. Rabbi Akiba used to say: Beloved is man that he was created in the image of God; but greater yet is that love inasmuch as it has been made known by the verse in Scripture (Genesis 9.6) "For God made man in his own image." Beloved are the Israelites that they are called children of God; but greater yet is that love inasmuch as this has been made known to them in the verse of Scripture (Deuteronomy 14.1): "You are the sons of the LORD your God." Beloved are the Israelites that there has been given to them the precious instrument of the world's creation; but greater yet is that love inasmuch as Scripture has made this known to them in the verse (Proverbs 4.2) "For I give you good precepts; do not forsake my teaching."

19. Rabbi Akiba said: All is foreseen, but freedom of choice is given. The world is judged in goodness, yet all is proportioned to one's work.

20. Rabbi Akiba used to say: All is given against a pledge, and the net is cast over all living; the shop stands open and the shopkeeper gives credit and the account book lies open and the hand writes. Every one that wishes to borrow let him come and borrow; but the collectors go their daily rounds and exact payment from man with or without his consent; for the collectors have that on which they can rely; and the judgment is a judgment of truth; and all is made ready for the feast.

21. Rabbi Eleazar ben Azaryah used to say: Where there is no Torah there is no culture; and where there is no culture there

is no Torah. Where there is no wisdom there is no reverence of God; and where there is no reverence of God there is no wisdom. Where there is no knowledge there is no discernment; and where there is no discernment there is no knowledge. Where there is no food (economic stability) there is no Torah; and where there is no Torah there is no food.

22. He used to say: He whose wisdom is more abundant than his works, to what is he like? To a tree whose branches are abundant but whose roots are few; and the wind comes and uproots it and overturns it, as it is written (Jeremiah 17.6) "He is like a shrub in the desert and shall not see any good come. He shall dwell in the parched places of the wilderness." But he whose works are more abundant than his wisdom, to what is he like? To a tree whose branches are few but whose roots are many; so that even if all the winds in the world come and blow against it, it cannot be stirred from its place, as it is written (Jeremiah 17.8) "He is like a tree planted by the water, that sends out its roots by the stream, and does not fear when heat comes, for its leaves remain green, and is not anxious in the year of drought, for it does not cease to bear fruit."

23. Rabbi Elazar Hisma used to say: The rules about bird offerings and the rules about uncleanness of women (menstruation) are essentials of the law; but astronomy and mathematics are incidentals to religious learning.

IV

1. Ben Zoma said: Who is wise? He who learns from all men, as it is written (Psalm 119.99) "I have more understanding than all my teachers."

Who is mighty? He who subdues his passions, as it is written (Proverbs 16.32) "He who is slow to anger is better than the mighty, and he who rules his spirit than he who takes a city."

Who is rich? He who rejoices in his portion, as it is written (Psalm 128.2) "You shall eat the fruit of the labor of your hands, you shall be happy, and it shall be well with you." "You shall be" refers to this world; and "it shall be well with you" refers to the world to come.

Who is honored? He that honors his fellow men as it is written (I Samuel 2.30) "For those who honor me I will honor, and those who despise me shall be lightly esteemed."

2. Ben Azzai said: Be eager to fulfil the highest duty and flee from transgression; for one duty induces another and one transgression induces another transgression. The reward of a

duty is a duty, the reward of one transgression is another transgression.

3. He also used to say: Despise no man and deem nothing impossible; for there is no man but has his day and there is no thing but has its place.

4. Rabbi Levitas of Jamnia used to say: Be exceeding lowly of spirit, for the hope of man is but the worm.

5. Rabbi Johanan ben Baroka said: Whosoever profanes the name of Heaven in secret will pay the penalty in public: in profaning the name it is all one whether it be done unwittingly or wantonly.

6. Rabbi Ishmael his son used to say: He who learns in order to teach will be enabled both to learn and to teach. But he who learns in order to practice will be enabled to learn, to teach, to observe, and to practice.

7. Rabbi Zadok his son used to say: Do not keep aloof from the community. Do not seek to influence the judges. Do not make the Torah a crown wherewith to aggrandize yourself nor use it as a spade wherewith to dig. As Hillel was wont to say: He who makes wordly use of the crown of the Torah shall perish. Thus you may infer that any one who exploits the words of the law removes himself from the world of life.

8. Rabbi Jose used to say: He who honors the law is himself honored by mankind. He who dishonors the law shall himself be dishonored by mankind.

9. Rabbi Ishmael his son said: He who shuns the office of judge rids himself of enmity, theft, and false swearing. He who presumptuously lays down the law is foolish, wicked, and arrogant.

10. He used to say: Judge not alone, for none may judge alone save one. And say not, "Accept my opinion," for it is for them to decide and not you.

11. Rabbi Jonathan said: He who fulfils the law in poverty shall in the end fulfil it in wealth. He who disregards the law in wealth shall in the end disregard it in poverty.

12. Rabbi Meir said: Engage not overmuch in business but occupy yourself with the law. Be humble in spirit before all men. If you neglect the law many causes for neglecting it will present themselves to you; but if you labor in the law then God has abundant reward to give you.

13. Rabbi Eliezer ben Jacob used to say: He who performs one commandment acquires for himself one advocate, while he who commits one transgression has gotten for himself one ac-

cuser. Penitence and good deeds are as a shield against punishment.

14. Rabbi Johanan the sandal-maker said: Every assembly that is for a hallowed purpose shall in the end be established. But any assembly that is not for a hallowed purpose shall not ultimately be established.

15. Rabbi Eleazar ben Shammua used to say: Let the honor of your pupil be as precious to you as your own; and the honor of your associate (colleague) as the respect due your teacher; and the respect towards your teacher as your reverence for God.

16. Rabbi Judah used to say: Be careful in teaching, for error in teaching amounts to deliberate sin.

17. Rabbi Simeon used to say: There are three crowns—the crown of the law, the crown of the priesthood, and the crown of kingship; but the crown of a good name excels them all.

18. Rabbi Nehorai said: Betake yourself to a place of the law, and say not that it will follow you or that your companions will establish it in your possession. Lean not upon your own understanding.

19. Rabbi Yannai used to say: It is not in our power to explain the well-being of the wicked or the sorrows of the righteous.

20. Rabbi Mattithyah ben Heresh used to say: Be first in greeting every man. Be rather a tail to lions than a head to foxes.

21. Rabbi Jacob used to say: This world is like a vestibule to the future world. Prepare yourself in the vestibule that you may enter into the banquet hall.

22. He also would say: Better is one hour of penitence and good deeds in this world than all the life of the world to come. Better is one hour of spiritual repose in the world to come than all the life of this world.

23. Rabbi Simeon ben Eleazar used to say: Appease not your fellow man in the hour of his anger, nor comfort him while his dead lies before him. Question him not in the hour of his vow. Strive not to see him in the hour of his disgrace.

24. Samuel the Younger used to quote the saying (Proverbs 24.17-18) "Do not rejoice when your enemy falls, and let not your heart be glad when he stumbles; lest the LORD see it and be displeased, and turn away his anger from him."

25. Elisha ben Abuyah used to say: He who learns as a child, to what is he like? To ink written on new paper. He who learns as an old man, to what is he like? To ink written on blotting paper.

26. Rabbi Jose bar Judah of Kefar ha-Babli said: He who learns from the young, to what is he like? To one that eats

unripe grapes and drinks wine fresh from his wine press. But he who learns from the aged, to what is he like? To one that eats ripe grapes and drinks old wine.

27. Rabbi Meir used to say: Look not on the flask but on what is in it; there may be a new flask that is full of old wine and an old flask that has not even new wine in it.

28. Rabbi Eleazar ha-Kappar used to say: Jealousy, lust, and ambition remove man from the world.

29. He also used to say: They who have been born are destined to die. They that are dead are destined to be made alive. They who live (after death) are destined to be judged, that men may know and make known and understand that he is God, he is the maker, he is the creator, he is the discerner, he is the judge, he is the witness, he is the complainant, and it is he that will in the future judge, blessed be he, in whose presence is neither guile nor forgetfulness nor respect of persons nor taking of bribes; for all is his. And know that everything is according to the reckoning. And let not your evil nature assure you that the grave will be your refuge: for despite yourself were you fashioned, and despite yourself were you born, and despite yourself you live, and despite yourself you die, and despite yourself shall you hereafter give account and reckoning before the supreme King of kings, the Holy One, blessed be he.

V

1. By ten divine fiats was the world created. Could it not have been created by one? What does Scripture wish to teach us? In order to emphasize the guilt of the wicked who mar his creation and the merit of the righteous who preserve it.

2. There were ten generations from Adam to Noah, to show how great was his long suffering, for every one of those generations provoked him continually until he brought upon them the waters of the Flood.

3. There were ten generations from Noah to Abraham, to show how great was his long suffering, for every one of those generations provoked him continually until Abraham, our father, came and received the reward of them all.

4. With ten temptations was Abraham, our father, tested. He stood steadfast in them all to show how great was his love of God.

5. Ten wonders were wrought for our fathers in Egypt and ten at the sea.

6. Ten plagues did the Holy One, blessed be he, bring upon the Egyptians in Egypt and ten more at the sea.

7. Ten times our ancestors in the wilderness tried the Holy One, blessed be he, even as it is said in Scripture (Numbers 14.22) "Who . . . have put me to the proof these ten times and have not hearkened to my voice."

8. Ten marvels were wrought for our fathers in the Temple: no woman miscarried from the odor of the flesh of the offerings; the flesh of the offerings never turned putrid; no fly was ever seen in the place of slaughter; the high priest never suffered a pollution on the Day of Atonement; rain never quenched the fire of the wood arranged on the altar; no wind prevailed over the pillar of smoke; never was a defect found in the omer or in the two loaves or in the showbread; though the worshipers stood pressed together yet they could freely prostrate themselves; never did serpent or scorpion do harm in Jerusalem; and no man said to his fellow, "There is no room for me to lodge in Jerusalem."

9. Ten things were created at twilight on the eve of the first Sabbath: the mouth of the earth (Numbers 16.32); the mouth of the well (Numbers 21.16); the mouth of the ass (Numbers 22.28); the rainbow; the manna; Aaron's staff; the Shamir; [2] writing; the inscription on the tablets of the Ten Commandments; and the tablets themselves. Some also include the evil spirits, the grave of Moses, the ram of Abraham; and others add the original tongs, for tongs must be made with tongs.

10. Seven marks characterize the clod and seven the wise man. The wise man does not speak before one who is greater than he in wisdom and he does not break in upon the speech of his fellow. He is not hasty in making answer. He asks what is relevant and answers according to the Halakah. He speaks on the first point first and on the last point last. Where he has heard no tradition he says, "I have not heard"; and he agrees to what is true. The opposites of these attributes are the marks of the clod.

11. Seven kinds of punishment come upon the world for seven classes of transgression. If some give tithe and some do not give tithe, there comes famine from drought. Some hunger while some have a sufficiency. When all resolve not to give tithes there comes famine from tumult and drought. And if they will not set apart dough offerings (Numbers 15.20) there comes an all-

---

[2] The Shamir is a worm associated with the legendary stories about King Solomon (Talmud, tractate Gittin 68a and Sotah 48b). It possessed the power to split stone. Consequently, it was used by Solomon in the building of the Temple inasmuch as there was supposed to have been a law against using any iron instrument in the building of the House of God—because iron is the symbol of war.

consuming famine. Pestilence comes upon the world because of crimes deserving of the death penalties enjoined in the law that are not brought before the court; and because of the transgressions of the laws of the seventh year produce (Leviticus 25.1-7). The sword comes upon the world because of the delaying of justice and the perverting of justice; and because of them that teach the law not according to the *Halakah*. Evil beasts come upon the world because of false swearing and the profaning of the name. Exile comes upon the world because of idolatry and incest and the shedding of blood; and because of neglect to give release to the soil during the sabbatical year.

12. At four periods pestilence increases: In the fourth year and the seventh year and in the year after the seventh year, and at the end of the Feast of Tabernacles every year. "In the fourth year"—because of neglect of the Poorman's Tithe in the third year (Deuteronomy 14.28-30). "In the seventh year"—because of neglect of the Poorman's Tithe in the sixth year. "In the year after the seventh year"—because of transgressing the laws of the seventh year produce. "At the end of the Feast of Tabernacles every year"—because of robbing the poor of the harvest gifts that are their due.

13. There are four types among men: He who says, "What is mine is mine and what is thine is thine"—this is the common type, though some say that this is the type of Sodom. He who says, "What is mine is thine and what is thine is mine"—he is an ignorant man. He who says, "What is mine is thine and what is thine is thine own"—he is a saintly man. And he who says, "What is thine is mine, and what is mine is mine own"—he is a wicked man.

14. There are four temperaments among men: Easy to provoke and easy to appease—his loss is canceled by his gain. Hard to provoke and hard to appease—his gain is canceled by his loss. Hard to provoke and easy to appease—he is a saintly man. Easy to provoke and hard to appease—he is a wicked man.

15. Four characteristics are found among students: Quick to learn and quick to forget, his gain is canceled by his loss. Slow to learn and slow to forget, his loss is canceled by his gain. Quick to learn and slow to forget, his is a happy lot. Slow to learn and quick to forget, his is an unhappy lot.

16. There are four types of almsgivers: He that is minded to give but does not wish that others should give—he begrudges what belongs to others. He that is minded that others should give but not that he should give—he begrudges what belongs to himself. He that is minded to give and also that others should

give—he is a saintly man. He that is minded not to give himself
and does not wish that others should give—he is a wicked man.

17. There are four types among those who attend the house
of study: He who goes and does not practice—he has the reward
of his going. He who practices but does not go—he has the reward of his practicing. He who goes and also practices—he is a
saintly man. He who neither goes nor practices—he is a wicked
man.

18. There are four types among those who sit in the presence
of the sages: the sponge, the funnel, the strainer, and the sieve.
"The sponge," which soaks up everything. "The funnel," which
takes in at this end and lets out at the other. "The strainer,"
which lets out the wine and retains the dregs. "The sieve," which
removes the coarse meal and collects the fine flour.

19. Whenever love depends upon some material consideration and the consideration passes away, then love passes away
too. But if love does not depend upon some ulterior interest
then love will never pass away. What is an example of the love
which depended upon some material advantage? That of Amnon
for Tamar. And what is an example of the love which did not
depend upon some ulterior interest? That of David and Jonathan.

20. Any controversy waged in the service of God shall in the
end be of lasting worth, but any that is not shall in the end lead
to no permanent result. Which controversy was an example of
being waged in the service of God? Such was the controversy
of Hillel and Shammai. And which was not for God? Such was
the controversy of Korah and all his company.

21. Whoever leads the masses in the right path will not occasion any sin; but whosoever leads the masses astray will not be
able to do penance for all the wrong he occasions. Thus Moses
was virtuous and he led the masses in the right path, and their
merit is ascribed to him, as it is written in Scripture (Deuteronomy 33.21) "With Israel he executed the commands and just
decrees of the LORD." But Jeroboam, the son of Nebat, sinned
and caused the multitude to sin, and so the sin of the masses is
ascribed to him as it says in Scripture (I Kings 15.30) "For the
sins of Jeroboam which he sinned and which he made Israel to
sin."

22. Whosoever possesses these three qualities belongs to the
disciples of Abraham our father: a generous eye, a humble
spirit, and a meek soul. But he who possesses the three opposite
qualities—an evil eye, a proud spirit, and a haughty soul—is of
the disciples of Balaam the wicked. How do the disciples of
Abraham differ from the disciples of Balaam? The disciples of

Abraham enjoy this world and inherit the world to come, as it is written (Proverbs 8.21) "Endowing with wealth those who love me and filling their treasuries." The disciples of Balaam inherit *Gehenna* and go down to the pit of destruction, as it says in Scripture (Psalm 55.23) "But thou, O God, wilt cast them down into the lowest pit; men of blood and treachery shall not live out half their days; but I will trust in thee."

23. Judah ben Tema used to say: Be strong as the leopard, swift as the eagle, fleet as the gazelle, and brave as the lion to do the will of your Father in Heaven. He also used to say: The impudent are for *Gehenna* and the affable for Paradise. (He used to pray): May it be thy will, O Lord our God and the God of our fathers, that the Temple be rebuilt speedily in our days, and grant our portion in thy law.

24. He used to say: At five years old a person should be fit to study the Scriptures, at ten years for the *Mishnah,* at thirteen for the commandments, at fifteen for the *Talmud,* at eighteen for the bridechamber, at twenty for one's life pursuit, at thirty for authority, at forty for discernment, at fifty for counsel, at sixty to be an elder, at seventy for gray hairs, at eighty for special strength (Psalm 90.10), at ninety for decrepitude, and at a hundred a man is as one who has already died and has ceased from the affairs of this world.

25. Ben Bag-Bag used to say of the Torah: Turn its pages and turn it again, for everything is in it. Pore over it, and wax gray and old over it. Stir not from it for thou canst have no better rule than it.

26. Ben Heh-Heh used to say: According to the effort is the reward.

VI [3]

The sages—blessed be he who chose them and their teachings —taught also the following in the style of the *Mishnah:*

1. Rabbi Meir used to say: He who occupies himself in the study of the law for its own sake merits many things; and, still more, the whole world is indebted to him. He is called friend, beloved, lover of God, lover of mankind. It clothes him with humility and reverence and fits him to become righteous, saintly, upright, and faithful. It keeps him far from sin and brings him near to virtue. From him men enjoy counsel and sound knowl-

---

[3] This sixth chapter of *Aboth* is called "Acquisition of the Law" or "The Baraitha of Rabbi Meir." Originally it was not a part of the canonical *Mishnah.* (On the meaning of *Baraitha see* p. 196.)

edge; as is suggested by Scripture (Proverbs 8.14) "I have counsel and sound wisdom, I have insight, I have strength." It gives
him rule and authority and insight into justice. To him are revealed the secrets of the law. He is made like a never-failing
spring and like a river that flows on with ever sustained vigor.
He becomes modest, patient, and forgiving of insult. It magnifies
him and exalts him above all things.

2. Rabbi Joshua ben Levi used to say: Every day a heavenly
voice goes forth from Mt. Horeb, proclaiming: "Woe to mankind
for their contempt of the law!" For he who occupies himself not
in the study of the law is said to be under divine censure. To
him may be applied the verse of Proverbs (11.22) "Like a
golden ring in a swine's snout is a beautiful woman without
discretion." Further, is his comment (Exodus 32.16) where
Scripture says: "And the tables were the work of God, and the
writing was the writing of God graven upon the tables," Rabbi
Joshua ben Levi declared that we ought not read *charut* (engraved) but *cheruth* (freedom).[4] Thereby making the text sug-
gest that no man is free unless he occupies himself with the
study of the Torah. Such a person progresses upward, a thought
suggested by the names in the Book of Numbers (21.19) "And
from Mattanah to Nahaliel and from Nahaliel to Bamoth." [5]

3. He who learns from his fellowman a single chapter or a
single *Halakah* or a single verse, or a single expression or even
a single letter, must show him honor. This we find exemplified
in David king of Israel who learned only two things from
Ahitophel, but called him his teacher, his guide, and his familiar
friend, as we find it written (Psalms 55.13) "But it is you, my
equal, my companion, my familiar friend." And is there not here
an inference from the less to the greater? If David king of
Israel, who learned but two things from Ahitophel, called him
his teacher, his guide, and his familiar friend, how much more
then must he that learns from his fellow a single chapter or a
single *Halakah* or a single verse or a single expression or even
a single letter pay him honor. And "honor" is naught else than
"the law," for it is written (Proverbs 3.35) "The wise will inherit
honor." And still again it says (Proverbs 28.10) "The blameless
will have a goodly inheritance." This is naught else than the

---

[4] A play upon words. This type of play was a device frequently em-
ployed by the rabbis to squeeze out of Scripture a fine homiletical thought.
[5] As words these place-names mean: Mattanah, gift; Nahaliel, heritage
of God; Bamoth, the heights. Consequently, Rabbi Joshua ben Levi interprets the verse to mean that from the gift of the Torah man gains the
heritage of God which leads him to the heights of lofty ideals.

law, for it is written (Proverbs 4.2) "For I give you good precepts; do not forsake my teaching."

4. This is the mode of living the study of the Torah (law)
entails: a morsel of bread and salt you must eat, and water by
measure you must drink; upon the ground you must sleep, and
a life of trouble you must live while you toil in the Torah. If
you do thus, then—"You shall be happy and it shall be well with
you" (Psalm 128.2) "You shall be happy" in this world, and "it
shall be well with you" in the world to come.

5. Seek not greatness for yourself, and crave not honor.
Practice more than you learn. Yearn not after the tables of kings,
for your table is greater than theirs and your crown nobler than
their crown, while the master of your work can be trusted to pay
you the reward of your labor.

6. Greater is the Torah than priesthood or royalty, for royalty
is attained through thirty qualifications and the priesthood
through twenty-four; but the Torah is attainable through forty-
eight, to wit: by audible study, by distinct pronunciation, by
understanding, by discernment of the heart, by awe, by reverence, by meekness, by cheerfulness, by ministering to the sages,
by attaching oneself to colleagues, by discussion with disciples,
by sedateness, by knowledge of the Scripture, by knowledge of
the *Mishnah*, by minimizing business, by minimizing worldy
interests, by minimizing indulgence, by minimizing sleep, by
minimizing conversation, by minimizing jesting, by patience, by
a good heart, by faith in the sages, by resignation under affliction, by knowing one's place, by rejoicing in one's lot, by setting
a limit to one's words, by not claiming merit for oneself, by
being one that is beloved, by loving God, by loving one's fellow-
men, by loving the ways of justice, by loving rectitude, by loving
reproof, by keeping oneself far from the pursuit of honor, by
not being arrogant in learning, by not delighting to lay down
legal decisions, by bearing the yoke with one's fellow student,
by judging him favorably, by leading him to truth and peace, by
being composed in one's study, by questioning and answering,
by hearing and adding to what one hears, by learning in order
to teach, by learning in order to practice, by making one's
master wiser, by fixing attention upon his discourse, and by re-
porting a thing in the name of him who said it. So thou hast
learned, that whosoever repeats a saying in the name of its
author brings salvation to the world, as it is implied in Scripture: "And Esther told the king in the name of Mordecai"
(Esther 2.22).

7. Great is the law which gives life to them that practice it

both in this world and in the world to come, as it is written
in Scripture (Proverbs 4.22) "For they are life to him who finds
them, and healing to all his flesh." And it further says in Scripture (Proverbs 3.8) "It will be healing to your flesh and refreshment to your bones." And it further says (Proverbs 3.18) "She
is a tree of life to those who lay hold of her; those who hold her
fast are called happy." And it also says (Proverbs 1.9) "For
they are a fair garland for your head, and pendants for your
neck." And it says (Proverbs 4.9) "She will place on your head
a fair garland, she will bestow on you a beautiful crown." And
furthermore it says (Proverbs 9.11) "For by me your days will
be multiplied and years will be added to your life." And it says
(Proverbs 3.16) "Long life is in her right hand; in her left hand
are riches and honor." And it says (Proverbs 3.2) "For length
of days, and years of life, and abundant welfare will they give
to you."

8. Rabbi Simeon ben Judah in the name of Rabbi Simeon
ben Yohai said: Beauty, strength, riches, honor, wisdom, old age,
the hoary beard, and children are comely for the righteous and
comely for the world, for it is written (Proverbs 16.31) "A hoary
head is a crown of glory; it is gained in a righteous life." And it
further says (Proverbs 20.29) "The glory of young men is their
strength but the beauty of old men is their gray hair." And it
says (Proverbs 14.24) "The crown of the wise is their wisdom."
And it says (Proverbs 17.6) "Grandchildren are the crown of
the aged and the glory of sons is their fathers." And it says
(Isaiah 24.23) "Then the moon will be confounded, and the sun
ashamed; for the LORD of hosts will reign on Mount Zion and in
Jerusalem, and before his elders he will manifest his glory."
Rabbi Simeon ben Menasya said: These seven qualities which
the sages have reckoned as comely for the righteous were all
of them fulfilled in Rabbi Judah "the Prince" and in his sons.

9. Rabbi Jose ben Kisma said: I was once walking by the
way and a man met me and greeted me and I returned his
greeting. He said to me, "Rabbi, from what place are you?"
I answered, "I come from a great city of sages and scribes." He
said to me, "If you will dwell with us in our place I will give
you a thousand thousand golden pieces and precious stones and
pearls." I answered, "If you gave me all the silver and gold and
precious stones and pearls in the world I would not dwell except
in a place where there is the Torah." And thus it is written
(Psalm 119.72) by David, king of Israel, "The law of thy
mouth is better to me than thousands of gold and silver pieces."
Moreover at the time of a man's departure, neither silver nor

gold nor precious stones nor pearls go with him, but only the Torah and good deeds; for it is written (Proverbs 6.22) "When you walk they (the Torah) will lead you; when you lie down, they will watch over you; and when you awake they will talk with you." When you walk it shall lead you—in this world; when you sleep, it shall watch over you—in the grave; and when you awake, it shall talk with you—in the world to come. Yea, further it is said in Scripture (Haggai 2.8), "The silver is mine, and the gold is mine, says the Lord of hosts."

10. Five possessions did the Holy One, blessed be he, acquire in this world; and these are they: (a) the law, (b) heaven and earth, (c) Abraham, (d) Israel and (e) the Temple. Whence do we learn this of the Law? Because it is written (Proverbs 8.22) "The LORD created me at the beginning of his work, the first of his acts of old." Whence do we learn this of heaven and earth? Because it is written (Isaiah 66.1), "Heaven is my throne and the earth is my footstool; what is the house which you would build for me and what is the place of my rest?" And it says (Psalm 104.24), "O LORD, how manifold are thy works! In wisdom hast thou made them all: the earth is full of thy creatures." Whence do we learn this of Abraham? Because it is written (Genesis 14.19), "And he blessed him, and said, Blessed be Abram by God Most High, maker of heaven and earth." Whence do we learn this of Israel? Because it is written (Exodus 15.16), "Till thy people, O LORD, pass by, till the people pass by whom thou hast purchased." And it says, "As for the saints in the land, they are the noble, in whom is all my delight" (Psalm 16.3). Whence do we learn this of the Temple? Because it is written (Exodus 15.17), "The place, O LORD, which thou hast made for thy abode; the sanctuary, O LORD, which thy hands have established." And it says (Psalm 78.54), "And he brought them to his holy land, to the mountain, which his right hand had won."

11. All that the Holy One, blessed be he, created in this world, he created only for his glory, as it says in Scripture (Isaiah 43.7) "Every one who is called by my name, whom I created for my glory, whom I formed and made."

"The LORD will reign for ever and ever" (Exodus 15.18).

APOCRYPHA TO THE TALMUD

In addition to the sixty-three tractates which compose the *Talmud* there are seven treatises which are connected with it as a kind of Apocrypha. These uncanonical treatises are:

1. *Aboth d'Rabbi Nathan:* A commentary on tractate *Aboth.* The ethical sayings of *Aboth* are here considerably enlarged and illustrated by numerous narratives.

2. *Sopherim:* This treatise is important for the Masoretic rules. It contains the regulations for the writing of the Pentateuch and the liturgical laws for the service on the Sabbath, Holidays, and Fast days.

3. *Ebel Rabbati:* This treatise deals with the laws and customs concerning burial and mourning. It is also known as *Semachoth.*

4. *Kallah:* Concerns itself with the subject of marriage. It also treats of the duties of the bride and the married woman.

5. *Derech Eretz:* Treats of prohibited marriages, and deals with ethical, social, and religious teachings.

6. *Derech Eretz Zuta:* Treatise on the conduct of life. It is replete with rules for the learned and maxims of wisdom.

7. *Perek Ha-Shalom:* It treats of the importance of peace.

ADDITIONS TO THE TALMUD

In addition to the sixty-three tractates of the *Talmud,* and the seven treatises which form a kind of Apocrypha, there are also "Seven Small Tractates" which arose after the *Talmud* was compiled and redacted. These "Seven Small Tractates" form a kind of subsidiary to the *Talmud.* They supply ready information upon seven subjects of almost daily importance to the people.

The "Seven Small Tractates" are:

1. *Sefer Torah:* Concerning the writing of the Torah.
2. *Mezuzah:* Concerning the writing on the doorpost.
3. *Tephillin:* Concerning phylacteries.
4. *Tzizith:* Concerning fringes.
5. *Abadim:* Concerning slaves.
6. *Kuthim:* Concerning Samaritans.
7. *Gerim:* Concerning proselytes.

COMMENTARIES ON THE TALMUD

The very nature of the *Talmud* gave rise to a large number of commentaries; for the brevity of its style—a system of shorthand notes—confronted the post-Talmudic sages with numerous difficulties. Oftentimes Talmudic expressions are elliptical and abound in technical language. Without the aid of expert commentators in every generation, much would have been for ever obscure. Commentaries on the Talmud may be divided into: (a) *Perushim*, (b) *Tosaphoth*, (c) *Chiddushim*, (d) *Hagahoth*. The *Perushim* are running commentaries accompanying the text. The *Tosaphoth* are supplements on Rashi's commentary. The *Chiddushim* (*novellae*) are explicit comments on certain passages of the *Talmud* text. The *Hagahoth* are marginal glosses.

A glance at the names of the most important contributors in this whole field of commentary will help our appreciation of the continuity of Talmudic explanation which goes back to the eleventh century.[1]

ELEVENTH CENTURY: Isaac Alfasi, Nissim ben Jacob, Gershom ben Judah, Hananel ben Hushiel, Solomon ben Isaac (Rashi)

TWELFTH CENTURY: Samuel ben Meir, Moses Maimonides (Rambam), Jacob ben Meir Tam, Isaac ben Asher

THIRTEENTH CENTURY: Meir Abulafia, Solomon ibn Adret, Meir of Rothenburg, Judah ben Isaac of Paris

FOURTEENTH CENTURY: Asher ben Jehiel, Yomtob ben Abraham, Joseph Habiba

FIFTEENTH CENTURY: Obadiah Bertinoro

SIXTEENTH CENTURY: Bezalel Ashkenazi, Solomon Luria, Joshua Boas, Solomon Syrileio (Palestinian *Talmud*)

SEVENTEENTH CENTURY: Samuel Edels, Meir Lublin (Maharam), Meir Schiff, Yomtob Lippman Heller, Joshua Benveniste (Palestinian *Talmud*)

EIGHTEENTH CENTURY: Ezekiel Landau, Jacob Emden, Elijah Vilna, Elijah Fulda (Palestinian *Talmud*), David Frankel (Palestinian *Talmud*), Moses Margoleth (Palestinian *Talmud*)

NINETEENTH CENTURY: Akiba Eger, Moses Sofer, Aryeh Loeb Yellin, Joshua I. Shapiro (Palestinian *Talmud*), Meir Marim (Palestinian *Talmud*)

TWENTIETH CENTURY: Joseph Engel, Israel Meir Hakohen, Louis Ginzberg (Palestinian *Talmud*)

---

[1] Before the eleventh century, there were explanatory notes of a fragmentary nature. Perhaps the earliest attempt at commentary began with the textual comments of Paltoi Gaon (ninth century).

THE HOUSE OF HILLEL [1]

HILLEL (30 B.C.–10 A.D.)

Came to Palestine from Babylonia in his mature years. Became head of the Sanhedrin and founder of the School of Hillel (liberal interpretation of the law) as opposed to the school of Shammai. Ancestor of the patriarchs who stood at the head of Palestinian Judaism until the fifth century.

SIMEON I "THE ELDER" (10–20 A.D.)

Nothing is known of him except his name and the fact that he was his father's successor as head of the Sanhedrin at Jerusalem.

GAMALIEL I (20–40 A.D.)

Head of the Sanhedrin at Jerusalem. This is the Gamaliel mentioned in the New Testament. He was the first to use the title "Rabban."

SIMEON II, SON OF GAMALIEL I (40–70 A.D.)

Head of the Sanhedrin at Jerusalem in the last two decades before the destruction of the Temple. Man of resolution and great courage. He opposed Josephus, the historian. Died during the siege of the Holy City.

JOCHANAN BEN ZAKKAI (60–95 A.D.)

The only non-member of the House of Hillel to be called "Rabban." Established the Academy-Council (*Beth-Din*) at Jamnia which was a continuation of the old Sanhedrin.

GAMALIEL II OF JAMNIA (90–110 A.D.)

He continued with success the work of Jochanan ben Zakkai at Jamnia despite the heavy hand of Roman rule.

SIMEON III, SON OF GAMALIEL II (110–165 A.D.)

His residence was at Usha. Distinguished organizer. Under his leadership the patriarchate attained a degree of honor previously unknown. He was against the use of fear as a factor in religion. In the interpretation of the law he carried forward the liberal traditions of the House of Hillel.

---

[1] Approximate dates of their active careers.

JUDAH I "THE PRINCE" (165–219 A.D.)

Redactor of the *Mishnah*. One of the most distinguished Jews of all times. The seat of his residence was first at Bet She'arim and then at Sepphoris.

GAMALIEL III (219–225 A.D.)

Worked on his father's great project, the *Mishnah*, and is credited with having much to do with its completion. Three sayings of this Gamaliel are incorporated in the "Sayings of the Fathers" (*Aboth* 2:2-4)

JUDAH II (225–250 A.D.)

Removed the seat of the patriarchate to Tiberias. Known for his reform of the divorce laws. Abrogated an old law which forbade Jews from using oil prepared by pagans. He would not however abrogate the prohibtion against using bread prepared by pagans.

GAMALIEL IV (250–265 A.D.)

Very little is known about him.

JUDAH III (265–320 A.D.)

Best known for the organization of a school system for the children of Palestinian cities. During his reign there was a protest against the number of fast days on the theory that the community should not be overburdened. While Judah III was still patriarch the Roman Emperor, Diocletian visited Palestine.

HILLEL II (320–365 A.D.)

Honored by the Roman Emperor, Julian. Hillel II instituted certain calendar reforms.

GAMALIEL V (365–380 A.D.)

This Gamaliel is celebrated in connection with perfecting the Jewish calendar.

JUDAH IV (380–400 A.D.)

Very little is known about him.

GAMALIEL VI (400–425 A.D.)

The last patriarch. When he died there were no heirs and the House of Hillel died out.

NAMES OF IMPORTANT FOUNDERS OF THE MISHNAH

It is not necessary to list here more than a few illustrious names to show the various generations of the founders of the *Mishnah*. Those sages are known as *Tannaim* (*Tanna*, means "teacher").

PRE-TANNAITIC GENERATIONS (300 B.C.–10 A.D.):

Men of the Great Assembly

First Pair
{ Jose ben Joezer

Jose ben Johanan

Second Pair
{ Joshua ben Perachyah

Nittai of Arbela

Third Pair
{ Judah ben Tabbai

Simeon ben Shetah

Fourth Pair
{ Shemayah

Abtalyon

FIRST GENERATION (10–80 A.D.):

Hillel, Shammai, Gamaliel I, Simeon II Son of Gamaliel I, Jochanan ben Zakkai

SECOND GENERATION (80–120 A.D.):

Gamaliel II (of Jamnia), Eliezer ben Hyrcanus, Elazar ben Azariah, Joshua ben Hananiah

THIRD GENERATION (120–140 A.D.):

Tarphon, Ishmael, Akiba, Ben Azzai, Ben Zoma

FOURTH GENERATION (140–165 A.D.):

Meir, Simeon ben Yochai, Simeon III, Son of Gamaliel II, Elazar ben Shaummua, Jose ben Halafta, Judah ben Ilai

FIFTH GENERATION (165–200 A.D.):

Judah "the Prince," Elazar ben Simeon, Jose ben Judah, Symmachus

SIXTH GENERATION (200–220 A.D.):

Gamaliel III, Hanina, Abba Areka (*Rab*), Simeon ben Halafta, Dosetai ben Yannai

NAMES OF IMPORTANT MAKERS OF THE GEMARA

Only a few of the more illustrious names of the founders and makers of the *Gemara* are here listed. These sages are known as *Amoraim*.

FIRST GENERATION (219–257 A.D.):

Palestinian	*Babylonian*
Chanina bar Chama	Abba Areka
Jonathan ben Eleazar	Mar Samuel
Joshua ben Levi	Assi I
Alexander	Mar Ukba
Oshaya	
Yannai Rubbah	

SECOND GENERATION (257–320 A.D.):

Palestinian	*Babylonian*
Johanan	Huna
Simeon ben Lakish	Judah bar Ezekiel
Aha I	Rab Chisda
Jose ben Hanina	Shesheth
Simlai	Nachman ben Jacob

THIRD GENERATION (320–375 A.D.):

Palestinian	*Babylonian*
Elazar ben Pedat	Rabba Huna
Hiyya ben Abba	Rabba bar Machmani
Simeon ben Pazzi	Joseph bar Chiya
Zera	Nachman bar Isaac
Abbahu	Papa

FOURTH GENERATION (375–427 A.D.):

Palestinian	*Babylonian*
Judah ben Shalom	Abbaye
Yudan	Ashi
Aha II	Raba
Berechiah	Zebid
Huna II	Dimi
Yannai the Younger	Rafram I
	Mar Zutra

FIFTH GENERATION (427–468 A.D.):

Palestinian	Babylonian
Tanhuma ben Abba	Mar Yemar
Jose bar Zabda	Idi bar Abin
	Ashi
	Rafram II

SIXTH GENERATION (468–500 A.D.):

Palestinian	Babylonian
	Rabina
	Jose

HEADS OF SURA AND PUMBEDITHA

A chronological list of the sages who headed these two great academies. Not all the heads are listed here but enough important names to give the reader a bird's-eye view of the parallel vitality of the two seats of learning which lasted for more than eight hundred years.

PERIOD OF THE GEMARA (*Amoraim*)

Sura	*Pumbeditha*
Abba Areka (d. 247)	Mar Samuel (d. 254)
Huna (d. 297)	Judah ben Ezekiel (d. 299)
Hisda (d. 309)	bar Nachmani (d. 330)
Rabba bar Huna (d. 322)	Joseph bar Hiyya (d. 333)
Papa (d. 375)	Abaye (d. 338)
Ashi (d. 427)	Raba (d. 352)
Maremar (d. 432)	Rafram II (d. 443)
Rabina II (d. 499)	Rab Jose (d. 520)

POST-GEMARA PERIOD (*Geonim*)

Sura	*Pumbeditha*
Mar R. ben Mar R. Huna (d. 609)	Mar R. Mari ben Mar R. Dimi (d. 609)
Mar R. Nehilai of Naresh (d. 697)	Mar R. Isaac (d. 660)
R. Mari ha-Levi ben R. Mesharsheya (d. 777)	Mar Rabba ben R. Dodai (d. 773)
Natronai ben Mar R. Hilai (d. 853)	Mar R. Zemach ben Mar Paltoi (d. 872)
Shalom ben Mar R. Mishael (d. 904)	R. Mebasser Kahana (d. 918)
Saadia (d. 928)	Chanieh ben Mar R. Yehudai (d. 938)
R. Joseph ben R. Jacob (d. 942)	Sherira (d. 968)
R. Samuel ha-Kohen ben Hofni (d. 1034)	Hai (d. 1038)

RULES OF INTERPRETATION

Methods had to be devised which would enable the sages to extend the limited sphere of Biblical law. The problem was: how to find in the old laws of the Pentateuch new decisions, especially for unprecedented cases. The earliest collection of methods (Rules of Interpretation) was ascribed to Hillel. He is said to have fixed seven norms of interpretation as standard in adjusting Biblical law to post-Biblical life.

1. THE INFERENCE FROM MINOR AND MAJOR: This rule is applied from the less important to the more important. Thus, if the easier thing is prohibited then the more difficult one is most certainly prohibited. The premise of the easier proposition is established, then the premise of the more difficult one, so that the conclusion flows from the two. This rule is also capable of being reversed—that is, an inference from the major to the minor. This rule in Hebrew is called *Kal v'Homer.*

2. THE ANALOGY OF IDEAS OR ANALOGOUS INFLUENCE: This rule infers from the similarity of two cases that the legal decision given for the one holds good for the other. By this rule various words, which occur in the Bible and have similar or identical connotations, are treated legally alike. Thus the entire sequence of ideas which attaches to a word in one passage is made to bear the same sequence of ideas in the other. Although a word may be bound up in Scriptural laws that are widely different, yet the law in question is made subject to the same regulations and applications (inasmuch as the same word occurs in both). This rule enabled the sages to establish a new law by analogy in the contents or the meaning of a word in two different Biblical passages. This rule in Hebrew is called *Gzerah Shawah.*

3. GENERALIZATION FROM ONE SPECIAL PROVISION: It is permitted to derive a general interpretation from one passage in Scripture. Other cases may be grounded upon this one passage if they are sufficiently similar. Thus the principal passage imparts a common character to the others under consideration. This rule is called in Hebrew *Binyan Ab mi-Katub Echad.*

4. GENERALIZATION FROM TWO SPECIAL PROVISIONS: A generalization may be drawn from two passages in Scripture. This rule is similar to rule 3. Whereas the former rule is based upon a deduction from only one Biblical passage, this rule generalizes from two special provisions. Thus, a decision in two laws having

191

a characteristic in common is applied to many other laws which have this same characteristic. This rule is called in Hebrew *Binyan Ab m'Shene Ketubim.*

5. GENERAL AND PARTICULAR: The determination of the general by the particular and vice versa: the particular by the general. If a given passage begins with a general statement and ends with a specific statement, the particular does not exceed the general and the law remains as outlined in the particular. If the passage, on the other hand, begins with a particular statement and ends with a general statement, the law is as asserted in the general, not in the particular. This rule is called in Hebrew *Klal u'Ferat.*

6. HARMONIZING PASSAGES: The explanation of a Biblical passage according to another of similar content. Thus, when two texts contradict each other, the meaning can be determined when a third text bearing on the subject is found which can be made to harmonize with the difficulties. This rule is called in Hebrew *Ka-yozeh bo m'Makom Aher.*

7. DEFINITION FROM THE CONTEXT: If a passage in Scripture is insufficiently clear, the subject matter of the context may be used to clarify the meaning.

Besides the seven rules of Hillel, which were widely adopted, other rules and methods were developed by succeeding generations of sages. Always the problem was: how to make new deductions from Biblical law. Thus, for example, Nahum of Gimzo originated a method called "Extension and Limitation." The illustrious Rabbi Akiba took up Nahum's method and greatly extended it. The underlying principle of Akiba's system revolved around the idea that every word in the Pentateuch, every syllable, every letter is of vital importance in defining a law. Akiba's system developed entirely new ways and means to find a Scriptural basis for new laws. It was an ingenious system having many merits but it also possessed many defects. Moreover, it was dangerous inasmuch as it opened wide the gates of interpretation to any one whose lively imagination could concoct some fanciful play upon words. Akiba's system took interpretation out of the field of rational approach and placed it in the field of mystical experience; for according to Akiba, the language of the Pentateuch differs from human language.

In opposition to Akiba, Rabbi Ishmael claimed that the Torah (Pentateuch) "speaks in the ordinary language of men." [1] There-

---

[1] Rabbi Ishmael ben Elisha was a distinguished Palestinian sage. He lived during the latter part of the first century A.D., and the early part of the second century. A contemporary of Akiba.

fore, according to Rabbi Ishmael, no special interpretative
weight or mystical significance ought to be assigned to words,
syllables, or individual letters. Rabbi Ishmael insisted that legal
deductions could be justified only by the spirit of the Biblical
text under consideration and not by fanciful play upon letters and
syllables. Consequently, Rabbi Ishmael would recognize as
standard rules of interpretation those norms laid down by Hillel.
From Hillel's norms Rabbi Ishmael developed additional rules,
but always in the direction of a rational approach. Rabbi Ishmael's famous thirteen rules are therefore elaborations of Hillel's
seven. Interestingly enough, Ishmael's thirteen rules for expounding the Torah were incorporated in the Jewish prayer
book and have been recited daily by the faithful over the centuries since they were formulated.

One of Akiba's later disciples, a sage by the name of Eliezer
ben Jose ha-Gelili, evolved thirty-two rules which were applied
mostly in the field of *Haggadah* rather than in the *Halakah*.
These thirty-two rules of interpretation deal primarily with syn-
tax, style, and the subject matter of the Bible. A number of
Eliezer's rules are adaptations of his predecessors.

NOTE ON MIDRASH LITERATURE

Midrash literature arose out of the need to penetrate into the spirit of the Scriptures, to go beyond the mere literal sense of Holy Writ. Changing conditions forced the Jews to derive interpretations from the Pentateuch which were not immediately obvious in the plain meaning of its text. Of necessity scriptural passages were made to yield far more than could be discerned on the surface.

In the Book of Nehemiah (8.2-8) there is to be found the earliest evidence of this kind of penetration for we are told that Ezra the Scribe, together with others, read distinctly to the people the Pentateuch (the law of God) "and gave the sense, so that the people understood the reading." This type of scriptural activity, once having been initiated, was carried on and continued by subsequent generations of scribes and sages. Their commentaries upon Scripture whether oral or written came to be called *Midrash* (*derash* meaning "to dig in" hence to penetrate, to deduce, to interpret).

Inasmuch as *Halakah* and *Haggadah* are two aspects of the Biblical writings it was inevitable that the penetration into Scripture should divide itself accordingly into: (a) *Midrash* on the *Halakah* and (b) *Midrash* on the *Haggadah*.

The earliest Midrashic literature is predominantly Halakahic in character. All *Midrash* which deals with *Halakah* (law) is concerned chiefly with the legal portions of the Pentateuch. Such *Midrash* seeks to find the rules and the principles whereby the sages could arrive at the proper decisions for new legal cases. It also gave the sages scriptural support for all those traditional practices of later origin which the people came to accept over and above the practices described in the Bible. The most important *Midrash* collections of the Halakahic class are:

Mekilta: A *Midrash* on Exodus. The word *Mekilta* means "measure," "rule," or "form."

Siphra, or "the Book": It is also known under the name *Torath Kohanim.* This *Midrash* is an interpretation of Leviticus.

Siphre, or "Books": These are Midrashic writings upon the books of Numbers and Deuteronomy.

In contradistinction to *Midrash Halakah* there is *Midrash Haggadah.* Midrashic literature which is chiefly Haggadahic in

194

character is of vast extent.[1] Century after century the Jews developed this kind of Biblical interpretation all the way from the fourth century before Christ down to the tenth A.D. Its richest period of development was unquestionably the Talmudic period, the age in which the *Mishnah* and *Gemara* came to be written. The most important collections in this class are:

Bereshit Rabbah: A running commentary on the Book of Genesis. Inasmuch as Genesis contains practically no legal (*Halakah*) matters, it can readily be seen that a commentary upon Genesis would be almost exclusively Haggadahic.

Shemot Rabbah: Midrashic commentaries on the Book of Exodus.

Vayikra Rabbah: Midrashic commentaries on the Book of Leviticus.

Bamidbar Rabbah: Midrashic commentaries on the Book of Numbers.

Debarim Rabbah: Midrashic commentaries on the Book of Deuteronomy.

Ekah Rabbati: Midrashic commentaries on the Book of Lamentations.

Midrash Shir ha-Shirim: Homiletical commentaries on the Song of Songs.

Midrash Ruth: Homiletical commentaries on the Book of Ruth.

Midrash Kohelet: Homiletical commentaries on the Book of Ecclesiastes.

Midrash Esther: Homiletical commentaries on the Book of Esther.

Tanchuma Yelammedenu: Two originally distinct works which came to be united: (1) *Midrash Tanchuma* the work of a celebrated Palestinian sage named Tanchuma, and (2) *Yelammedenu.* Together these two Midrashic collections contain a large variety of homilies dealing with the Five Books of Moses (Pentateuch).

Pesikta d'Rab Kahana: So-called because it is based upon the "sections" (*pesikta*) of Scripture which form the lessons read on the Sabbath and festivals. This collection is attributed to Rab Kahana (died about 280 A.D.).

---

[1] The student of Midrashic literature will be greatly helped by the English translation of the entire *Midrash Rabbah.* This translation was accomplished by a group of Jewish scholars in England and published by the Soncino Press. The work appears in 10 volumes (with complete index) edited by H. Freedman and M. Simon. London 1939.

NOTE ON BARAITHA

The *Baraitha* (the word means "extraneous") constitutes a great mass of traditional material which was not included in the *Mishnah* compiled by Rabbi Judah "the Prince." Judah's compilation was accepted as authoritative and it alone became canonical. But there existed other collections of similar materials. Certain traditions were excluded from the authoritative teachings which nevertheless continued to be transmitted as relevant data although not incorporatd in the *Mishnah* text. These "excluded" collections are called *baraitha*—that is, extraneous. *Baraitha* do not stand in opposition to the authoritative tradition as found in the *Mishnah;* they constitute a kind of supplement. Being supplementary materials they never achieved the exalted status of Rabbi Judah's *Mishnah* however widely used and discussed.

The relation of the *baraitha* materials to the *Mishnah* is similar to that of the Apocrypha to the canonical Old Testament. *Baraitha* materials are made up of both *Halakah* and *Haggadah.* The important *baraitha* collections are: *Sifra, Sifre, Mekilta,* and *Tosefta.* In addition to these collections there is scattered about in both *Talmuds* (Babylonian and Palestinian) a considerable amount of *baraitha* material; these "Talmudic *baraitha*" exist in the form of isolated sections and are easily distinguishable from the general Talmudic text. Frequently in the *Talmud* the sages opened up their debates by quoting an extraneous (*baraitha*) tradition which appears to take a different view of the legal question under discussion. Much ingenuity was then generated by the debaters to harmonize the *Mishnah* text with a *baraitha* tradition.

One of the best known *baraitha* writings is the sixth chapter of tractate *Aboth.* Eleven paragraphs make up this supplement which is called "Acquisition of the Law" and sometimes "The *Baraitha* of Rabbi Meir." The opening sentence of these eleven paragraphs starts off with a saying of Rabbi Meir which accounts for the title "The *Baraitha* of Rabbi Meir." Actually, however, many more sages are represented by famous sayings. A glance at the superscription which stands at the very beginning of these eleven paragraphs shows that they were considered a

196

baraitha collection, for the superscription starts off: "The sages taught . . . in the style of the *Mishnah*." When a *baraitha* is introduced in the *Talmud* it always begins with the words—"The sages taught."

NOTE ON THE TOSEFTA

The story of the *Tosefta* is closely related to the story of the *Mishnah*. When the editorial board, under the direction of Rabbi Judah "the Prince," had completed its work in 220 A.D. there were other Mishnaic collections extant embodying similar legal materials. These omitted collections, which did not become a part of the canonical *Mishnah,* were nevertheless preserved as outside (*baraitha*) materials—that is, valuable traditions not incorporated into the authoritative *Mishnah*. They came to be known collectively as *Tosefta,* meaning the supplement or the "addition."

Like the *Mishnah,* the *Tosefta* is divided into six orders. Its arrangement largely parallels the *Mishnah* while its style is more diffuse. Besides offering to the reader independent materials the *Tosefta* gives many amplifications thereby filling out the brevity of the *Mishnah* text.

ATTACKS UPON THE TALMUD

The attacks upon the *Talmud* have been of a varied nature, most of them leading to public burnings and desecration. There are three principal reasons why the *Talmud* has been subjected to indignities:

1. Since it forms the main teaching of the Jewish religion, it has been regarded as the supreme obstacle in preventing Jews from being converted to Christianity.

2. Since the *Talmud* interprets the Old Testament by reshaping ancient Biblical laws to meet the needs of post-Biblical times, it has been charged with the falsification of Scripture.

3. Since the *Talmud* is a non-Christian production, it has been accused of harboring an evil and irreverant attitude towards Christ and the Church.

For many centuries the *Talmud* was regarded as mysterious and a source of blasphemous statements against Christianity. This suspicion was not only grossly untrue but it was magnified and distorted by ignorance of the *Talmud*. The inability of Christian scholars to read the *Talmud* made matters worse.

A new attitude toward the *Talmud* was very slow in developing. It was on May 24, 1510 that the Emperor Maximilian of Austria rescinded his edict to burn the *Talmud* and appointed Johann Reuchlin, the legal adviser of the Dominicans, to examine it. Reuchlin is said to have been the only Christian in Europe at that time familiar with the Hebrew language. Reuchlin stated that from personal investigation he had arrived at the conclusion that there was nothing blasphemous in the *Talmud* and that, therefore, it was senseless to burn it. He opposed the destruction of books "written by Christ's nearest relations." As an alternative to burning the *Talmud,* he suggested that at every German university two professors of Hebrew should be appointed. In 1520 Pope Leo X permitted the *Talmud* to be printed by Daniel Bomberg at Venice. This became the first complete edition of the *Talmud*.

After thirty years, the Vatican, which had permitted the *Talmud* to appear in print, undertook numerous campaigns to destroy it. A prominent feature of these campaigns was the public disputation in which Jews were compelled to defend and justify Talmudic teachings.

Attacks upon the *Talmud* have always been a part of the

stock-in-trade of nearly every anti-Semitic movement. In modern times perhaps the most notorious attack was published by Dr. Alfred Rosenberg, the "philosopher" of Adolph Hitler's Third Reich. Dr. Rosenberg's book entitled *Immorality in the Talmud* was competently analyzed by the Rev. Herbert Danby, Regius Professor of Hebrew in the University of Oxford.[1]

---

[1] *Immorality in the Talmud* by Dr. Alfred Rosenberg with a Foreword by the Rev. Herbert Danby, issued by Friends of Europe, London 1937. The reader's attention is also called to chapter ten of H. L. Strack's *Introduction to Talmud and Midrash*. Both Strack and Danby are Christians whose knowledge of the *Talmud* has greatly benefited world scholarship.

BURNINGS OF THE TALMUD

A chronological survey of the important dates dealing with both the confiscation and burning of the *Talmud*. Included in this survey are the dates of significant attacks and calumnies.

1. The apostate Nicholas Donin of La Rochelle, France, laid before Pope Gregory IX a formal accusation against the *Talmud* charging that it contained blasphemies against God, Jesus, and Christianity. The Pope gave orders for the seizure of all copies of the *Talmud*. On March 3, 1240, while the Jews of France were in their synagogues, their books were seized.

2. Paris, June, 1242. Twenty-four cartloads of Hebrew books were consigned to the flames. This was the first public official burning of the *Talmud*.

3. Barcelona, July, 1263. Public disputations leading to burnings.

4. Pope Clement IV in 1264 orders the death penalty upon any person caught harboring a copy of the *Talmud* in his house.

5. On November 30, 1286 Pope Honorius IV writes to the Archbishop of Canterbury and York against the *Talmud* denouncing it as "that damnable book" and requesting the bishops "vehemently to see that it be not read by anybody, since all other evils flow out of it."

6. In 1299 and again in 1309 the *Talmud* was burned publicly in Paris.

7. Toulouse, France, 1315. Public burning.

8. Rome, 1322. *Talmud* burned publicly by order of Pope John XXII.

9. May 11, 1415. Pope Martin V issued a bull forbidding Jews to study or teach the *Talmud* and ordering the destruction of all copies.

10. Spain, 1490. Torquemada ordered large scale burnings.

11. Germany, 1509. Confiscations carried out by the Dominicans.

12. Johann Reuchlin succeeded in 1510 in getting Emperor Maximilian to rescind the royal edict to burn the *Talmud*.

13. Wittenberg, 1544. Martin Luther atacked the Jews and the *Talmud* in his book *Von den Juden und Ihren Luegen* (*Concerning the Jews and Their Lies*). In this book he brands the *Talmud* as "nothing but godlessness, lies, cursing, and swearing." He repeatedly urged that all synagogues be burned. He advised that the houses of Jews be torn down, their books taken from them, and their rabbis be prohibited from teaching.

14. Rome, August 12, 1553. Pope Julius III issued an edict demanding the burning of the *Talmud*. The papal decree was carried out in Rome, Venice, Barcelona, Romagna, and other places.

15. Rome, 1554. The censorship of the *Talmud* and other Hebrew books is introduced by a Papal bull.

16. Rome, 1558. The *Talmud* is ordered burned in public by Cardinal Ghislieri.

17. Rome, 1559. The *Talmud* is placed on *Index Expurgatorius*.

18. Cremona, Italy, 1569. The Jewish library of the city was closed and plundered. It is estimated that twelve thousand Talmudical books were burned.

19. Rome, 1593. Pope Clement VIII renewed the interdiction against reading or owning the *Talmud*.

20. Frankfort, Germany, 1700. Johann A. Eisenmenger published an attack upon the *Talmud*, entitled *Judaism Unmasked*. It has long been the source book of anti-Semitic misinformation down to the middle of the 20th century.

21. Poland, 1757. Bishop Dembowski ordered all copies of the *Talmud* found in the diocese of Podolia to be confiscated and burned.

22. Munster, Germany, 1871. August Rohling, Catholic theologian and anti-Semitic author, published *The Talmud Jew* (*Der Talmudjude*) which quickly became a standard work for anti-Semitic authors.

23. Germany, 1883. Dr. Justus (alias Aaron Briman) who had been publishing anonymous pamphlets against the Jews brings out *Der Judenspiegel* (*The Mirror of the Jew*), a compilation of a hundred Talmudic laws purporting to show Jewish animosity towards Christians.

24. St. Petersburg, 1892. The notorious Justin Pranaitis published his monograph *The Christian in the Jewish Talmud*. It was in 1912 during the trial of Mendel Beilis that Pranaitis offered his services to the Czarist government in order to slander the *Talmud* and prove Beilis guilty of ritual murder by reason of Talmudic teachings.

25. Breslau, 1935. Walter Forstat, a Nazi "expert" on Jewish literature published *The Basic Principles of the Talmud* (*Die Grundlagen des Talmud*). Much of this kind of propaganda against Judaism led the German people to approve the ghastly horrors of the Third Reich against minorities.

26. Germany, 1935. Dr. Alfred Rosenberg, close friend and associate of Hitler published a booklet entitled *Immorality in the Talmud* (*Unmoral in Talmud*).

GENERAL BIBLIOGRAPHY

ABRAHAMS, I. *Studies in Pharisaism and the Gospels* (2 vols.), Cambridge, 1917–24.

———. *Short History of Jewish Literature*, London, 1910.

AMRAM, D. W. *The Jewish Law of Divorce*, Philadelphia, 1896.

AVERBACH, C. *The Talmud: A Gateway to the Common Law*, Cleveland, 1950.

BADER, G. *Our Spiritual Heroes*, New York, 1935.

BAECK, L. *The Pharisees*, New York, 1947.

———. *The Essence of Judaism*, New York, 1948.

BARON, S. W. *Social and Religious History of the Jews* (Vol. 1), New York, 1937.

BERNFELD, S. *Foundations of Jewish Ethics*, New York, 1929.

BEVAN, E. R. *Jewish Parties and the Law*, Cambridge, 1932.

BLACKMAN, PHILIP (Editor). *The Mishnah*, Hebrew text with English Translation (6 vols.), London, 1951–54.

BOKSER, B. Z. *Pharisaic Judaism in Transition*, New York, 1935.

———. *Wisdom of the Talmud*, New York, 1951.

CHARLES, R. H. *Apocrypha and Pseudepigrapha*, Oxford, 1913.

COHEN, A. *Everyman's Talmud*, London, 1931.

COHON, B. D. *Ethics of the Rabbis*, Boston, 1932.

DANBY, H. *The Mishnah* (English translation), Oxford, 1933.

DEUTSCH, G. *Theory of the Oral Tradition*, Cincinnati, 1896.

EPSTEIN, RABBI I. AND OTHERS (Editors). *Talmud*, English Translation (Soncino Edition, 35 vols.), London, 1935–52.

EPSTEIN, L. M. *Marriage Laws in Bible and Talmud*, Cambridge, 1942.

——. *Sex Laws and Customs in Judaism*, New York, 1948.

FELDMAN, A. *Parables and Similes of the Rabbis*, Cambridge, 1924.

FINKELSTEIN, L. *The Pharisees* (2 vols.), Philadelphia, 1938.

FREEDMAN, H. AND SIMON, M. (Editors). *Midrash* (Soncino Edition, English Translation of *Midrash Rabbah*, 10 vols.), Index, London, 1939.

FRIEDLANDER, G. *Rabbinic Philosophy and Ethics*, London, 1912.

——. *Laws and Customs of Israel* (4 vols.), London, 1921.

GAER, J. *Lore of the Old Testament*, Boston, 1951.

GASTER, M. *Exempla of the Rabbis*, London, 1924.

GINZBERG, L. *A Commentary on the Palestinian Talmud*, New York, 1941.

——. *The Legends of the Jews* (7 vols.), Philadelphia, 1909–37.

GOLLANCZ, H. *Pedagogics of the Talmud*, London, 1924.

GRAYZEL, S. *A History of the Jews*, Philadelphia, 1947.

HERFORD, R. T. *The Pharisees*, London, 1924.

——. *Ethics of the Fathers*, New York, 1930.

——. *Judaism in the New Testament Period*, London, 1924.

——. *Talmud and Apocrypha*, London, 1933.

HERTZ, S. H. *Sayings of the Fathers* (Hebrew text with English translation), New York, 1945.

HERZOG, I. *Main Institutions of Jewish Law* (2 vols.), London, 1936.

HIGGER, M. *Jewish Utopia in Rabbinic Literature*, New York, 1932.

——. *Intention in Talmudic Law*, New York, 1927.

HIRSCH, W. *Rabbinic Psychology*, London, 1947.

HOENIG, S. B. *The Great Sanhedrin*, New York, 1952.

HOROWITZ, G. *The Spirit of Jewish Law*, New York, 1953.

Jewish Apocryphal Literature Series, Philadelphia, 1948–52.

KADUSHIN, M. *Organic Thinking in Rabbinic Thought*, New York, 1938.

——. *The Rabbinic Mind*, New York, 1952.

KAPLAN, J. *The Redaction of the Babylonian Talmud*, New York, 1933.

KOHLER, K. *Jewish Theology*, New York, 1918.

LAUTERBACH, J. Z. *Midrash and Mishna*, New York, 1916.

——. *Rabbinic Essays*, Cincinnati, 1951.

——. *Mekilta* (Critical text with English translation, 3 vols.), Philadelphia, 1931–35.

LAZARUS, M. *Jewish Ethics*, Philadelphia, 1900.

MALTER, H. *The Treatise Ta'anit of the Babylonian Talmud*, Philadelphia, 1928.

MARCUS, R. *Law in the Apocrypha*, New York, 1927.

MARMORSTEIN, M. *The Doctrine of Merits in Old Rabbinical Literature*, London, 1920.

——. *The Old Rabbinic Doctrine of God*, London, 1927.

MIELZINER, M. *Introduction to the Talmud*, New York, 1925.

——. *Legal Maxims and Fundamental Laws of the Civil and Criminal Code of the Talmud*, Cincinnati, 1898.

MONTEFIORE AND LOWE. *A Rabbinic Anthology*, London, 1938.
MONTEFIORE, G. S. *The Old Testament and After*, London, 1921.
———. *Rabbinic Literature and Gospel Teachings*, London, 1930.
MOORE, G. F. *Judaism in the First Centuries of the Christian Era* (3 vols.), Cambridge, 1927–30.
NEWMAN, L. *Semikah (Ordination) The Study of the Origin of Ordination, Its History, Function in Rabbinic Literature*, Manchester, 1950.
———. *Talmudic Anthology*, New York, 1945.
OESTERLEY, W. O. E. *A Short Survey of the Literature of Rabbinical and Medieval Judaism*, London, 1920.
———. *Religion and Worship of the Synagogue*, London, 1911.
PATAI, R. *Man and Temple in Ancient Jewish Myth and Ritual*, London, 1947.
RAISIN, J. S. *Sect, Creed, and Custom in Judaism*, Philadelphia, 1907.
RAPPOPORT, A. S. *Folklore of the Jews*, London, 1937.
SADOWSKY, S. *Rabban Gamaliel ben Simeon*, New York, 1941.
SCHECHTER, S. *Some Aspects of Rabbinic Theology*, New York, 1910.
———. *Studies in Judaism* (First Series, 1896; Second Series, 1908; Third Series, 1924).
SILVERSTONE, H. *A Guide to the Talmud*, Baltimore, 1942.
SIMON, M. *Jewish Religious Conflicts*, London, 1950.
STRACK, H. L. *Introduction to the Talmud and Midrash*, Philadelphia, 1931.
TAYLOR, C. *Sayings of the Jewish Fathers*, Cambridge, 1897.
UNTERMAN, I. *The Talmud*, Philadelphia, 1952.
WAXMAN, M. *History of the Jewish Literature*, New York, 1930.
WRIGHT, D. *The Talmud*, London, 1932.
ZEITLIN, S. *The History of the Second Jewish Commonwealth*, Philadelphia, 1933.
———. *The Pharisees and Their Opponents*, New York, 1939.
———. *Religious and Secular Leadership*, Philadelphia, 1943.
ZUCROW, S. *Adjustment of Law to Life in Rabbinic Literature*, Boston, 1928.

GLOSSARY

Abadim, slaves
Abodah Zarah, idolatry
Aboth, Sayings of the Fathers
Alenu, the opening word of the "Adoration" prayer
Al peh, by the mouth—that is, oral (tenor)
Amoraim, sages of the *Gemara*
Arakin, evaluations
Aramaic, a language related to Hebrew

Baba Bathra, last gate
Baba Kamma, first gate
Baba Metzia, middle gate
Bamidbar Rabbah, a *Midrash* commentary on Numbers
Baraitha, extraneous traditional material
Bekoroth, first born
Berachoth, blessings
Bereshit Rabbah, a *Midrash* commentary on Genesis
Beth-din, a court
Beth-El, house of God
Beth ha-Midrash, house of interpretation
Betzah, egg
Bikkurim, first fruits
Binyan ab mi-Katub Echad, a rule permitting a general interpretation
    from one passage of Scripture
Binyan ab mi-Shene Ketubim, a rule of interpretation permitting a
    generalization drawn from two passages of Scripture

Chagigah, festival offering
Challah, dough
Charut, engraved
Cheruth, freedom
Chiddushim, comments on *Talmud* text (novellae)
Chullin, profane things

Debarim Rabbah, a *Midrash* commentary on Deuteronomy
Demai, doubtful
Derech Eretz, prohibited marriages
Derech Eretz Zuta, conduct of life
Dina d'malchuta dina, the law of the land is the law

Ebel Rabbati, customs of burial and mourning
Eduyoth, testimonies
Ekah Rabbati, a *Midrash* commentary on Lamentations
Erubim, combinations
Essenes, Jews who followed an ascetic way of life

Gehenna, hell
Gemara, commentary on the *Mishnah*
Gerim, proselytes
Gittin, divorces
Gzerah Shawah, a rule of interpretation based upon an analogy of
   words

Hagahoth, commentaries on the *Talmud* (marginal glosses)
Haggadah, history, parables, folklore
Hakam, wise man
Halakah, legal rules
Horayoth, decisions

Kallah, bride
Kal V'Homer, a rule of interpretation which is the inference from
   minor to major and vice versa
Karaites, a sect of Jews
Kaylim, vessels
Ka-yozeh bo m'Makom Aher, a rule of interpretation which seeks to
   harmonize passages of Scripture
Kerithuth, excisions
Kethuboth, marriage deeds
Kiddushin, betrothals
Kilayim, mixtures
Kinnim, birds' nests
Klal u'ferat, a rule of interpretation: deduction of particular from the
   general
Kodashim, sacred things
Kuthim, Samaritans

Lulaf, palm branch

Maaseroth, tithes
Maaser Sheni, second tithe
Makkoth, stripes
Makom, place, "God"
Makshirin, preparations
Megillah, scroll
Me'ilah, trespass
Mekilta, literally "a measure." The name used for a *Midrash* commentary on Exodus
Menahot, meal offerings
Meturgeman, a translator
Mezuzah, literally "a door-post." Applied to a roll of parchment which is placed in a wood or metal container and affixed to the upper right hand post of entrance to a house
Middoth, measurements
Midrash, literally digging. A term applied to the expositions of Scripture
Midrash Haggadah, expositions that deal with nonlegal matters
Midrash Halakah, expositions which deal with legal matters
Midrashim, plural of the word *Midrash*
Midrash Kohelet, an exposition or commentary on Ecclesiastes
Midrash Shir ha-Shirim, an exposition or commentary on the Song of Songs
Mikwa'oth, reservoirs
Mishnah, the text of the *Talmud*
Mitzvah, noble act
Moed, festivals
Moed Katan, minor festivals

Nashim, women
Nasi, prince (a title), the president of the Sanhedrin
Nazir, nazirite
Nedarim, vows
Negaim, leprosy
Nezikin, damages
Niddah, menstruant

Ohaloth, tents
Orlah, uncircumcized

Parah, heifer
Peah, corner
Perek ha-Shalom, chapters of peace
Perushim, running commentaries upon the *Talmud* text
Pesikta, homilies of a *Midrash* nature
Pesikta d'Rab Kahana, Midrashic homilies of Rabbi Kahana

Pharisees, adherents of the Oral Law
Pilpul, casuistic arguments
P'sachim, Passover sacrifices

Rab, master, a rabbi, a teacher
Rabbi, my master, my teacher
Rosh Hashana, New Year

Saboraim, scholars
Sadducees, priestly aristocracy
Sanhedrin, high court
Seder, order. The *Talmud* is divided into six Orders
Sefer, a book
Sefer Torah, the book of the Torah, the Pentateuch
Semachoth, joys (*Ebel Rabbati*)
Shabbat, Sabbath
Shamir, worm
Shebu'oth, oaths
Shekalim, shekels
Shekinah, the divine presence
Shema, the first word of the Jewish confession of faith: "Hear, O
    Israel, the Lord our God, the Lord is one"
Shemot Rabbah, *Midrash* commentary on Exodus
Sheviith, sabbatical year
Sifra (Siphra), a halakic *Midrash* on Leviticus
Sifre (Siphre), a halakic *Midrash* on Numbers and Deuteronomy
Sopherim, scribes
Sotah, adulteress
Succa, booths

Ta'anith, fasting
Tamid, daily sacrifice
Tanna, a sage of the *Mishnah*
Tannaim, plural form of *tanna*
Tanchuma, collections of *Haggadah* on the Pentateuch
Tanchuma Yelammedenu, one of the *Tanchuma* collections
Targum, Aramaic version of Scripture
T'bul Yom, immersed at daytime
Temurah, exchange
Tephillin, phylacteries
Terumoth, heave offerings
Toharoth, purifications
Torath Kohanim (same as *Sifra*)
Tosaphoth, critical and explanatory glosses on the *Talmud*
Tosefta, supplements or additions to the Talmudic law, a collection of
    baraitot
Tzizith, fringes

Uktzin, stalks

Vayikra Rabba, a *Midrash* commentary on Leviticus

Yadayim, hands
Yahweh, God, Jehovah
Yebamoth, sisters-in-law
Yoma, day

Zabim, sufferers with gonorrhea
Zebachim, sacrifices
Zeraim, seeds
Zugoth, pairs. Leaders of the two branches of the Sanhedrin